Poli*** *** **

Parish

Politics in the Parish

The Political Influence of Catholic Priests

GREGORY ALLEN SMITH

Georgetown University Press

Washington, D.C.

Georgetown University Press, Washington, D.C. www.press.georgetown.edu
© 2008 by Georgetown University Press. All rights reserved. No part of this book
may be reproduced or utilized in any form or by any means, electronic or mechani-
cal, including photocopying and recording, or by any information storage and
retrieval system, without permission in writing from the publisher.

Chapter 3 is a revised and expanded version of "The Influence of Priests on the
Political Attitudes of Roman Catholics," *Journal for the Scientific Study of Religion*
44 (3): 291–306. Used by permission of Blackwell Publishing.

Library of Congress Cataloging-in-Publication Data

Smith, Gregory Allen.
    Politics in the parish : the political influence of Catholic priests / Gregory Allen
Smith.
        p. cm.—(Religion and politics series)
    Includes bibliographical references (p.   ) and index.
    ISBN 978-1-58901-193 9 (alk. paper)
    1. Priests—United States—Political activity—History—20th century.
2. Catholic Church—United States—Political activity—History—20th
century.   3. Christianity and politics—United States.   I. Title.

    BX1407.P63S65 2008
    322'.10973–dc22   2007020030

15 14 13 12 11 10 09 08   9 8 7 6 5 4 3 2
First printing

Printed in the United States of America

Contents

Illustrations

Acknowledgments

I could not have completed this project or this program of study without the support and assistance of myriad people. Most notably, I am deeply grateful for the guidance of my two closest mentors, Steven Finkel and Paul Freedman. They graciously offered helpful comments, questions, and suggestions at every step of this project since its inception almost six years ago. I greatly appreciate the interest that they have taken in my work, and their support of my pursuit of academic, professional, and personal goals.

I am also very thankful for the advice and support of James Ceaser and Gerald Fogarty, who kindly served on my dissertation committee. Mr. Ceaser and Father Fogarty were both involved with this project from the very early planning stages, and their assistance and suggestions were integral to completing and improving this research.

The support of many people at the University of Virginia was instrumental in bringing this project to fruition. I am particularly grateful to the Department of Politics (and especially to Steven Finkel, who was the department director of graduate studies when I first came to the university, and to Herman Schwartz, who was the director of graduate studies for the bulk of my time at the university) for generous financial support that made attending the university possible for me. I am also grateful to the Center on Religion and Democracy at the University of Virginia (and especially to its director, James Davison Hunter, to its former associate director,

Steven Jones, and to the current associate director, Slavica Jakelic), which supported this research by providing me with a yearlong dissertation fellowship, several research grants, and a vibrant community that provided crucial intellectual stimulation. Larry J. Sabato and the Center for Politics provided me with numerous teaching and research assistantships and showed great kindness and generosity to both me and my family during our time at the university. I am indebted to the helpful staff at the University of Virginia Research Computing Support Center, and especially to Yakup Asarkaya and Kathy Gerber, without whose help I may not have been able to master the statistical and software-related skills necessary to employ multilevel modeling techniques. Finally, I greatly appreciate all of the assistance and support provided by the staff at the University of Virginia Department of Politics, especially Debbie Best and Cassandra Thomas.

Since leaving the university, my colleagues at the Pew Research Center—especially Luis Lugo, Sandra Stencel, Scott Keeter, John Green, David Masci, and Tim Shah—have provided me with vital support and feedback on various components of this research.

I am grateful for the consistent support, encouragement, advice, and critique provided by Georgetown University Press, especially that of its director, Richard Brown, and that of the editors of this series, John Green, Ted Jelen, and Mark Rozell. A number of others have also provided very helpful comments on portions of this research in a variety of forms, including Geoffrey Layman, Laura Olson, Lynn Sanders, and several anonymous reviewers.

I will always be grateful to Dr. Roe Buchanan for planting the seeds of intellectual curiosity from which this project grew. I was fortunate to be a student in Dr. Buchanan's history classes for three years in high school, during which time he taught me (to the extent that I am able) to write clearly, pushed me to think critically and independently, and demonstrated how interesting and fun it is to study human events. It is no exaggeration to say that Dr. Buchanan's instruction opened up a world to me that I might not otherwise have discovered, and I thank him for the profound influence he has had on my life.

A significant portion of the analysis that follows is based on the Notre Dame Study of Catholic Parish Life, and I acknowledge the American Religion Data Archive (ARDA) for making the data from that study available. Data from the Notre Dame Study were originally collected by Jay Dolan, David C. Leege, Phillip Murnion, Mark Searle, and Michael R. Welch.

I am deeply grateful to the dioceses and parishes that agreed to participate in this study. I thank His Eminence Theodore Cardinal McCarrick, former Archbishop of Washington, as well as Reverend Monsignor Godfrey Mosley, Vicar General of the Archdiocese of Washington, for permission to pursue this project. In the Diocese of Richmond, I am grateful to the Most Reverend Francis Xavier DiLorenzo, Bishop of Richmond, as well as to Anne Edwards, Chancellor of the Diocese of Richmond, for their support of this work. And in the Diocese of Arlington, I thank the Most Reverend Paul S. Loverde, Bishop of Arlington, and Reverend Robert J. Rippy, Chancellor of the Diocese of Arlington, for allowing me to pursue this research. I am also supremely grateful to the pastors (who cannot be named, to protect their anonymity) of the parishes that participated in this study, and to all of the parish priests who participated in this project, as it would not have been possible to complete this research without their cooperation and support. It was obvious to me that all of the priests that I spoke with during the course of this project were supremely and lovingly devoted to the service of the Church and her people, and I thank them for that as well.

It would have been impossible for me to complete this project without the love and support of my family. My father, Daniel A. Smith, and my late mother, Mary Catherine Smith, demonstrated for me (and my siblings) from an early age the value of hard work, the importance of perseverance, the sacredness of family and commitment, and the power of faith and hope. They told me and my siblings that we could do anything we set our minds to, and we believed them. My extended family has also been supportive of me and of this research for years, which I greatly appreciate.

Finally, I am deeply grateful to (and for) the four most important people in my life: my wife, Holly; sons, Marcus and Nicholas; and daughter, Victoria. Marcus was at home with me for much of the time that I was writing this book. His presence helped me to maintain a sense of perspective, and his encouragement was much appreciated. Finally, this project could not have been completed without the unwavering support of Holly, to whom this work is dedicated.

All of these individuals, and many more, have been crucial to the completion of this book, but they are not responsible for any errors that follow; the blame for those lies solely with me.

Introduction

Religion has always played an important role in American politics. Many of the earliest European settlers in the New World were motivated to cross the Atlantic by religious concerns, and the political institutions they established were influenced by their moral and religious convictions. The centrality of religion in American life continued through the development of the colonies and the establishment of the United States as an independent nation. By the 1830s Alexis de Tocqueville, by all accounts one of the most prescient observers of American society and culture, argued that for Americans religion should "be considered as the first of their political institutions, for although it did not give them the taste for liberty, it singularly facilitates their use thereof" (1833, 292). Kenneth Wald, one of the leading scholars of contemporary American religion and politics, has argued that "by forming an important strand in American culture, religion has helped to define the context of American political life" (1997, 42). From the time of the earliest European settlements in the New World, then, religion has played an important role in American politics.

In recent years, however, there seems to have developed a consensus within the scholarly community that religious influence in American politics, and in the politics of the developed world more generally, was waning and that religion was destined for eventual irrelevance. For example, Wald points out that many scholars, influenced by modernization and Marxist theories of cultural development, which "confidently forecast the demise of religion, . . . predicted that religious

1

controversy would eventually disappear from the political agenda" (1997, 7; see also Lenski 1961). However, the decline of religious influence in culture and politics has failed to materialize, at least in the United States. In fact, recent developments, including the rise of the Christian right as an organized and influential force on the political stage and the eruption of what some have identified as the "culture wars," have sparked a renewed interest in research geared toward understanding the intersection of religion and American politics. Furthermore, just as a decline in the importance of religion in American politics has failed to occur thus far, a decline does not appear to be on the horizon. Indeed, many of the most long-standing issues on the political agenda, including abortion and school prayer, are at least to some extent religious in nature. In addition, many of the new issues confronting political leaders and citizens alike—from the debate over gay marriage to the heated controversies over the appropriateness (and constitutionality) of placing the Ten Commandments, nativity scenes, and other religious symbols in public places—clearly have religious overtones. A comprehensive understanding of American politics, therefore, requires a careful consideration of the interplay of religion and politics.

Understanding the politics of Roman Catholics is a crucial component of an overall understanding of American religion and politics. National surveys indicate that approximately one-quarter of all Americans identify themselves as Catholic, making Roman Catholicism the single largest religious tradition in the United States (Froehle and Gautier 2000, 3). As such, Catholics have the potential to wield enormous political power and influence. Among American Catholics, 34 percent indicate that they attend Mass at least once a week, with another 26 percent saying that they attend Mass almost every week or once or twice a month (Froehle and Gautier 2000, 23; see also the Center for Applied Research in the Apostolate 2005). Thus, a substantial proportion of American Catholics is regularly exposed to the teachings—including the political teachings—of the Church.

Due to its hierarchical structure, which (at least in theory) permits the delivery of a unified and consistent teaching, its considerable resources, and its weekly access to millions of citizens, the Catholic Church is a potential heavyweight in the American political arena. Indeed, over the past century (and especially in more recent decades, as anti-Catholic bigotry has declined) Catholic leaders have worked hard to promulgate specific positions on various political issues and to convince both Catholics and non-Catholics alike of the wisdom of those positions. Specifically, the Church, through papal encyclicals, pastoral letters emanating from the United States Conference of Catholic Bishops (USCCB), and other documents, has articulated clear teachings on at least five issues of contemporary cultural and political significance in the United States: aid to the poor and disadvantaged in society (on which the Church takes a liberal stand, in that it favors devoting increased attention and resources to helping the downtrodden); capital punishment (which the Church opposes); international relations (especially with regard to war and the use of military force, on which the Church is more cautious, and thus more liberal, than most American conservatives); abortion (which the Church opposes); and sexual morality (on which the Church, by disallowing artificial contraception and by continuing to affirm the sinfulness of homosexuality, may safely be considered conservative). The Church's teachings on each of these issues will be considered in more detail in chapter 1, but for now a discussion of Joseph Cardinal Bernardin's development of a consistent ethic of life provides a brief and clear articulation of what an authentically Catholic politics might look like.

Joseph Cardinal Bernardin served the Church among other capacities as the leader of the Archdiocese of Chicago from 1982 to 1996, and he was also influential in the USCCB. Bernardin developed an intellectual framework in which he encouraged Catholics, when thinking about politics and making electoral decisions, to consider and attempt to implement the Church's teachings on all of the

issues mentioned above. He argued that these political issues should
be looked at not as separate, unrelated topics, but rather as parts of a
single political question, one on which Catholics should be unified in
the course of embracing a consistent ethic, or "seamless garment," of
life. In order to demonstrate the links that Bernardin drew between a
number of political issues, it is worth quoting him at length. In the
Gannon Lecture at Fordham University in December of 1983, he
stated:

> If one contends, as we do, that the right of every fetus to be born should
> be protected by civil law and supported by civil consensus, then our
> moral, political and economic responsibilities do not stop at the mo-
> ment of birth. Those who defend the right to life of the weakest among
> us must be equally visible in support of the quality of life of the power-
> less among us: the old and the young, the hungry and the homeless, the
> undocumented immigrant and the unemployed worker. Such a quality
> of life posture translates into specific political and economic positions
> on tax policy, employment generation, welfare policy, nutrition and
> feeding programs, and health care. Consistency means we cannot have it
> both ways: We cannot urge a compassionate society and vigorous public
> policy to protect the rights of the unborn and then argue that compas-
> sion and significant public programs on behalf of the needy undermine
> the moral fiber of the society or are beyond the proper scope of govern-
> mental responsibility (12).

Bernardin went on in this lecture to link questions regarding foreign affairs and military policy to the consistent ethic of life, arguing
that "reversing the arms race, avoiding nuclear war and moving toward a world freed of the nuclear threat are profoundly 'pro-life' issues" (14). In short, Bernardin's work clearly articulates principles
that might be held by someone who sought to follow Church teachings across the spectrum of important contemporary political issues.
Such a person, it is safe to say, would adopt what has become the
politically conservative position on abortion, and what have become

more politically liberal positions on economic issues, capital punishment, and foreign affairs.

Bernardin did more than simply outline the fundamental principles of an authentically Catholic politics. He also sought to inspire a more thoroughgoing agreement with the principles of the seamless garment of life among American Catholics (as well as the American populace generally) and to promote pro-life policies across a wide range of political issues. As he put it in his Gannon Lecture, "a consistent ethic of life must be held by a constituency to be effective. The building of such a constituency is precisely the task before the Church and the nation" (13). On this count, Bernardin and his successors have apparently come up short.[1] Although Catholic politics remains something of an enigma, it is possible to affirm with confidence that American Catholics have not adopted Bernardin's consistent ethic of life in large numbers. With regard to foreign affairs and military policy, for example, a 2004 Pew Research Center survey found that a majority of Catholics favor either maintaining defense spending at current levels (54 percent) or increasing it (21 percent); only one in five Catholics expressed support for cutting back on defense spending (Pew Research Center 2005b). A 1999 Gallup survey of American Catholics found that nearly one-quarter of respondents disagreed or strongly disagreed with "further reductions in nuclear weapons" (Gallup 1999). With regard to economic issues, the picture is less clear, as a 2005 Pew survey revealed that 70 percent of Catholics favor providing more generous government assistance to the poor (Pew Research Center 2005a). But a Pew survey from 2002 found that nearly one-half of all Catholics agree that the "current welfare system changes things for the worse by making able-bodied people too dependent on government aid" (Pew Research Center 2002). In Gallup's 1999 survey of Catholics, roughly 50 percent expressed support for "further cutbacks in welfare programs" (Gallup 1999). With regard to capital punishment, nearly 60 percent of American Catholics favor the death penalty for persons convicted of murder (Pew Research Center 2006b).

Finally, Catholics have clearly failed to embrace the totality of Bernardin's seamless garment when it comes to abortion. One study, for example, reports that among American Catholics fully 52 percent believe that abortion should be legal "in many or all cases" (D'Antonio et al. 1996, 62). Pew polling from 2006 found that 44 percent of all Catholics (and 50 percent of white, non-Hispanic Catholics) believe that abortion should either be generally available or legal with more limitations than are currently in place; only 17 percent of Catholics, by contrast, say that abortion should never be permitted (Pew Research Center 2006a). If the Church had been successful in promoting adherence to a consistent ethic of life such as that enunciated by Bernardin, one would expect to see much more opposition to abortion, and much less support for military spending, capital punishment, and welfare cutbacks among Catholics than is evident in these surveys. Moreover, just as it seems that Catholics have not rushed to embrace the tenets of the seamless garment of life in their attitudes on various political issues, neither have they supported candidates for political office who embrace the seamless garment. Of course, there are not many—and perhaps not any—candidates for high political office who embrace the principles of the seamless garment, due in large part to the fact that the issues of the seamless garment cut across familiar political party divisions in the United States (Republicans tend to be more in line with Church teachings on abortion and sexual morality, while Democrats tend to be more sympathetic to Church teachings on the other issues).

It is therefore clear that American Catholics do not march in lockstep with their Church and many of its leaders on political issues. How, then, do Catholics reconcile their religious and political beliefs when they approach political issues and make electoral decisions? There have been several attempts by scholars in recent years to answer this question; these explanations are discussed in more detail in the next chapter. For now, it is sufficient to point out that some scholars have offered accounts of Catholic politics that rely primarily on secular and demographic explanations (Gerner 1995; Leege et al. 2002; Prender-gast 1999; Reichley 1986; but see Penning 1986). These accounts contend that Catholics have become more Republican and politically conservative during recent decades largely as a result of their assimilation into American culture and rising socioeconomic status. Other scholars have looked for, and found, potential religious explanations for Catholic political attitudes and voting decisions (Leege 1988; Leege and Welch 1989; Wald, Kellstedt, and Leege 1993; Welch and Leege 1988, 1991; Wilcox, Jelen, and Leege 1993). These accounts of Catholic political behavior and attitudes (that is, both the secular and religious accounts) are informative and instructive insofar as they go. However, recent advances in research on religion and politics and in the subfields of political communication and voting behavior suggest that there is more to the story. For instance, the role of Catholic priests, who are the representatives of the Church with whom Catholics are likely to have the most extensive and intimate contact, has rarely figured in empirical investigations of Catholics' political views.

Recent research on political decision making has demonstrated the importance of elite actors in providing citizens with political information and heuristics that are used by citizens in forming opinions and making political choices. This book reports on the results of a study designed to consider and investigate the extent to which Catholic priests (as opposed to the Church hierarchy) influence the political opinions of their parishioners. In theory, the potential for priestly influence is great. Priests have regular access to a presumably receptive and relatively captive audience. Furthermore, while the institutional Church may fail to provide citizens with political guidance that can realistically be followed (since there is no powerful political group or entity, such as a political party, that agrees with the Church across the spectrum of political issues), individual priests, by emphasizing Church teachings on some issues while de-emphasizing others, may provide more forthright and easily interpretable political cues than does the institutional Church.

This book investigates in two main ways the extent to which Catholic priests influence the political attitudes and voting decisions of their parishioners. First, it reviews and analyzes the Notre Dame Study of Catholic Parish Life, looking for evidence of priestly influence. The Notre Dame Study consists of data from surveys administered to pastors and parishioners at a nationally representative sample of thirty-six Catholic parishes. Though the survey is not ideal for investigating priestly influence in that it queries pastors as to their own personal political attitudes and opinions (as opposed to asking them what they actually say to their parishioners), it is the only publicly available survey of its kind, matching relatively large numbers of parishioner respondents with their pastors. As such, the Notre Dame Study provides a good opportunity for conducting initial tests of priestly influence, and it suggests that priests may in fact be politically influential, especially in their ability to shape their parishioners' opinions on a number of sociopolitical issues.

Second, this book investigates the nature and extent of priestly influence through case studies of several Catholic parishes from the Virginia, Maryland, and Washington, D.C., region. Through interviews with the pastors, surveys of priests, and analysis of public statements made by pastors at each parish, I document the tone and content of political messages delivered by priests at each parish. This information is combined with data gleaned from surveys administered to a sample of parishioners from each parish. By comparing survey results across parishes, each of which is headed by a priest who delivers political messages that are unique in both tenor and content, a portrait emerges that indicates that priests may indeed be politically influential, but that the political influence of the clergy is likely to be modest in magnitude and to operate through indirect as well as direct channels.

The research and findings presented here serve three main purposes. First, drawing on the extensive scholarly literature on political communication and religion and politics, I develop a theory of how and why Catholic priests might plausibly be expected to exercise significant political influence. Second, the results of a variety of tests of priestly influence provide a new and improved understanding of the political attitudes of American Catholics, and, by providing an enhanced understanding of the politics of adherents to such a large religious tradition, they advance our understanding of American politics in general. Third, by providing an account of the ways in which the political attitudes and voting decisions of American Catholics are influenced by their parish priests, this book advances the growing subfield of religion and politics, one of the primary shortcomings of which is that, while religious leaders have often been assumed to wield substantial influence with their congregations, this influence has not been empirically demonstrated.[2]

Plan of the Book

Chapter 1 opens with a discussion of the theoretical background that makes it reasonable to suspect that priests exercise significant political influence with their parishioners. More specifically, chapter 1 draws heavily on work in the subfields of religion and politics, political communication, and voting behavior to show how, and under what circumstances, priests might be looked to as political leaders and cue-givers. In addition, chapter 1 provides a more complete explication of Church teachings on contemporary political issues, and it contains an explanation of the precise mechanisms through which priests are able to exercise political influence. Chapter 2 analyzes data from the Notre Dame Study of Catholic Parish Life. This analysis indicates that Catholic priests may have the potential to influence the opinions of their parishioners with regard to a variety of political issues, including political ideologies.

Chapter 3 provides a more detailed description of the methodology employed in carrying out the case studies of local Catholic parishes. It also documents the variety and heterogeneity (in both style and substance) of the political messages to which parishioners

at different parishes are exposed by discussing the results of interviews conducted with pastors at each of the parishes participating
in the case studies. Chapter 4 provides additional empirical support
for the claims made in chapter 3 by summarizing the results of a
content analysis of parish bulletins along with information from
surveys administered to priests at each parish. Chapter 5 looks closely
at the survey data collected at each of the parishes included in the
case studies. It documents both the potential for, and the limitations on, priestly influence by showing that priestly political influence, though important, is largely subtle and indirect. Finally, the
concluding chapter summarizes the salient findings presented in the
preceding chapters, considers the implications for political scientists
and political actors alike, and provides some suggestions for potentially fruitful avenues of future research.

Notes

1. But see Perl and McClintock 2001. They argue that evidence that opinions regarding abortion are linked to opinions regarding capital punishment and welfare
reform among some Catholics suggests that the consistent ethic of life may in fact be
somewhat influential.

2. This book constitutes an early step on the road to understanding the political influence of clergy in the United States, and it takes a close look at Catholics
for two reasons. First, because of their numbers, Catholics have the potential to
wield significant power in American politics. Second, the fact that Catholic
parishioners do not hire or fire their priests helps to alleviate concerns about the
direction of any apparent influence that is observed. Of course, this is not to argue
that investigating clergy influence by looking specifically at Catholics provides
perfect assurance that findings consistent with priestly influence are, in fact, evidence of influence flowing from priests to parishioners, and not in the opposite
direction. Bishops and other diocesan officials charged with assigning priests to
parishes may, for instance, attempt to match priests with compatible parishes. Additionally, there are some Catholics who choose to attend Mass at parishes other
than their own territorial parish, and some who engage in this practice may do so
precisely because of certain characteristics of the priests at particular parishes. It
may also be the case that some Catholics who disapprove of their parish priests
may cease attending Mass altogether. For these reasons, a certain degree of caution
must be exercised in interpreting correlations between priests' political attitudes
or public messages and the political attitudes of their parishioners as evidence of

priestly influence. But while these concerns are important and must be borne in mind when investigating clergy influence, they are relatively less serious when one considers the Catholic case, since parishioners do not play a direct role in choosing their priests, than when one considers clergy influence in other denominations.

chapter one
A Theory of Priestly Influence

 It is plausible to suspect that Catholic clergy may be important sources of political influence for American Catholics, but there are also reasons to think that the ability of clergy to wield political influence may be sharply limited. It is not the case, for instance, that messages from elites are always received and correctly perceived by those exposed to them. Nor is the importance of religion in American politics self-evident. Before embarking on a more elaborate theory of priestly influence on the political attitudes of Catholic parishioners, therefore, it is necessary to consider the existing literature on political communication and voting behavior, as well as recent developments in the subfield of religion and politics. This discussion will demonstrate how the theory and models to be subsequently proposed emerge from these literatures and help to determine why, and under what circumstances, the theory proposed here may be applicable.

Political Communication and Persuasion

Although the question of interest here concerns the extent to which—and the circumstances under which—Catholic priests influence the political attitudes and behavior of their parishioners, the theoretical justification of the study comes largely from the literature on political communications (especially from research on the effects of mass media) and from research on voting behavior (more specifically, from recent research that has sought to demonstrate the rationality of American voters).

Researchers in the early and middle parts of the twentieth century, spurred by rapid progress in the field of communications technology, undertook numerous investigations into the effects of messages emanating from the mass media on the attitudes and beliefs of the general public. They expected to find evidence that the public was greatly influenced by information carried in the mass media, and they were concerned about the implications for democratic government posed by attempts at propaganda and persuasion. Their expectations, and their fears, however, were not realized. Early research into the effects of mass media found little evidence of discernible influence on the beliefs and attitudes of the public. With regard to politics, the work of researchers in the Columbia school indicated that the mass media in general, and political campaigns in particular, did not exercise large persuasive influence over a vulnerable public, but rather reinforced preexisting considerations (Berelson, Lazarsfeld, and McPhee 1954; Lazarsfeld, Berelson, and Gaudet 1944). By 1960, Klapper was able to review and summarize the existing body of research on media effects and to argue persuasively that any effects the media had on public opinion were minimal (Klapper 1960). For years thereafter, research into media effects on political attitudes and behavior waned as the "minimal effects" model of media influence held sway.

By the 1970s, however, research into media effects reemerged as a field of widespread scholarly inquiry. The notion that information carried in the media, to which virtually the entirety of the American population was continually exposed, could actually have no effect on attitudes and beliefs seemed unlikely. In an effort to improve upon earlier scholarly efforts to detect large and dramatic media influences on attitudes and beliefs, researchers began to refine their efforts to document more subtle media effects. One of the earliest studies to uncover evidence of media effects determined that one possible influence of media was to perform an agenda-setting function with regard to politics (McCombs and Shaw 1972). In their study of undecided voters in the 1968 presidential general election campaign, McCombs and Shaw discovered a high degree of correlation between topics covered in the media and problems identified by voters as the most important issues of the campaign. Although these results were tentative—there was no way to be sure that the correlation between media coverage and public opinion evidenced the media's influence rather than the media's response to public interest in certain topics—they were consistent with the agenda-setting hypothesis. The work of McCombs and Shaw implied that, whereas the media may not have the ability to change individual opinions on issues in one direction or another, they may have the ability, by covering some topics and ignoring others, to influence the degree to which the public considers some problems and issues to be of high importance and others to be of relatively less importance.

This rekindled research into media effects was continued and refined through the 1980s and 1990s. Iyengar and Kinder, for instance, built and expanded upon the foundations laid by McCombs and Shaw and others to demonstrate conclusively the existence of the agenda-setting influence of mass media (Iyengar and Kinder 1987). Whereas McCombs and Shaw were simply able to demonstrate a correlation between media coverage and the degree of importance accorded certain problems by the general public, the experimental design employed by Iyengar and Kinder left no doubt as to the direction of causality in the agenda-setting process. In their experiments, participants who viewed segments of news programs later reported considering those issues covered in the news programs to be of the utmost importance on the contemporary political agenda. Furthermore, these experimental results were borne out by analysis of public opinion polls and content analysis of information simultaneously carried in the mass media.

In addition to firmly establishing the existence of the agenda-setting effect, Iyengar and Kinder also uncovered a more subtle potential effect of the mass media on public opinion: the priming effect. They demonstrated that "by calling attention to some matters while ignoring others," the media "influences the standards by which governments, presidents, policies, and candidates for public office are judged" (1987, 63). Media priming is highly significant for politics in general, and may even have the potential to affect electoral outcomes (Krosnick and Kinder 1990; Mendelsohn 1996; Valentino 1999; Valentino, Hutchings, and White 2002).

This burgeoning research on media effects is directly relevant to this book's focus on the influence of priests on the political attitudes and behavior of their parishioners. In addition to demonstrating the effects of exposure to information carried in mass media, these studies implicitly demonstrate the effectiveness and influence of messages emanating from political elites. Messages disseminated by the media originate from elites, whether they be trusted anchormen, investigative reporters, public officials, or political activists. Whereas early research cast doubt on the potential impact of mass media and instead posited that interpersonal communications were of greater importance in shaping political attitudes (Berelson, Lazarsfeld, and McPhee 1954; Lazarsfeld, Berelson, and Gaudet 1944), these new findings suggest that elite communications can be of paramount importance in explaining political beliefs and behavior. Moreover, if elite messages mediated through television, radio, and print have the capacity to influence public opinion, there is no theoretical reason to suspect that elite messages that are not so mediated should not have similar effects. And while the work of McCombs and Shaw, Iyengar and Kinder, and other researchers served to rekindle interest in the search for media effects, more recent research has delved even more deeply into the processes and circumstances through which elite communications can be expected to influence public opinion (Lodge, Steenbergen, and Brau 1995; Popkin 1994; Sniderman, Brody, and Tetlock 1991; Zaller 1992). This more advanced research provides additional reason to suspect that Catholic priests may be able to influence Catholic parishioners' attitudes and political behavior.

While the early reconsideration of the "minimal effects" model of media influence indicated that media effects may be subtle but are certainly not minimal, other work suggests that media effects should more accurately be characterized as neither minimal nor subtle (Entman 1989; Dalton, Beck, and Huckfeldt 1998; Zaller 1992, 1996). Zaller, for instance, argues that significant media effects exist but remain largely hidden because of research poorly designed to reveal them. He points out, for example, that anticipating large shifts in opinion as the result of persuasive media communications (as much of the media effects literature does) is usually inappropriate, since most of the time there is more than one message prevalent in the media (Zaller 1996). His own research provides support for the proposition that the media is highly important, and perhaps even decisive, in shaping public opinion.

But Zaller does more than assert and provide evidence to demonstrate that the mass media are vitally important in shaping public opinion; he also provides a theoretical justification for why and how this is so (Zaller 1992). Using previous research on the nature of public opinion as his point of departure (especially Converse 1964; Achen 1975), Zaller asserts that individuals do not possess opinions about public issues of political importance. Instead, they form opinions on specific issues only when conditions demand that they do so (as in the context of responding to a survey). The opinion formulated in response to any particular stimuli is a product of considerations, or reasons "that might induce an individual to decide a political issue one way or the other," that are already present in the mind (Zaller 1992, 40). Individuals are likely to have a large number of various and conflicting considerations in their mind at any given time. With regard to abortion, for example, most people are likely to possess several pro-choice and several pro-life considerations (very few, if any, individuals will have all pro-choice or all pro-life considerations). When asked a question about abortion, the individual's response will be determined by the considerations that are brought to the front of the mind; if more pro-choice considerations are brought to the front of the mind, the individual will give a pro-choice response, and vice versa. According to Zaller, the process through which considerations are brought to the front of the mind is not random. Instead, the accessibility of various considerations is determined in part by how recently they have been activated. If recent media content has highlighted pro-choice considerations, then pro-choice considerations are likely to be accessed when an individual is asked his or her opinion about abortion. Even the wording and order of survey questions can influence the likelihood that certain considerations, and not others, will be activated.

Although Zaller's model of opinion formation is one of the most innovative and influential developments of the last decade in political science, it has not necessarily carried the day. Lodge and his colleagues, for instance, argue that an online model of opinion formation, in which individuals utilize new information to update their opinions and then discard the actual information itself, is a more accurate description of opinion formation than is Zaller's (Lodge, Steenbergen, and Brau 1995).[1] Nevertheless, Zaller's work provides an important justification for the theory and hypotheses of interest in this book. It is my assertion that Catholic priests have the potential to influence the considerations of their parishioners. For instance, when responding to survey questions about abortion, choosing which political party to identify with, and deciding whom to vote for in an election, parishioners whose priest emphasizes Church teachings on abortion as opposed to Church teachings on economic issues are more likely to have more pro-life considerations—and to have more pro-life considerations that are cognitively accessible—than parishioners from other parishes.

While Zaller focuses on the influence of the media, other recent research on political decision making and voting behavior demonstrates the wide range of sources from which citizens are able to draw information used to make political decisions. Much of this recent research is a reaction to the earlier prevailing school of thought regarding political attitude formation and decision making typified by the work of Converse (1964). In "The Nature of Belief Systems in Mass Publics," Converse set the tone for a generation of researchers by documenting the ways in which Americans form and possess (or, perhaps more accurately, fail to form and possess) political attitudes. He pointed out that responses to opinion surveys demonstrated an astonishingly high degree of instability. Individuals gave responses to questions that were highly variable over time, and their responses to some questions often appeared to be almost wholly independent of their answers to other, theoretically related, questions. Converse concluded that a large proportion of the American populace essentially did not possess well-formed attitudes with regard to most political issues.

To be sure, Converse's thesis did not go unchallenged for long. Achen, for instance, argued that the response instability observed by Converse was not so much a product of citizens' nonattitudes as it was a function of unreliable survey questions (Achen 1975). Sullivan, Piereson, and Marcus made a similar argument, pointing out that the apparent increase in ideological constraint observed in the period immediately following Converse's work was caused not by the highly charged political atmosphere of the mid- to late 1960s (as many suggested), but by improvements in survey questions (Sullivan, Piereson, and Marcus 1978). Scholars in recent years have proposed a more subtle challenge to the notion, implicit in Converse's work, that citizens and voters are irrational (Page and Shapiro 1992; Popkin 1994; Sniderman, Brody, and Tetlock 1991).[2] This school of thought argues that, while voters may not exhibit attitude consistency and think ideologically in the ways desired by some democratic theorists, they are nonetheless able to make sense of the political world and make reasonable political decisions. Perhaps the most important work in this vein for the purposes of this discussion is that of Samuel Popkin. In *The Reasoning Voter*, Popkin argues that experiences from everyday life can and should be expected to provide individuals with political information, as well as with cues that are helpful in making political decisions. He points out that "political information is acquired while making individual economic decisions and navigating daily life: shoppers learn about inflation of retail prices; home buyers find out about the trends in mortgage-loan interest rates; owners of stock follow the

Dow-Jones averages" (Popkin 1994, 24). It is my expectation, and a logical implication of the work of Popkin and others, that one such potential source of political information and cue-giving for American Catholics is their parish priests. Indeed, given their frequency of exposure to messages delivered by priests (recall from the introductory chapter that approximately 60 percent of Catholics report attending Mass at least once a month) it would be surprising if priests did not constitute an important source of political information and cue-giving.

In sum, recent research in political communication and voting behavior provides support for the idea that Catholic priests may be a significant source of political influence for Catholic parishioners. Research in political communication has demonstrated the ability of elite actors, if not actually to cause frequent and fundamental attitude change, at least to influence the contents of the political agenda and the considerations upon which political attitudes and electoral decisions are formed. In addition, recent work in the field of voting behavior has demonstrated the ability of citizens to collect information and cues during the course of their everyday activities. Both findings lead to the highly plausible assertion that priests have the potential to be politically influential.

Of course, this is not the first, nor will it be the last, assertion that religion, and religious communication, can influence the political behavior of citizens. Indeed, there is a rich literature addressing the interaction of religion and politics. I turn now to a discussion of this literature so as to demonstrate the ways in which the questions addressed here represent an outgrowth of, but also a different and new direction in, the existing research on religion and politics.

The Importance of Religion in American Politics

As pointed out in the introduction, religion has always been an important factor in American politics, and there is every indication that this will continue to be true for the foreseeable future. Indeed, the rise of the Christian right in the 1980s and the waging of a culture war in recent decades, pitting competing worldviews against each other, suggest that religious issues will be at the heart of American politics well into the twenty-first century.[3] Accordingly, the ways in which religious beliefs and practices influence the political attitudes and behavior of Americans have, in recent years, attracted much attention from scholars, and the salient findings of their research deserve attention here. I focus particularly on the growing literature on the contextual effects of religious affiliation on political behavior, for that literature, like this project, focuses explicitly on the intersection of religion and political communication.

The contemporary literature addressing the influence of contextual effects on political opinions and attitudes is largely an outgrowth of the work of the Columbia school, which posited that group affiliation was one of the keys to understanding the political behavior of Americans (Berelson, Lazarsfeld, and McPhee 1954; Lazarsfeld, Berelson, and Gaudet 1944). With the publication of *The American Voter* in 1960, however, much work in political science adopted a more individualistic approach to the study of political behavior (Campbell et al. 1960). More recently, a small but growing group of scholars, influenced by the Columbia school, dissatisfied with the limitations of analysis of individual attitudes, and desirous of obtaining a better understanding of the origins of such attitudes, has undertaken research to determine the ways in which the behavior and attitudes of individuals are influenced by their surrounding environments or contexts. For practical reasons, much of this literature considers the effects of geographic context (such as neighborhood context or county context) on political attitudes. Data regarding the political context of a neighborhood or county are simply more readily available than are data regarding the political context of potentially important environments such as the workplace or social networks (but see Finifter 1974; Huckfeldt and Sprague 1995). That said, an important (and growing) subset of the literature on political contexts seeks to understand the importance of churches, as political contexts, for shaping individual attitudes (Djupe and Gilbert 2002a, 2002b, 2006; Gilbert 1993; Huck-feldt and Sprague 1995; Huckfeldt, Plutzer, and Sprague 1993; Jelen 1992; Wald, Owen, and Hill 1988). Wald, Owen, and Hill, for instance, in their study of more than twenty Protestant congregations in the Gainesville, Florida area, find that the level of theological conservatism of one's congregation is a strong predictor of individual political conservatism (1988). They find that congregational theological conservatism "remains a powerful predictor of moral conservatism" even after controlling for other potential influences on moral political conservatism, including party identification, race, age, educational attainment, and marital status (543).

As part of their broader consideration of contextual effects on political behavior, Huckfeldt and Sprague and colleagues investigate the potential for churches to exercise such contextual effects. They determine that, for Protestants, the partisanship of particular congregations has a strong influence on the partisanship of individuals over and above the influence exercised by neighborhood contexts (Huckfeldt and Sprague 1995; Huckfeldt, Plutzer, and Sprague 1993). Similarly, parish context emits a strong influence on individual attitudes toward abortion (at least for Protestants), though "the effect of parishes is . . . mediated by exposure. Regular attenders (of church services) are more likely to be affected than infrequent attenders" (Huckfeldt, Plutzer, and Sprague 1993, 377). This evidence, which documents the importance of political communication in a religious context in shaping individuals' political attitudes, provides direct support for the notion that clergy may be consequential sources of political communication and influence.

Christopher Gilbert, like Huckfeldt and Sprague and colleagues, relies on the unique opportunities provided by the South Bend Community Study data as the basis for his book, *The Impact of Churches on Political Behavior* (1993). Gilbert's extensive study confirmed many of the findings suggested by previous work, particularly that the context of the congregation to which an individual belongs (that is, aggregate measures of congregational attitudes and the attitudes of those identified as discussion partners) can, in many situations, exercise considerable influence on the political attitudes of individuals. He demonstrates, for instance, that though church context appears not to play a formidable role in influencing party identification, "the voting behavior of the church as a whole . . . plays a strong role in determining individual voting choices. This influence does not vary across religions; it is very consistent in direction and quite consistent in intensity" (88). Gilbert also shows that church context can be an important predictor of individual attitudes with regard to certain political issues, arguing that "church context significantly affects attitudes on issues that have an explicit moral or religious dimension—abortion and school prayer, for example" (109). Similarly, Djupe and Gilbert's studies of Episcopalian and Evangelical Lutheran Church in America congregations reveal that mean church opinion and discussion-partner ideology are both positively correlated with individuals' attitudes on gay rights, school prayer, and abortion (Djupe and Gilbert 2002b). They also show that participation in small church groups facilitates civic skill building, especially for individuals who feel similar to others in the small group in which they participate, and for individuals who feel religiously isolated from their neighbors (Djupe and Gilbert 2006). In short, as Gilbert argues, much evidence suggests "that churches are significant sources of political cues, and that churches do affect the political actions and beliefs of their members" (1993, 171).

Clearly, much recent research has definitively established the influence of religious contexts on political behavior. Much of the research on context effects generally, however, and on religious contexts specifically—and with regard to context in Catholic parishes especially—begs the question of where the context comes from. That is, how is the context of a particular congregation established? Is it simply a product of the aggregation or interaction of the beliefs and attitudes brought to it by individual congregants? It seems likely that religious elites, including pastors and priests, might play an important role in establishing the context in a given congregation, and especially in Catholic parishes, where priests are not chosen by their parishioners.

This is a concern that has been considered by scholars working on contextual effects. Wald and colleagues, for instance, point out that "there are ample opportunities for church authorities to communicate political messages through direct channels such as sermons, pastoral messages, adult education classes, poster displays, and church publications" (Wald, Owen, and Hill 1988, 532–33). Other scholars have asserted the importance of clergy as political leaders as well, even though this capacity has not been empirically demonstrated (Beatty and Walter 1989; Djupe and Gilbert 2002c, 2003; Jelen 2003; Kohut et al. 2000; Layman 2001). Beatty and Walter, for instance, in their 1988 study, describe "clergy as the gatekeepers of the group process; they help to shape the religion and politics connection, and they communicate that connection or translation to their congregations or religious groups" (1989, 130). More recently, in a study of the politics of Catholic priests, Jelen points out that "there exist ample reasons to study the political attitudes and activities of Roman Catholic priests. Priests provide the most consistent contact between a Church hierarchy that is occasionally politically assertive, and a laity that, by its very size, constitutes an important electoral force in American elections. The extent and nature of the cues provided by Catholic priests are at least potentially quite consequential for politics in the United States" (Jelen 2003, 592).

Of course, these assertions are entirely plausible. Indeed, it is the very reasonableness of these assertions that make this project necessary and useful. The fact remains, nonetheless, that the political influence of clergy, including Catholic clergy, has yet to be fully and empirically demonstrated (but see Bjarnason and Welch 2004; Smith 2005). To be sure, there have been previous efforts to discern whether or not religious elites wield political influence with their adherents. Huckfeldt, Plutzer, and Sprague, for instance, examine the extent to which the theological position of churches (as opposed to the political opinions of congregants or parishioners) influence individual attitudes about abortion. They find that, when Catholics and non-Catholics are considered separately, there is relatively little correlation between the theological positions of churches on abortion and the attitudes toward abortion expressed by church members. They demonstrate that "the theological position of the church explains, at maximum, 2% of the variation in parishioner attitudes," and show that their original contextual measure "provides much more statistical purchase than the clergy-reported theological position" (Huckfeldt, Plutzer, and Sprague 1993, 379). Their analysis, however, does not take into account the messages actually delivered by clergy to parishioners, which is problematic. Consider, for example, a situation in which a church or church leaders are, for theological reasons, opposed to legalized abortion. If this opposition is rarely expressed, or if other political concerns are addressed with more emphasis or regularity (as often happens in Catholic parishes), it is not reasonable to suspect that the theological position of the church will have a significant impact on the attitudes of church members. In other words, to investigate the influence of religious elites in explaining political attitudes of individuals, it is necessary to consider the content of the messages coming from church leaders.

This shortcoming of the religion and politics literature, in which the potential for a high degree of clergy influence has been assumed rather than demonstrated, has been recognized by several leading scholars. Jelen, for example, points out that "considerably less is known" about the consequences of clergy political activity as opposed to the factors motivating clergy political activity (2001, 16–17). Similarly, Guth, addressing the subfield of religion and politics generally, acknowledges that "although there is still much to be done in delineating the political *choices* made by clergy, the most obdurate problem is discovering the *consequences* of their activity" (2001, 41). Finally, Fetzer asserts that "although the possibility of pastoral influence is intuitively appealing and often hypothesized . . . , surprisingly little empirical research seems to have directly tested its validity" (2001, 177). Fetzer, however, goes on to demonstrate empirically that Anabaptist ministers do in fact appear to exercise significant influence over their congregants' beliefs regarding war and pacifism.

In a similar vein, a recent article by Bjarnason and Welch suggests that Catholics' attitudes regarding capital punishment may be influenced by their pastors (2004). They persuasively argue in part that "parishioners as a whole can be expected to be less supportive of the death penalty when their parish priest is personally more strongly opposed to such punishment" (Bjarnason and Welch 2004, 106). Indeed, their analysis demonstrates that parishioners who belonged to parishes headed by pastors who were strongly opposed to capital punishment were, on average, significantly more opposed to capital punishment than were their counterparts in parishes headed by pastors who were less adamantly opposed to the death penalty. This project, like the work of Fetzer and Bjarnason and Welch, begins to alleviate this shortcoming in the religion and politics literature by attempting directly to assess the influence of priestly communications on the attitudes and political behavior of Catholic parishioners. It is also the case that, to truly get a handle on the extent of contextual effects in religious communities, it is essential to consider the extent to which the context is a product of elite leadership. This book begins to do that as well.

There are, then, several reasons to suspect that messages delivered to parishioners by Catholic priests may be influential in shaping the political attitudes of individual Catholics. The political communications literature suggests that elite communications, generally speaking, potentially have a variety of dramatic political effects. The literature on religion and politics, and on the contextual effects of religion in particular, further indicates that religious variables continue to be of fundamental importance in understanding political behavior. That said, however, several explanations of Catholic political attitudes and behavior currently exist. To complete the demonstration of the usefulness of this project, it is necessary to consider where these existing explanations come up short, and why a new investigation of Catholic political behavior is important.

Current Explanations of Catholic Political Behavior

There are several competing explanations of Catholic political attitudes and voting habits. Many scholars argue that the Catholic vote has become less monolithically Democratic due in large part to simple changes in Catholic demographics (Gerner 1995; Leege et al. 2002; Prendergast 1999; Reichley 1986; but see Brewer 2003; Penning 1986).[4] For much of the early part of the twentieth century, the Catholic population was poorer, less well-educated, and included more recent immigrants as compared with the rest of the population. Largely as a result, Catholics were much more likely than many other groups to vote Democratic. Over time, however, as Catholics caught up with the rest of the population in terms of wealth and education, so too did Catholic voting patterns come to resemble more closely those of the rest of the country. Gerner points out that, according to William Dinges, the conservative political trend among Catholics "is a by-product of Catholic upward mobility. Larger numbers of educated and affluent Catholics have 'produced a class transformation that leads inevitably to more of them voting Republican'" (1995, 19).

This explanation of Catholic voting habits is certainly helpful and informative. It leaves out, however, the extent to which religion may be important in shaping Catholics' political attitudes and behavior. But as Wald points out, the United States is "an advanced industrial society in which religion" exercises "a tenacious hold on the public mind and strongly [influences] the conduct of political life" (1997, 8). This should hold true for Catholics as well as for other religious groups; thus, any comprehensive examination of Catholic voting patterns must include some account of the influence of the religion itself.

Indeed, there are many studies of Catholic political attitudes that consider the impact of religious aspects of Catholicism on political variables. Wilcox, Jelen, and Leege, for example, attempt to differentiate between the religious identities of Catholics, utilizing the 1989 National Election Studies (NES) Pilot Study, which asked Catholics whether they considered themselves to be traditionalist Catholics (i.e., supportive of pre-Vatican II doctrine and liturgy), post-Vatican II Catholics (i.e., "supportive of the reforms" of Vatican II), ethnic Catholics (i.e., Irish, Polish), or charismatic Catholics. They determined that "charismatic and traditionalist Catholics take significantly more conservative positions on the moral traditionalism scale than do other Catholics, while post-Vatican II Catholics take more liberal positions" (1993, 82). Additionally, Catholics who identified themselves as charismatic, traditionalist, or post-Vatican II all took "more conservative positions on social issues" than did Catholics who refused to adopt a label. Although the small number of Catholics in the sample for the 1989 NES Pilot Study requires that Wilcox, Jelen, and Leege's results be interpreted as "preliminary," their results suggest that knowing the "specific identity of a Catholic" can provide important additional purchase over and above that gained from simply knowing whether one is Catholic or not (1993, 90–91).

Wald, Kellstedt, and Leege determined that for Catholics, as for those of other religions, involvement in church activities was a key predictor of certain political attitudes. Specifically, they found that while Catholics "were significantly more pro-choice than the nonreligious," they "turned against liberal abortion laws as a consequence of high levels of church involvement" (1993, 134). Their research confirmed that "the message transmitted by the church was apparently perceived and internalized by the strongly involved congregant" (134).

In another study, Kellstedt and Smidt investigated the link between views of the Bible and political attitudes. Using NES data, they examined two groups of religious people: those who considered the Bible to be the actual, literal word of God, and those who believed the Bible to be the inspired word of God. They found that, across several religious traditions, one's view of the Bible was significantly related to party identification and presidential vote choice. For Catholics specifically, one's view of the Bible was related to one's attitude about abortion. Those Catholics who considered the Bible to be the actual word of God were significantly more opposed to abortion than were those Catholics who considered the Bible to be the inspired word of God (Kellstedt and Smidt 1993).

Leege—and later Leege and Welch—asserted that Catholic political attitudes are related to certain foundational religious beliefs (Leege 1988; Leege and Welch 1989). Using data from the Notre Dame Study of Catholic Parish Life, they characterized Catholics as either individualist, communitarian, integrated (somewhere between individualist and communitarian), or anomalous. These classifications were based upon respondents' answers to questions about the fundamental problem of human existence, how religion responds to that problem, and what the solution to the problem is. Those who "used me, my problems, my salvation as the frame of reference were classified as religious individualists." Conversely, Leege and Welch classified "those for whom relationships, intergroup conflict, and community concerns were clearly the frame of reference" as "religious communitarians" (Leege 1988, 725). They found that, for Catholics, religious individualism was related to social conservatism, whereas religious communitarianism was related to social liberalism. More specifically, they determined that religious individualists were more conservative than were religious communitarians with regard to "women's rights, male-female family roles, the threat of secular humanism, and sexuality" (Leege 1988, 726). Although their measure of religious communitarianism and individualism is not the only, nor the best, predictor of Catholic attitudes across all political issues (demographic variables like income, for example, remain important factors in determining support for disarmament and defense spending), the work of Leege and Welch clearly demonstrates that religious beliefs and considerations have the potential to influence the political attitudes of Catholics.

Finally, Leege and Welch determined that Catholics' sociopolitical attitudes can also be predicted by both religious imagery and religious evangelicalism. With regard to religious imagery, they found that "those parishioners who view God as judgelike (as opposed to God as companion, savior, or father) are much more likely to take conservative positions on most of the issues we studied" (Welch and Leege 1988, 547). Furthermore, just as a judgelike image of God was related to social conservatism, so too was evangelicalism. Catholics who indicated that they read the Bible on their own, study the Bible as part of a group, pray with friends or family, share religious beliefs with other Catholics, and say grace before meals were classified as evangelically oriented. Leege and Welch concluded that "Catholics who practice evangelical-style patterns of devotion take more 'conservative' positions on issues relating to abortion, premarital cohabitation, and the male's role as sole economic 'breadwinner' for the family" (Welch and Leege 1991, 40).

These are all persuasive explanations for Catholic political attitudes and behaviors. But most of them leave unexamined the question of the importance and political significance of the role of the parish priest, who is a central actor in the religious life of Catholic parishioners. Parish priests, by virtue of their status as the most frequent point of contact between the Church itself and Catholic parishioners, might plausibly be expected to be a source of guidance and influence, on Catholic political attitudes as well as on the religious beliefs that so much research demonstrates are politically consequential. A consideration of Catholic political attitudes that takes into account the impact of messages emanating from parish priests will provide a more complete understanding of the politics of this important group.

A Theory of Priestly Influence on Catholic Politics

Existing research on political communications demonstrates the importance of elite influence on individual political attitudes. The religion and politics literature, especially that dealing with religious contexts, indicates the potential influence of religious factors on political beliefs (although, as already mentioned, it leaves unanswered the question about the extent of elite influence in establishing a particular context). This project draws on, and contributes to, the literature on elite political communications by considering the extent to which, and the circumstances under which, priests influence the political beliefs and attitudes of their parishioners. In addition, it advances the field of political behavior generally, and the literature on religion and politics specifically, by investigating a new theory of Catholic political behavior.

Of course, the Catholic Church is not primarily a political institution. The Church does not endorse particular candidates for public office, nor is it officially affiliated with any political party. That said, the institutional Church does expend considerable effort in attempting to provide both Catholics and non-Catholics alike with guidance in formulating opinions and making political and electoral decisions. As Pope John XXIII wrote in his encyclical *Mater et magistra*, "though the Church's first care must be for souls . . . she concerns herself too with the exigencies of man's daily life, with his livelihood and education, and his general, temporal welfare and prosperity" (1961, 159–60). Popes regularly publish encyclical letters that address important public policy questions facing not only the United States, but all nations. In the United States, the U.S. Conference of Catholic Bishops (USCCB) issues pastoral letters and, more frequently, makes less formal public statements on myriad public issues. In addition, in each presidential election year since 1976, the U.S. bishops have issued a statement elucidating the Church's views on currently salient issues and political problems, and urging Catholics to consider such concerns in making electoral decisions. Finally, the *Catechism of the Catholic Church*, a "statement of the Church's faith and of Catholic doctrine" and "a sure norm for teaching the faith and thus a valid and legitimate instrument for ecclesial communion," provides general statements regarding Church teaching on various social and political issues (*Catechism* 1997, 5–6).

In many ways and through many outlets, therefore, the Church has articulated clear positions on many issues of public concern. Church teaching on each of five issue domains (economic issues, capital punishment, foreign affairs, sexual morality, and abortion) is particularly relevant for contemporary American politics. Throughout its two thousand-year history, the Catholic Church has been committed to the idea that the poor and downtrodden should receive care and assistance from those with the means to help them. As Pope John Paul II wrote, "the church's social teaching finds its source in sacred scripture . . . and especially in the Gospel and the writings of the apostles. From the beginning it was part of the church's teaching" (1981, 322). Over the course of the last century Catholic popes have published a series of encyclical letters designed specifically to address the challenges posed by the modern economy and to elaborate on Catholic social teaching. Beginning with Pope Leo XIII's 1891 encyclical letter *Rerum novarum*, the Church has consistently held that, when circumstances require, the state has a duty to provide for the material well-being of those in need. According to Leo XIII, "when there is a question of defending the rights of individuals, the poor and badly off have a claim to especial consideration. The richer class have many ways of shielding themselves, and stand less in need of help from the state; whereas the mass of the poor have no resources of their own to fall back upon, and must chiefly depend upon the assistance of the State. . . . It is for this reason that wage-earners, since they mostly belong in the mass of the needy, should be specially cared for and protected by government" (41). Furthermore, in considering some of the problems posed by the capitalist system—especially the tendency for working people and wage earners to be relatively (sometimes grindingly) poor and owners of capital to be relatively well off—*Rerum novarum* held that "the public administration must duly and solicitously provide for the welfare and the comfort of the working classes; otherwise, that law of justice will be violated which ordains that each man shall have his due" (39).[5]

Over the course of the twentieth century, a succession of Catholic popes built upon the foundations laid by Leo XIII in *Rerum novarum* by continuing to urge both private citizens and public authorities to care for the poor. In *Pacem in terris*, published in 1963, Pope John XXIII argued that all persons have a right to all that is necessary for subsistence and good health. "Beginning our discussion of the rights of man," he wrote, "we see that every man has the right to life, to bodily integrity, and to the means which are suitable for the proper development of life; these are primarily food, clothing, shelter, rest, medical care, and finally the necessary social services. Therefore a human being also has the right to security in cases of sickness, inability to work, widowhood, old age, unemployment, or in any other case in which he is deprived of the means of subsistence through no fault of his own" (1963, 228).

John XXIII went on to affirm that individuals possess both the "right . . . to an opportunity to work" and the "right to a wage determined according to criteria of justice, and sufficient, therefore, in proportion to the available resources, to give the worker and his family a standard of living in keeping with the dignity of the human person" (1963, 230–31). These rights, furthermore, are to be ensured by government, for "if any government does not acknowledge the rights of man or violates them, it not only fails in its duty, but its orders completely lack juridical force" (238). More recently, Pope John Paul II, in his 1991 encyclical *Centesimus annus*, wrote that "society and the State must ensure wage levels adequate for the maintenance of the worker and his family, including a certain amount for savings" (1991, 470).

Catholic social teaching has been applied specifically to the American situation by the USCCB, perhaps most famously in their 1986 pastoral letter *Economic Justice for All*. In that document, the U.S. bishops argued that "when people are without a chance to earn a living, and must go hungry and homeless, they are being denied basic rights. Society must ensure that these rights are protected" (USCCB 2000, 17). The letter went on to advocate an increase in the minimum wage, and to argue that, with regard to welfare programs, "national minimum benefit levels and eligibility standards in cash assistance programs" should be established (82). Clearly, then, the institutional Church, including a succession of popes and American bishops, have adopted and promoted clear teachings with respect to economic issues, advocating consistently on behalf of the poor and disadvantaged.

In addition to its advocacy on behalf of increased societal and governmental attention to the plight of the poor, the Church has also in recent decades been a fervent opponent of capital punishment. The Church concedes that, "assuming that the guilty party's identity and responsibility have been fully determined, the traditional teaching of the Church does not exclude recourse to the death penalty, if this is the only possible way of effectively defending human lives against the unjust aggressor" (*Catechism* 604–05). Two paragraphs later, however, the *Catechism*, drawing on *Evangelium vitae*, stipulates that "today, in fact . . . the cases in which the execution of the offender is an absolute necessity 'are very rare, if not practically non-existent' " (605). Pope John Paul II was a dedicated opponent of the death penalty. He wrote in *Evangelium vitae*, for instance, that "modern society in fact has the means of effectively suppressing crime by rendering criminals harmless without definitively denying them the chance to reform" (1995, 20). A similar point was made by the U.S. bishops in their 1980 statement on capital punishment, in which they argued that "in the conditions of contemporary American society, the legitimate purposes of punishment do not justify the imposition of the death penalty. Furthermore, we believe that there are serious considerations which should prompt Christians and all Americans to support the abolition of capital punishment" (Nolan 1984, 430).

When it comes to issues of foreign policy and national defense, the position of the Church is less clear. On the one hand, the Church acknowledges and respects the right and duty of nations to provide militarily for their own defense. Although the Church is therefore not an advocate of absolute pacifism, the general thrust of Catholic teaching has in recent decades (and in contrast to earlier periods in American history) been more in line with the thinking of foreign policy doves than with that of hawks. Thus in their 1983 pastoral letter *The Challenge of Peace*, published during the height of the U.S.–Soviet arms race, the American bishops urged caution and restraint upon both nations (USCCB 1983). Although the letter stopped short of calling for a unilateral freeze in the development of nuclear weapons, it did encourage the two superpowers to negotiate a bilateral freeze and to agree to reductions in existing arsenals. More generally, the Church has sought to be an advocate for peace, and to encourage nations to think of war and military conflict only as a last resort and as a legitimate option only insofar as the reasons for military action correspond to Catholic just war teaching.

The Church's position on abortion is well-known. According to the *Catechism of the Catholic Church*, "since the first century the Church has affirmed the moral evil of every procured abortion. This teaching . . . remains unchangeable" (606). The *Catechism* goes on to affirm the role of government in prohibiting abortions by claiming that "the inalienable right to life of every innocent human individual is a constitutive element of a civil society and its legislation" (607). The Church's opposition to abortion has also been proclaimed and expounded upon both in papal encyclical letters and in statements issued by the USCCB. Pope John Paul II, for instance, in his 1995 encyclical letter *Evangelium vitae*, asserted that "laws which authorize and promote abortion and euthanasia are . . . radically opposed not only to the good of the individual but also to the common good; as such they are completely lacking in authentic juridical validity" (1995, 53). He went on to claim that "there is no obligation in conscience to obey such laws; instead there is a grave and clear obligation to oppose them by conscientious objection" (53). Similar sentiments have been expressed by the USCCB. For instance, in their November 1985 statement, "Pastoral Plan for Pro-Life Activities: A Reaffirmation," the U.S. bishops wrote that "a comprehensive public policy program on behalf of the unborn must include . . . goals" such as "a constitutional amendment providing protection for the unborn child to the maximum degree possible" (Nolan 1989, 207). These statements demonstrate the institutional Church's clear and consistent position regarding the illegitimacy of legalized abortion.

The Church's teachings on sexual morality, including extramarital sex and contraception, are equally forceful. The Church teaches that adultery is "an injustice," and that "fornication is carnal union between an unmarried man and an unmarried woman" that "is gravely contrary to the dignity of persons and of human sexuality which is naturally ordered to the good of spouses" (*Catechism* 632, 624). In addition, the Church explicitly forbids the use of contraceptives, even within marriage, holding that " 'every action which, whether in anticipation of the conjugal act, or in its accomplishment, or in the development of its natural consequences, proposes, whether as an end or as a means, to render procreation impossible' is intrinsically evil" (*Catechism* 629).

In short, the institutional Church has promulgated clear and consistent teachings on a wide variety of contemporary sociopolitical issues. It is thus plausible to postulate that Church leaders may be quite influential in shaping the political attitudes and voting decisions of American Catholics. However, parish priests, even more than the pope, bishops, and the institutional Church as a whole, may be in a better position to exercise political influence than is the Church hierarchy. There are two important reasons for this. First, recall the ideological direction of the Church's teachings on the issues discussed above. On some issues, like abortion and sexual morality, the Church holds a position that is similar to that held by political conservatives and Republicans. On the other issues (aid to the poor, capital punishment, foreign policy), the teachings of the Church are more similar to the positions held by political liberals and Democrats. When it comes to contemporary political issues in the American context, therefore, Church teachings essentially cut across major political divisions (Byrnes 1991; Jelen 1993; Reichley 1986; Steinfels 2003). As Peter Steinfels aptly remarks, "Catholic leadership and organized activists have deep differences with both major parties. They find themselves being abandoned by some of the Church's traditional allies and courted by some of its traditional critics" (2003, 68). The fact that Church teachings do not mesh well with the platforms of either of the two major political parties may make it difficult for Americans to look to Catholic doctrine for political guidance.[6] The second reason that priests might be expected to be more influential than the Church hierarchy is simple access: church-going Catholics hear from their parish priests on a weekly basis, whereas the Church hierarchy's public statements and published writings are much more infrequent occurrences (though see Wald 1992 for a discussion of the potential influence of the Bishops' peace pastoral). Priests, then, perhaps even more than members of the Church's hierarchy, are in a position to wield significant political influence.[7]

Importantly, previous research suggests that Catholic priests seek to realize this potential by publicly discussing political and social issues with their parishioners. In their 1989 study, for instance, Beatty and Walter reported that Catholic clergy were quite likely to report discussing social and political issues in church. A sample of clergy were asked, "How often do you say anything about politics or speak out on political or social issues in church?" (1989, 137–38). Responses ranged from (1) never to (4) very frequently. Among Catholic priests, the mean score on this question was a relatively high 2.97. In a more recent survey of Catholic priests, Jelen also reports a high level of political speech emanating from priests. In his survey, for instance, more than 55 percent of Catholic priests report urging their congregations to register and vote, nearly 50 percent report praying publicly about an issue, and nearly 45 percent report touching on a controversial issue in a sermon (Jelen 2003, 599). The evidence suggests, then, that priests often do convey political messages to their congregations.

Priests are somewhat limited, however, in the mechanisms available to them to exercise such influence. The Catholic Church is an exceedingly hierarchical organization. Its positions on these social and political issues are well established, and openly dissenting from these positions may be difficult for Catholic priests. It is important to be clear, therefore, about the ways in which priests can be expected to be politically influential. Catholics are unlikely to hear, for instance, their parish priest openly advocate support for legal abortion, or opposition to efforts (including governmental efforts) to help the poor. Nevertheless, it is true that priests at different Catholic parishes may choose to emphasize either the issues on which the Church takes a conservative position or issues on which the Church adopts a more liberal position. Priests in some parishes, while never actually refuting the official Church position on economic issues or capital punishment, may place much greater emphasis (from the pulpit, in public announcements, in their prayer petitions) on issues like abortion and sexual morality (on which the Church takes a conservative position) while paying less attention to issues on which the Church takes a liberal stance. Conversely, priests in other parishes may place emphasis on economic issues almost to the exclusion of issues like abortion and sexual morality. In addition, priests also have the potential to exercise fairly wide latitude in the way they present or frame issues when addressing their parishioners (Iyengar 1991; Kinder and Sanders 1996; Nelson 2004; Nelson and Kinder 1996). It is by their choice of topic and the manner in which they address political issues that Catholic priests have the potential to be of great influence in shaping the politics of Catholic parishioners.

By emphasizing some issues while downplaying others, priests may exercise political influence through one or both of two potential avenues. First, it is entirely plausible to expect priests to exercise some degree of direct influence with regard to their parishioners' voting behavior and political attitudes. Priests who emphasize issues on which the Church takes a conservative stand may be expected to exercise a politically conservatizing influence with their parishioners, while priests who emphasize issues on which the Church takes a more liberal position may be expected to exercise a politically liberalizing influence with their parishioners. Accordingly, the analyses that follow will begin by investigating whether or not parishioners' politics can be linked directly with priestly messages.

In addition to exercising direct influence, however, priests might also be expected to play an important role in shaping Catholic politics through a more indirect route. Recall that much of the literature on religion and politics discussed above documents various links between individuals' religious beliefs and their political opinions (see, for instance, Leege and Kellstedt 1993; Leege and Welch 1989; Wald et al. 1988; Welch and Leege 1988, 1991; Welch et al. 1995). It may be that in addition to (or instead of) exercising direct political influence, priests wield political influence indirectly, through their influence on religious attitudes that in turn affect parishioners' politics. Indeed, it may be more plausible to expect priests to exercise political influence indirectly, through their influence on religious attitudes, than it is to expect them to wield direct political influence. Priests are, after all, religious elites, and not political or journalistic authority figures, and are presumably looked to for primarily religious, and not political, instruction and guidance. The chapters that follow examine both potential routes of priestly influence (direct and indirect).

Notes

1. This is not to imply that the memory-based process of opinion formation and the on-line model are necessarily contradictory or mutually exclusive. See, for instance, Taber 2003.

2. Of course, the matter of the rationality (or lack thereof) of citizens and voters is not a settled debate. See, for instance, Althaus 1998; Bartels 1996; Delli Carpini and Keeter 1996; Kuklinski et al. 2000; Kuklinski and Quirk 2000.

3. See Hunter 1991. For Hunter, the term *culture war* clearly does not imply the existence of a religious war. He points out that "The divisions of political consequence today are not theological and ecclesiastical in character but the result of differing worldviews. That is to say, they no longer revolve around specific doctrinal issues or styles of religious practice and organization but around our most fundamental and cherished assumptions about how to order our lives—our own lives and our lives together in this society" (42). Nevertheless, the culture war clearly has a religious component. As Hunter later points out, "at the heart of the new cultural realignment are the pragmatic alliances being formed across faith traditions" (47). Wuthnow makes a related point, arguing that the important religious division in contemporary American society is not denominational division, but is rather the division of religious conservatives against religious liberals (1988).

4. Although it is true that Catholics' loyalty to the Democratic Party has waned over the years, the magnitude of Catholics' drift towards the Republican Party should not be overstated, as it does not constitute a full-scale realignment of Catholic voters into the Republican fold. For a full discussion of this point, see Brewer 2003.

5. It should be pointed out that, though *Rerum novarum* and the social encyclicals that followed it constitute a critique of the capitalist economic system and urge capitalist nations to grant increased attention to the plight of the poor, they do not represent an endorsement of socialism. Indeed, much of *Rerum novarum* is devoted to justifying the right, within limits, of citizens to own private property.

6. See, for instance, the 2004 version of the U.S. bishops' statement on political responsibility. The statement is effective in raising a number of questions that Catholics might consider when deciding how to vote, but it does not provide direct guidance as to which political parties or candidates Catholics should support (USCCB 2003).

7. Of course none of this is to suggest that the Church hierarchy is an unimportant source of influence for American Catholics. See, for instance, Wald 1992. Devout Catholics, in particular, might reasonably be expected to receive and internalize political cues from the institutional Church (from Catholic periodicals, television programs, contact with other Catholics, and other sources) even if such cues are not explicitly relayed by the priests at their own parish.

chapter two
An Initial Look at Priestly Influence

 The Notre Dame Study of Catholic Parish Life

Even a cursory investigation of the extent to which Catholic priests possess the ability to influence the political attitudes of their parishioners requires two separate types of information. First, one must know something of the political attitudes of (at least a sample of) Catholic parishioners; second, one must know something about the political beliefs of the priests assigned to the parishes to which those parishioners belong. Clearly, this is a high threshold, as most surveys, even those dealing explicitly with the religious dimensions of politics, do not meet these criteria. Surveys tend to be based either on a sample of individuals from one or several religious denominations, or on a sample of clergy. In fact, there is only one large, publicly available study, the Notre Dame Study of Catholic Parish Life, that combines survey data gathered from pastors and parishioners at a nationally representative sample of American Catholic parishes. Thus, the Notre Dame Study provides an initial opportunity to investigate the extent to which priests have the potential to wield political influence with their congregations.[1]

The Notre Dame Study was carried out in several waves between 1982 and 1984, and it focused on thirty-six parishes selected as a representative sample of all American Catholic parishes. For each of the thirty-six parishes, researchers undertook investigations into four separate aspects of parish life; specifically, researchers conducted observations of the liturgy (that is, to observe the characteristics of the celebration of the Mass in each parish) and they administered surveys to a sample of pastors, parishioners, and parish staff. Of primary interest here are the surveys of pastors and parishioners. The Notre Dame Study obtained usable survey responses from pastors at thirty-five of the thirty-six parishes, and from a total of 2,667 parishioners.[2]

The Notre Dame Study of Catholic Parish Life was not designed primarily to investigate the politics of Catholics or Catholic parishes. Instead, it "was launched with the idea of combining analysis of parish structure, leadership, and performance with study of parishioners' views and behavior. . . . It involved sociology, history, liturgy, doctrine, and spirituality, together with an analysis of organizational structure and decision making as a community, and a survey of parishioners' beliefs, practices, and communal faith experiences" (Castelli and Gremillion 1987, 6). While the study was designed to investigate a broad array of subjects, it included a small subset of items concerning the political attitudes and behavior of pastors and parishioners. They were queried, for instance, as to their political ideology and party identification, and were asked for their opinions regarding a number of important and controversial political and social issues, including abortion, capital punishment, national defense, and a number of other subjects. It is this subset of questions that is of primary interest here.

While the results of the Notre Dame Study provide the best (and perhaps the only) opportunity for an initial exploration of the potential for priestly influence on Catholic politics, it must be pointed out that there are several aspects of the study that make it less than ideal for these purposes. First, although the surveys administered to pastors included questions designed to measure the pastors' political attitudes and opinions, the study does not contain information regarding the messages delivered by pastors to their parishioners. That is, although the study provides one with a solid idea of what pastors believe, it does not provide one with information about what pastors actually say in their homilies, announcements, and public prayers. As a result, evidence of priestly influence from the Notre Dame Study is necessarily based on the assumption, and not the knowledge or demonstration, that pastors' political beliefs are conveyed to their parishioners.

Second, though the parishioner surveys contain questions regarding partisanship and issue positions, they provide less information about actual political behavior. Parishioners were not asked, for instance, about the frequency with which they vote or participate in and volunteer for political campaigns, nor were they asked about their normal voting decisions (that is, whether they normally vote for Democrats, Republicans, or other political candidates). This potential aspect of priestly influence, therefore, cannot be investigated with data drawn from the Notre Dame Study. Third, the data collected in the Notre Dame Study are over twenty years old. Although I do not believe that the political climate has changed so much in twenty years as to lead one to expect wholly different results were the study conducted today, it would be preferable to have more recent data.

Despite these weaknesses, the Notre Dame Study provides a unique opportunity to investigate the influence of priests on the political attitudes of Catholics. When the data on pastors' attitudes and beliefs are combined with the results of the parishioner surveys, it is possible to determine the extent to which pastors and parishioners share similar political views.

Of course, asserting that priests have the potential to influence the political attitudes of their parishioners necessarily implies that the political beliefs of Catholic priests (or, more accurately, the political messages delivered by priests) are heterogeneous. That is, if all priests thought alike (and agreed with the Church hierarchy on all political issues) and said the same things to their parishioners, it would be much more interesting to examine the influence of the Church hierarchy, as opposed to priests, on Catholic parishioners. Recall that the very notion that Catholic priests are likely candidates to wield political influence stems from the fact that, unlike the Church hierarchy, which espouses clear teachings regarding many political topics and urges attention to a wide variety of political issues, individual priests may be more heterogeneous in their thinking and may emphasize certain po-litical issues while paying less attention to others. This assumption that priests display important and substantial variation in their political beliefs is borne out by the results of the Notre Dame Study. The poli-tics of Catholic priests with regard to partisanship, political ideology, and a number of political issues are reported in tables 2.1, 2.2, and 2.3 below. Although these tables suggest that priests are not so heteroge-neous in their political beliefs as is the general population (or even the population of Catholics), it is clear that there is substantial variation among priests on many topics of political importance.

Table 2.1 indicates that a majority of priests indicate that they are politically independent, support a party other than the Republicans or Democrats, or have no political party preference. More than one-quarter of pastors, however, indicate support for the Democratic Party, while less than 10 percent indicate an affinity for the Republican Party. There is more variation when it comes to the ideological lean-ings of Catholic pastors. A majority of pastors report that they are ide-ologically moderate, but one-fifth of all pastors indicate that they are politically liberal, and nearly one-fifth indicate that they are politically conservative. Clearly, the Catholic pastors included in the Notre Dame Study are not an entirely homogeneous group with regard to political ideology.

The extent of political heterogeneity of Catholic priests is perhaps most evident in examining pastors' positions on eleven important so-cial and political issues: abortion, capital punishment, defense spend-ing, nuclear weapons, gun control, racial integration in public schools (busing), the Equal Rights Amendment (ERA), mandatory prayer in public schools, requiring equal time for the teaching of creationism as opposed to evolution, and allowing homosexuals to teach in public schools. Table 2.3 indicates that, with regard to two political issues, there is indeed remarkable unity among Catholic priests. Most obvi-ously and very importantly, there is near unanimity when it comes to abortion, with all of the pastors in the two most conservative cate-gories on this issue.[3] There is also a high degree of unity with regard to

Table 2.1 Party Identification of Pastors

	Party Identification (N)	Party Identification (%)
Democrat	10	29
Independent/Other/No Preference	22	63
Republican	3	9

Source: Notre Dame Study of Catholic Parish Life, Pastor's Sample, www.thearda.com.

support for a joint freeze between the United States and the Soviet Union on the development of nuclear weapons; fewer than 6 percent of priests in the sample (only two priests) opposed a joint freeze.

On the other political issues, however, there is substantial variation in pastors' opinions. For instance, with regard to capital punishment, despite the institutional Church's consistent opposition to the imposition of the death penalty, nearly one-third of pastors report favoring or strongly favoring the execution of convicted murderers. Similarly, nearly 30 percent of pastors support increased spending for national defense, even though the institutional Church, in documents like *The Challenge of Peace*, clearly supports the liberal position on this issue. A similar pattern holds across the rest of the political issues addressed by the Notre Dame Study, with a substantial proportion of pastors supporting either side of each issue.

In short, the results of the Notre Dame Study's survey of pastors indicates that there exists significant heterogeneity in the political opinions of Catholic priests. If it is assumed that priests convey their

Table 2.2 Political Ideology of Pastors

	Ideology (N)	Ideology (%)
Liberal	7	20
Moderate/Other/Refused	22	63
Conservative	6	17

Source: Notre Dame Study of Catholic Parish Life, Pastor's Sample, www.thearda.com.

Table 2.3 Issue Positions of Pastors (%)

	Abortion	Death Penalty	Defense Spending	Unilateral Freeze	Joint Freeze	Gun Control	Busing	ERA	School Prayer	Evolution	Homosexual Teachers
Most Liberal	0	25	29	21	74	37	0	12	6	16	3
	0	44	41	29	21	40	46	29	36	22	55
	23	22	29	24	6	14	36	41	49	50	26
Most Conservative	77	9	0	27	0	9	18	18	9	13	16

Source: Notre Dame Study of Catholic Parish Life, Pastor's Sample, www.thearda.com.

particular opinions to their parishioners, then an important prerequisite for attempting to investigate priestly influence has been met. Thus, I turn now to a discussion of the hypotheses to be tested, followed by a consideration of the results of this initial examination of priestly political influence.

Hypotheses

Although the data from the Notre Dame Study are limited in the extent to which they permit investigation of priestly influence on the political behavior of parishioners (since the study did not include questions pertaining to voting decisions or turnout), they do permit hypothesis testing with regard to the effect of priests on the political ideology, party identification, and issue opinions of their parishioners. Accordingly, I begin with an examination of the direct influence of priests on individual political ideology and partisanship, posing the following two hypotheses:

Hypothesis 1: Parishioners in parishes with a liberal pastor will be, on average, more liberal than parishioners in parishes with moderate pastors. Similarly, parishioners in parishes with a conservative pastor will be, on average, more conservative than parishioners in parishes with moderate pastors.

Hypothesis 2: Parishioners in parishes with a liberal pastor will be, on average, more Democratic with regard to partisanship than will parishioners in parishes with a moderate pastor. Similarly, parishioners in parishes with a conservative pastor will be, on average, more Republican than will parishioners in parishes with moderate pastors.

After analyzing the extent to which pastors seem to influence the political ideology and partisanship of their parishioners, I proceed to a consideration of the potential for pastors to influence directly their parishioners' attitudes with regard to a wide variety of important sociopolitical issues. I test for such influence in each of two ways: first, by examining the extent to which pastors' positions on various issues can be used to predict the positions of their parishioners (Bjarnason and Welch 2004); and second, by examining the extent to which pastors' ideology can be used to predict the issue positions of their parishioners. I also consider the extent to which the influence of pastors on the political opinions of their parishioners is conditioned by characteristics of the homilies delivered by the pastor. More specifically, I propose and test the following three hypotheses:

Hypothesis 3: The pastor's issue position will be a significant predictor of the issue positions held by parishioners.

Hypothesis 4: Parishioners in parishes with liberal pastors will be, on average, more liberal in their stances on a variety of sociopolitical issues than will parishioners in parishes with a moderate pastor. Similarly, parishioners in parishes with a conservative pastor will be, on average, more conservative in their stances on a variety of sociopolitical issues than will parishioners in parishes with a moderate pastor.

Hypothesis 5: The influence of pastors (both liberal and conservative) on the issue positions held by their parishioners will be conditioned by the quality of the homilies delivered by the pastor. That is, liberal pastors with above average homily quality and effort will have a greater liberalizing effect on parishioners' issue positions, and conservative pastors with above average homily quality and effort will have a greater conservatizing effect on parishioners' issue positions, than will pastors who deliver homilies of average or below average quality and effort.

Recall from chapter 1 that Catholic priests might plausibly be expected to exercise political influence in each of two ways: by directly influencing their parishioners' political attitudes (a possibility considered by each of the five hypotheses outlined above); or by indirectly influencing their parishioners' political attitudes via their role in shaping their parishioners' religious beliefs and values. I examine the extent of priests' apparent indirect political influence in several ways. First, in the course of investigating the direct political influence of parish priests, one individual-level religious variable—willingness to accept political guidance from the church—emerged as a consistent and powerful predictor of parishioners' political attitudes. Demonstrating a link between pastor characteristics and parishioners' willingness to accept church guidance would suggest that priests may sometimes exercise political influence indirectly through their influence on this politically important religious attitude. Accordingly, I propose the following hypothesis:

> Hypothesis 6: Catholics in parishes in which the pastor places great emphasis on preaching, and in which the pastor is supportive of a high degree of parish political involvement, will be more likely to accept guidance from the church on political issues than will parishioners from other parishes.

Finally, the work of Welch and Leege (1988) demonstrates that religious imagery (that is, the extent to which one perceives God as a judge, as a father, as a companion, and as the creator) is an important predictor of political attitudes. Therefore, I consider the extent to which these politically important religious views can be predicted by characteristics of one's local pastor, specifying the following hypothesis:

> Hypothesis 7: Catholics in parishes where the pastor accepts certain religious imagery (such as the image of God as judge and God as father) will be more likely to accept those images as accurate descriptions of God than will parishioners in parishes where the pastor rejects those descriptions.

Results

I test each of the hypotheses outlined above by specifying a series of hierarchical linear models.[4] I turn now to a presentation and consideration of the results.

Pastor Influence on Political Ideology and Partisanship

I begin by considering the influence of pastors on the political ideology and partisanship of their parishioners. These variables— ideology and partisanship—are two of the bedrocks of American political behavior, known to influence and predict everything from voter turnout and vote choice to opinions on specific political issues. Demonstrating that parishioners' ideology and partisanship can be predicted by pastors' ideology will provide reason to suspect an important role for priests in influencing the politics of American Catholics. To test hypotheses 1 and 2, which posit that parishioners' ideology and partisanship are influenced by the political ideology of their pastor, I specify two separate hierarchical linear models. In the first model, the dependent variable is parishioners' political ideology—a five-category variable with responses ranging from (1) very liberal to (5) very conservative. In the second model, the dependent variable is parishioners' party identification. This is a three-category variable, with Democrats coded 1; Independents, others, and those with no party preference coded 2; and Republicans coded 3.

In addition to a number of sociodemographic and geographic control variables,[5] there are two key independent variables in each model.[6] *Liberal pastor* is coded 1 for pastors who indicated that their political ideology is either liberal or very liberal, and 0 for all other pastors. *Conservative pastor* is coded 1 for pastors who indicated that their political ideology is conservative, and 0 for all other pastors. This arrangement makes parishioners in parishes with moderate pastors the baseline for comparison. Results for these models are reported in table 2.4.

The results reported in table 2.4 provide solid support for hypothesis 1 (that parishioners' ideology will be influenced by their pastors' ideology), but do not provide support for hypothesis 2 (that parishioners' party identification will be influenced by their pastor's ideology). The results for the ideology model indicate, for example,

Table 2.4 Influence of Pastors on Political Ideology and Partisan Identification of Parishioners (Hierarchical Linear Models)

	Ideology	Party
Parish-level Predictors		
Liberal Pastor	−.210***	.075
Conservative Pastor	−.107	−.015
Northeast	−.031	−.061
South	.099	−.161
City/Suburbs	−.087*	.003
Individual-level Predictors		
Party Identification	.289***	—
Ideology	—	.256***
Age	.002	−.002*
Male	.059*	.083**
Race	.264***	.336***
Income	.013*	.045***
Education	−.029***	.031***
Talk with Pastor	−.001	.013
Volunteering in Parish	−.005	.010
Accept Church Guidance	−.011***	−.004
Mass Attendance	.032**	−.000
Intercept	2.811***	.642***
Unexplained Parish Variance	.00722*	.04390***
Unexplained Residual Variance	.52648	45379
Explained Parish Variance	82.98%	51.63%
Explained Ind-level Variance	9.34%	11.73%
Observations	1975	1975

*p<.1; **p<.05; ***p<.01

that in parishes with liberal pastors, the parish mean score with regard to political ideology is .210 units lower (i.e., more liberal) than the parish mean score on the political ideology variable in parishes with moderate pastors, even when controlling for a host of other political and demographic variables known to have the potential to be significant predictors of political attitudes. This difference, furthermore, is highly significant ($p = .001$). Table 2.4 also indicates that, considered as a whole, the model specified here performs quite respectably, as it explains more than 80 percent of the between-parish explainable variance in political ideology, and almost 10 percent of the individual-level explainable variance. In sum, table 2.4 strongly suggests that liberal pastors may have a substantial influence on their parishioners' political ideology.

While the results reported in table 2.4 suggest that liberal pastors exercise a significant, liberalizing influence on their parishioners' ideology, the same appears not to be true for their conservative counterparts. The coefficient for *conservative pastor* fails to attain statistical significance, and it is not in the expected direction. The model indicates that in parishes with conservative pastors, the parish mean score on the political ideology dependent variable is .107 units lower (that is, more liberal) than in parishes with moderate pastors. However, since this coefficient fails to attain statistical significance, it is impossible to infer from these results that conservative pastors have any effect at all on their parishioners' ideology. Subsequent analyses in this chapter will continue to suggest that conservative pastors do not seem to influence their parishioners' attitudes in a significant way, and may even alienate their parishioners. The potential reasons for this are discussed below.

While table 2.4 thus provides support (albeit limited to liberal pastors) for the hypothesis that parishioners' political ideology is influenced by their pastor's ideology, the model for party identification fails to support the hypothesis that pastors possess the ability to influence their parishioners' partisanship. The coefficients for both *liberal pastor* and *conservative pastor* fail to attain statistical significance, suggesting that neither liberal nor conservative pastors exercise significant influence on their parishioners' party identification. Notice as well that the model for party identification, considered as a whole, performs much less admirably than does the model for political ideology. The party identification model explains only just over 50 percent of the between-parish variance in party identification, and the remaining between-parish variance (that is, the between-parish variance that remains even after this model is specified) is significant at the .01 level. Table 2.4 suggests, then, that parishioners' partisanship is not substantially affected by the political beliefs of their pastors.

To summarize, the models reported in table 2.4 provide solid support for hypothesis 1 but do not support hypothesis 2. The results show that parishioners in parishes with liberal pastors are significantly more politically liberal than are parishioners in parishes with moderate pastors, which suggests that liberal pastors may possess a strong influence on their parishioners' ideology. Parishioners' partisanship, by contrast, appears not to be influenced by characteristics of their pastor; parishioners in parishes with conservative pastors are no more Republican, and parishioners in parishes with liberal pastors are no more Democratic, than are parishioners in parishes with moderate pastors. I turn now to an analysis of pastor influence on parishioners' issue positions to better sort out the likely influence of pastors on the political attitudes of Catholic parishioners.

Pastor Influence on Parishioners' Issue Positions

In addition to asking parishioners about their general political ideology and their partisanship, the Notre Dame Study queried Catholics as to their attitudes regarding a number of social and political issues. Specifically, parishioners were asked whether or not they favored or opposed capital punishment, increased defense spending, a unilateral freeze on the development of nuclear weapons, a joint freeze on the development of nuclear weapons, registration of all firearms, busing to achieve school integration, the Equal Rights Amendment (ERA), mandatory prayer in public schools, equal time for the teaching of creationism and evolution, and allowing homosexuals to teach in public schools. In addition, parishioners were asked their opinion about the legitimacy of abortion, and about the extent to which their parish (but, unfortunately, not the local or national government) should be involved in providing aid to the poor.

Though the Notre Dame Study was conducted in the 1980s, many of these political and social issues retain a prominent place on the political agenda even in the twenty-first century. Abortion, for instance, continues to be one of the defining issues of the culture wars, and the question of the extent to which homosexuals are to have access to the same rights, privileges, and opportunities as heterosexuals remains prominent as well. Although the question of whether homosexuals should be allowed to teach in public schools is no longer at the forefront of the political agenda, the question of whether gay and lesbian couples should be permitted to legally marry was a key issue in the 2004 presidential campaign. Similarly, Americans continue to debate—and will most likely continue to debate for the foreseeable future—issues like capital punishment, defense spending, gun control, prayer in schools, and whether or not to present alternatives to Darwinian evolution in public schools.

Some of the other issues posed in the Notre Dame Study's survey of parishioners, by contrast, no longer figure prominently in American politics. It must be pointed out, however, that these issues were quite important in the context of the early 1980s. Perhaps most importantly, in the realm of foreign policy the United States and its allies continued to wage a cold war against the USSR, and the question of how best to manage the cold war was a perennial concern in politics and elections. For instance, the question of whether or not the United States should implement a "freeze" on the development of nuclear weapons, either unilaterally or in conjunction with a similar freeze on the part of the Soviet Union, was hotly debated. Indeed, as Plotkin describes in his account of the 1984 election, by the early 1980s "a well-organized movement emerged" in the United States "seeking a nuclear freeze. This movement dovetailed with similar groups abroad, particularly in Germany and England, which protested the deployment of Cruise and Pershing missiles in Western Europe" (Plotkin 1985, 55). Concerns about national defense and nuclear weapons were by no means restricted to movement organizers or participants; a *Los Angeles Times* exit poll conducted during the 1984 election revealed that 19 percent of the public indicated that "foreign relations" were important to them in deciding whom to vote for, and 18 percent said the same about "nuclear arms control." According to the poll, only "government spending" and the federal budget deficit exceeded or rivaled these national security concerns in importance (Keeter 1985, 96).

The items measuring parishioners attitudes on these political issues provide an opportunity to assess the extent to which parishioners' issue attitudes are influenced by the political beliefs of their pastors and, by extension (given the salience of these particular issues in the context of early-1980s U.S. politics), to measure the political relevance of Catholic clergy. Accordingly, I specified twelve new models, designed to test hypothesis 3, that pastors' issue positions will be a significant predictor of parishioners' issue positions. The dependent variables for the twelve models are parishioners' reported attitudes on each issue, coded such that low values indicate liberal responses, and high values indicate conservative responses.[7]

The key independent variable in each of the models is the pastor's opinion, coded in exactly the same way as the dependent variable.[8] Thus, for each of the models, I expect the coefficient for *pastor's opinion* to be statistically significant and positive, which would suggest that in parishes where the pastor is conservative on the issue, the parish mean score on the dependent variable is higher (i.e., more conservative) than in other parishes. In addition, these models include a variety of other independent and control variables, all coded in the same way as in table 2.4. The results of the models investigating the extent to which parishioners' issue attitudes can be effectively predicted by pastors' issue attitudes are presented in table 2.5.

A glance at table 2.5 reveals the consistent inability to predict parishioners' issue positions with pastors' issue positions. In eight of the twelve models, the relationship between pastor's opinion and parishioner's opinion fails to attain statistical significance, and in two of the models (school prayer and evolution), the coefficient for *pastor's opinion* is statistically significant in the wrong direction. That is, these two models indicate that, with regard to school prayer and the teaching of creationism, the mean parish score on these variables is significantly lower (that is, more liberal) in parishes with pastors who hold conservative opinions on these issues. In only two of the models, those for capital punishment and defense spending, are the coefficients for *pastor's opinion* statistically significant and in the expected

Table 2.5 Influence of Pastor's Issue Position on Parishioners' Issue Positions (Hierarchical Linear Models)

	Abortion	Death Penalty	Defense Spending	Poor Aid	Unilateral Freeze	Joint Freeze	Gun Control	Busing	ERA	School Prayer	Evolution	Homosexual Teachers
Parish Level												
Pastor's												
Opinion	-.051	.049*	.112**	.032	.026	-.010	-.010	.061	.028	-.112***	-.084***	.044
Northeast	.035	-.131*	.076	-.014	.006	.015	-.447***	-.157	-.131	.502***	.153**	-.010
South	.087*	-.036	.345***	-.180	.162	.233***	.031	.159	-.002	.407***	-.212***	.026
City/Suburb	-.008	.009	.048	.006	-.101	-.036	-.554***	-.030	-.040	.121***	.043	-.223***
Individual Level												
Party	.024	.047	.190***	.327***	.152***	.056***	.091***	.084***	.152***	.024	.026	.054**
Ideology	.046***	.104***	.115***	.386***	.148***	.058***	.139***	.117***	.224***	.038	.034	.136***
Age	.003***	-.003**	.001	-.003	.001	.001	.001	.001	.005***	.002	-.008***	.008***
Male	-.047*	.160***	.200***	.230**	.274***	.018	.331***	.054	.086**	-.072*	-.064	.175***
Race	.135***	.216**	.220**	.561***	.222**	.147**	.061	.477***	.225**	-.522***	-.006	.154*
Income	-.006	.018**	.028**	-.023	.042***	.013*	.004	.023***	.005	-.003	-.020*	-.001
Education	-.018**	-.019	-.034**	.078**	-.009	-.007	.019	-.006	-.014	-.088***	-.061***	-.058***
Talk with Pastor	.018	-.082***	-.026	-.049	-.071**	.008	.005	.051*	.003	.109***	.084***	.077***

Volunteer in Parish	.055***	-.053***	-.013	.021	-.008	-.040***	-.022	-.039***	.060***	.019	.005	-.020
Accept Church Guidance	.008***	-.020***	-.016***	-.049***	-.017***	-.010***	-.008**	-.013***	-.007**	-.007**	-.001	-.006*
Mass Attendance	.065***	-.020	.000	.071	-.015	-.034**	-.006	-.001	.023	.028*	.013	.017
Intercept	2.613***	2.712***	1.885***	6.025***	2.279***	1.509***	1.862***	2.316***	1.352***	3.153***	2.814***	2.551***
Parish Variance	.00233*	.00759**	.01857***	.07586**	.02000***	.00316	.04848***	.02913***	.01547***	.00126	.00220	.00817**
Individual Variance	.25129	.64687	.56614	5.03197	.66173	.46173	.81459***	.55379	.63030	.55093	.60597	.56973
Explained Parish Variance	42.18%	67.51%	70.32%	54.07%	67.28%	76.80%	72.66%	67.81%	66.32%	98.33%	83.06%	81.58%
Explained Individual Variance	7.96%	6.61%	10.18%	5.37%	10.58%	2.72%	5.99%	4.83%	9.71%	7.35%	3.85%	9.86%
Observations	1966	1730	1885	1859	1883	1901	1959	1861	1885	1836	1844	1730

*p < .1; ** p < .05; *** p < .01

direction. It is tempting to conclude that, at least when pastors' influence is investigated in this way, pastors appear not to wield much influence with regard to their parishioners' issue positions.

There are two reasons, however, to be cautious in jumping to this conclusion. First, the statistically significant and correctly signed *pastor's opinion* coefficient in the defense spending model may be of greater importance than it first appears. As mentioned previously, the Notre Dame Study parishioner surveys were administered in late 1983 and early 1984. Just prior to this, in July of 1983, the United States Conference of Catholic Bishops (USCCB) released its pastoral letter *The Challenge of Peace: God's Promise and Our Response.* Although the bishops' pastoral letter stopped short of calling for a unilateral freeze by the United States on the development of nuclear weapons, its emphasis and tone were clearly more in line with the liberal, or dovish, position on national defense than with the conservative, or hawkish, perspective. Furthermore, research suggests that the pastoral letter had a very significant, though short-lived, impact on the views of American Catholics regarding government spending for national defense. Specifically, in the aftermath of the pastoral letter, there was a sharp increase in the percentage of American Catholics who reported opposition to increased defense spending (Wald 1992). It is significant, then, that at the same time that there appears to have been a national movement of Catholics toward a more liberal position on defense spending in response to a statement of the Church hierarchy (the USCCB), the data suggest that there existed an independent effect of pastor's opinion on parishioners' views on this issue, distinct from a more general Church hierarchy influence on Catholics' attitudes.

A second reason to hesitate before concluding that pastors are not influential is that it is implausible to assume that pastors publicly address, on a regular basis, all or even most of the issues examined here. Though one might expect to hear priests mention the Church's teaching on some of the issues quite frequently, it would frankly be nearly impossible for any pastor to regularly and specifically address each of the twelve issues. In other words, it is unlikely that pastors will regularly express (in their homilies and other public announcements) opinions on each of these issues, and it is therefore also unlikely that parishioners will learn about, much less be influenced by, their pastor's (un-expressed) opinions on many of these political issues. Parishioners may, however, plausibly be expected over the course of time to be made more familiar with their pastor's general ideological leanings and be-liefs, as opposed to his specific issue positions. In other words, it may be pastors' ideology, and not pastors' issue positions, that influences parishioners' issue opinions.

In order to test the proposition (hypothesis 4) that liberal pastors will influence their parishioners to hold liberal opinions on a variety of political issues, and that conservative pastors will have the opposite effect on their parishioners, I specify twelve new models. The dependent variables in the models are identical to those described (and re-ported in table 2.5), as are most of the independent and control variables. Instead of using pastor's opinion on each issue as the key explanatory variable, however, I include two dummy variables, one for liberal pastors, and one for conservative pastors. These variables are coded in precisely the same way here as they were for table 2.4. For these new models, I expect the coefficients for *liberal pastor* to be statistically significant and negative, and the coefficients for *con-servative pastor* to be statistically significant and positive. The results of the new models are reported in table 2.6.

It is immediately obvious from a glance at table 2.6 that models specified in this way are much more suggestive of significant pastor influence on the political attitudes of their parishioners than are the models reported in table 2.5. Indeed, table 2.6 provides relatively strong support for hypothesis 4. For instance, in six of the twelve models (those for capital punishment, defense spending, unilateral freeze, busing, the ERA, and allowing homosexual teachers) the coef-ficient for *liberal pastor* is statistically significant and in the expected direction. That is, across a wide variety of political issues, the parish mean score is significantly lower (i.e., more liberal) on the dependent

Table 2.6 Influence of Pastor's Ideology on Parishioners' Issue Positions (Hierarchical Linear Models)

	Abortion	Death Penalty	Defense Spending	Pocr Aic	Unilateral Freeze	Joint Freeze	Gun Control	Busing	ERA	School Prayer	Evolution	Homosexual Teachers
Parish Level												
Liberal												
Pastor	-.030	-.111*	-.185**	-.212	-.136*	-.017	.009	-.304***	-.165**	-.083	-.079	-.114*
Conservative												
Pastor	-.069	.003	.052	-.176	-.001	.040	.002	-.130	-.034	.047	-.008	-.046
Northeast	.047	-.170**	.074	-.040	-.034	.006	-.444***	-.234***	-.173**	.328***	.035	-.008
South	.092**	-.061	.283***	-.218	.114	.164**	.030	.195**	-.014	.297***	-.222***	.131*
City/Suburb	-.016	.010	.000	-.052	-.119*	-.057	-.552***	-.018	-.046	.089	.047	-.177***
Individual												
Level												
Party	.025	.045*	.188***	.332***	.159***	.055**	.091***	.080***	.160***	.017	.029	.075***
Ideology	.043***	.098***	.119***	.379***	.146***	.062***	.139***	.118***	.221***	.044*	.026	.129***
Age	.003***	-.004***	.001	-.003	.002	.001	.001	.002	.005***	.002	-.008***	.008***
Male	-.049**	.169***	.206***	.233**	.261***	.016	.331***	.047	.089*	-.086**	-.069*	.174***
Race	.108**	.220**	.200**	.49*	.211**	.142**	.056	.444***	.206**	-.485***	-.032	.063
Income	-.006	.016*	.027**	-.024	.038**	.013*	.004	.022***	.006	-.002	-.021**	-.006
Education	-.017**	-.020*	-.031***	.07***	-.005	-.006	.019	-.005	-.014	-.088***	-.058***	-.052***
Talk with Pastor	.017	-.072**	-.027	-.049	-.071**	.005	.005	.044*	.007	.115***	.069**	.067**
Volunteer in Parish	.055***	-.054***	-.019	.021	-.011	-.038***	-.022	-.039***	.057***	.019	.006	-.021

Accept Church Guidance

Mass Attendance	.008***	−.022***	−.017***	−.049***	−.016***	−.010***	−.008**	−.013***	−.007**	−.007**	−.000	−.005*
Intercept	.065***	−.011	−.002	.072	−.013	−.032**	−.006	−.005	.020	.027*	.013	.015
	2.656***	2.732***	1.963***	6.210***	2.324***	1.502***	1.863***	2.461***	1.431***	3.200***	2.887***	2.648***
Parish Variance	.00240**	.00618**	.01953***	.08332***	.01766***	.00443**	.05112***	.01603***	.01175***	.01157***	.00749**	.01120***
Individual Variance	.25131	.65453	.56665	5.0295E	.66849	.45715	.81454	.54867	.62586	.54809	.59952	.56796
Explained Parish Variance	40.45%	72.73%	67.84%	49.56%	59.77%	66.31%	71.18%	82.36%	73.48%	85.08%	46.69%	73.60%
Explained Individual Variance	7.95%	6.65%	10.63%	5.42%	10.38%	2.72%	6.03%	4.92%	10.03%	7.76%	3.53%	9.87%
Observations	1966	1935	1936	1859	1934	1952	1959	1943	1936	1953	1926	1925

* p < .1; ** p < .05; *** p < .01

variable in parishes with a liberal pastor than it is in parishes with a moderate pastor. Moreover, these findings are maintained even though the models control for other potential explanations, including the geographic region and location of the parish.

The models also perform quite well when considered as a whole, explaining between 68 percent (defense spending) and 82 percent (busing) of the between-parish variance in opinion regarding these issues, and between approximately 5 percent (busing) and more than 10 percent (defense spending, unilateral freeze, ERA) of the individual-level variance. It should also be pointed out that, though table 2.6 reports results for twelve separate models (and, therefore, twelve different dependent variables), it is reasonable to expect only ten of the models to reveal significant pastor influence: there is very limited variance in the abortion dependent variable (roughly 95 percent of parishioners in the Notre Dame Study are in the two most conservative categories on this item); in addition, the dependent variable for the aid to the poor model asks respondents not for their opinion regarding governmental aid to the poor (which, in attempting to gauge the political influence of pastors, is what is really of interest), but rather asks them the extent to which they think their parish should be involved in providing aid to the poor. Given that there is thus limited potential to observe significant pastor influence on these two variables (abortion and aid to the poor), the findings reported in table 2.7 are even more suggestive. On six of ten issues on which significant pastor influence can reasonably be expected, the evidence is consistent with what one would expect if significant pastor influence were taking place. Specifically, parishioners in parishes with liberal pastors are, on average, significantly more liberal than their counterparts in parishes with moderate priests.

Finally, however, it should also be noted that, just as was found with regard to political ideology and partisanship, conservative pastors appear not to wield the same degree of influence on specific political issues as their more liberal colleagues. Indeed, table 2.6 reveals that the coefficient for *conservative pastor* fails to attain statistical significance in all twelve models. These data suggest, then, that the potential for priestly influence is restricted to liberal priests.

Data from the Notre Dame Study also afford a limited opportunity to test hypothesis 5, which contends that the influence of pastors will be conditioned in part by the characteristics of the homilies they deliver; thus I conclude this section with a consideration of this hypothesis. To test the hypothesis, I specified a series of new models, using the same dependent variables included in table 2.6. In addition to the *liberal pastor* and *conservative pastor* independent variables, the new models tested for interactions between pastor ideology and homily quality (as rated by the parishioners in each parish) as well as for interactions between pastor ideology and preaching effort (as measured by each pastor's indication of the amount of time and importance he attaches to preaching and the amount of enjoyment he derives from preaching).[9] I hypothesized that pastors who deliver high-quality homilies will exercise a greater degree of influence than pastors who deliver homilies of lesser quality, and that pastors who devote great effort to preaching will be more effective speakers, and so be more influential with their parishioners, than will pastors who do not put forth much effort in preaching.

For the most part, pastor influence was not conditioned by characteristics of the homily. That is, generally speaking, there was no interaction between pastors' ideology and the homily characteristics variables. There were, however, two important exceptions, reported in table 2.7 below.

The results reported in table 2.7 suggest that at least with regard to busing and the teaching of creationism and evolution, the influence of pastors is mediated by the characteristics of the homilies they deliver. First, consider the new model investigating pastors' influence on parishioners' opinions regarding the teaching of creationism. Recall from table 2.6 that there was no direct effect of pastors' ideology on parishioners' opinions on this issue. As reported in table 2.7, however, the interaction between *liberal pastor* and *preaching effort* is

Table 2.7 A Closer Look at Pastors' Influence on Parishioners' Issue Positions
(Hierarchical Linear Models)

	Busing	Evolution
Parish-level Predictors		
Liberal Pastor	−.198**	−.065
Conservative Pastor	−.160*	.028
Homily Quality	.006	—
Liberal Pastor* Homily Quality	−.148***	—
Conservative Pastor* Homily Quality	−.023	—
Preaching Effort	—	.043
Liberal Pastor* Preaching Effort	—	−.176**
Conservative Pastor* Preaching Effort	—	.022
Northeast	−.216***	.046
South	.248***	−.209***
City/Suburb	−.011	.065
Individual-level Predictors		
Party Identification	.076***	.021
Ideology	.117***	.035
Age	.002	−.008***
Male	.046	−.055
Race	.368***	.001
Income	.022***	−.021**
Education	−.004	−.057***
Talk with Pastor	.052**	.072***
Volunteer in Parish	−.038***	.004
Accept Church Guidance	−.014***	.001
Mass Attendance	−.006	.008
Intercept	2.523***	2.841***
Parish-level Variance	.01255***	.00583*
Individual-level Variance	.54768	.59283
Explained Parish Variance	86.19%	59.77%
Explained Individual Variance	5.09%	3.73%
Observations	1943	1880

$^*p < .1; ^{**}p < .05; ^{***}p < .01$

statistically significant (at the .05 level) and in the expected direction,
suggesting that liberal pastors who expend above-average effort in
preaching have a more liberalizing influence on their parishioners'
views regarding the teaching of creationism than do liberal pastors
who expend less effort in preaching.

The model predicting parishioners' opinion on busing displays similar results with regard to liberal pastors. *Liberal pastor* has a significant, negative coefficient, as does the interaction between *liberal pastor* and *homily quality*. This suggests that with regard to busing, parishioners in parishes with liberal pastors are, on average, more liberal than parishioners in parishes with moderate pastors, and this liberalizing effect of liberal pastors is magnified in parishes where the pastor gives high-quality homilies.

Table 2.7 also contains some puzzling findings. In the busing model the coefficient for *conservative pastor* is statistically significant and negative, indicating that parishioners in parishes with conservative pastors are, on average, more liberal in their views on busing than are parishioners in parishes with moderate pastors. Once again, expectations of pastor influence seem to be confirmed only for liberal pastors, while conservative pastors appear to lack such influence, and even to run the risk of alienating their parishioners. Of course, it is entirely possible that Catholic priests who identified themselves as politically conservative were nevertheless supportive of school integration, and may even have mentioned this to their parishioners. Confusing results such as these would be much easier to interpret were there data on what priests said in addition to data on what priests thought. These findings are discussed in more detail below.

Taken as a whole, then, the results reported in tables 2.6 and 2.7, which show that pastor ideology is a significant predictor of parishioners' opinions on a wide variety of political issues, suggest that pastors do, indeed, influence the political attitudes of their parishioners. More specifically, on many issues, Catholic parishioners who attend Mass at parishes with a liberal pastor are significantly more liberal than Catholics in parishes with moderate pastors. Indeed, on six of twelve issues there is a direct, independent, liberalizing effect of attending a parish with a liberal pastor, and on a seventh issue (the teaching of creationism in public schools) parishioners appear to be influenced by liberal pastors who expend above-average effort on preaching.

With regard to both political ideology and specific political issues, therefore, it appears that Catholic pastors may have the potential to influence the attitudes of their congregants.

The Indirect Political Influence of Pastors

Chapter 1 suggested that Catholic priests might be plausibly expected to wield direct political influence with their parishioners, and to exercise political influence indirectly through their influence on certain religious attitudes held by parishioners. The Notre Dame Study makes it possible to consider several avenues through which priests may exercise indirect political influence. First, parishioners' willingness to accept political guidance from the Church emerged in many of the models presented thus far as an important predictor of Catholics' political attitudes, which makes it important to consider whether priests exercise political influence through their ability to shape their parishioners willingness to accept political guidance from the Church. Second, other scholars have used the Notre Dame Study to identify several politically important religious attitudes. Specifically, Welch and Leege demonstrated that religious imagery (that is, the ways that parishioners conceptualize or imagine God) is important in shaping certain political attitudes (Welch and Leege 1988). These politically important religious attitudes constitute another potential avenue through which clergy may exercise indirect political influence.

The analyses presented thus far indicate that one religious variable in particular is a consistent predictor of various political attitudes among Catholics; the models reported in tables 2.4 through 2.7 reveal that the variable measuring individuals' willingness to accept guidance from the church on political issues is a consistent, highly significant predictor of political attitudes. Across a wide variety of political issues, from abortion to capital punishment to defense spending and nuclear weapons, parishioners who indicate a high degree of willingness to accept political guidance from the Church are significantly more likely than others to adopt political positions espoused by the Church. With respect to abortion, for instance, Catholics who look to the Church for guidance are more conservative than other Catholics. On other issues, including capital punishment and defense spending, Catholics who are willing to accept political guidance from the Church are more liberal than other Catholics. The importance of this variable in predicting the political attitudes of Catholics, as demonstrated by its consistent performance, suggests the potential utility of investigating whether or not it too can be predicted by pastor characteristics. Specifically, as outlined above in hypothesis 6, it is reasonable to expect that parishioners in parishes with a pastor who exerts maximum effort in preaching and who is highly political should be more willing to accept guidance from the Church than should parishioners in other parishes.

To test this hypothesis, I specified a new model. The dependent variable—*willingness to accept church guidance*—is a twenty-one-item summated scale (alpha = .903) indicating the extent to which the individual thinks three persons or institutions (the pope, the Catholic bishops, parish priests) may appropriately speak out on seven sociopolitical issues (aid to poor countries; eliminating poverty in the United States; birth control; equal opportunities regardless of sex; sex and violence on TV; action for world disarmament; and racial integration). The scale ranges from (0), for parishioners who say that none of the three persons or institutions may appropriately speak on any of these issues, to (21), for parishioners who believe that each of these three persons or institutions may appropriately speak on each of these issues. In addition to several familiar individual-level independent and control variables, the model includes a parish-level variable measuring pastors' effort in preaching (described previously), and a new parish-level variable, *political involvement,* measuring each pastor's degree of social and political involvement in the secular arena.[10]

I expect the coefficients for both of these pastor-level variables, and the coefficient for the interaction of these two variables, to be statistically significant and positive. Parishioners in parishes where the pastor expends great effort in preaching, who are thus assumed to be exposed to more well-thought-out and well-crafted homilies than are other parishioners, should as a result be more inclined to accept guidance from the Church. Parishioners in parishes with pastors with a high degree of enthusiasm for political involvement should become accustomed to seeing their pastor and their parish involved in politics, and so be more inclined to accept church guidance on political issues than parishioners in other parishes. Finally, I expect these two variables to work together: parishioners in parishes with pastors who expend great effort in preaching and who are highly political should be even more willing to accept church guidance on political issues than parishioners in parishes where the pastor either puts great effort into preaching or is highly political. The results of this new model are reported in table 2.8.

The results reported in table 2.8 provide partial support for hypothesis 6. Although the coefficient for *preaching effort* is significant and in the expected direction, the coefficient for *pastor's political involvement* is not statistically significant. The interaction term, however, is significant and in the expected direction, suggesting that the influence of each of these two variables on parishioners' willingness to accept guidance from the Church is conditioned by the other. Furthermore, the model does a respectable job of explaining between-parish variance in willingness to accept church guidance, accounting for over 76 percent of this variance, though it performs less well in explaining individual level variance. In general, table 2.8 suggests that priests may exercise political influence indirectly, through their influence on their parishioners' willingness to accept political guidance from the Church.

While the utility of investigating parishioners' willingness to accept church guidance as an avenue through which priests might be expected to exercise political influence was suggested by the analyses presented in this chapter, other potential avenues of indirect priestly influence are suggested by the existing religion and politics literature. Most prominently, in a 1988 article Welch and Leege used data from the Notre Dame Study to demonstrate that the images Catholics associate with God are correlated with certain political attitudes (Welch and Leege 1988). By using factor analytic techniques, Welch and Leege were able to determine the extent to which parishioners accepted four

Table 2.8 Pastors' Influence on Parishioners' Willingness to Accept Guidance from the Church (Hierarchical Linear Models)

	Accept Church Guidance
Parish-level Predictors	
Pastor's Preaching Effort	.490**
Pastor's Political Involvement	.156
Preaching Attention* Involvement	.465*
Individual-level Predictors	
Age	−.030***
Male	−.197
Race	−.212
Income	.132**
Education	.583***
Mass Attendance	.320***
Intercept	5.516***
Parish-level Variance	.28552**
Individual-level Variance	30.93028
Explained Parish Variance	76.78%
Explained Individual Variance	5.27%
Observations	2010

*p < .1; **p < .05; ***p < .01

different potential images of God: God as judge, God as father, God as companion, and God as savior. They determined that all four images were related to certain political attitudes. Parishioners who viewed God as a companion were significantly more conservative than other parishioners in their views about prayer in schools, increased defense spending, and cohabitation outside of marriage. Parishioners who viewed God as a father held significantly more liberal opinions than did other parishioners with respect to capital punishment and defense spending, and were more conservative in their approach to parenting. Those who imagined God as a savior were more conservative in their opinions about abortion and cohabitation than were other parishioners. Most importantly, parishioners who viewed God as a judge were more conservative than other parishioners with respect to a large majority of the fourteen dependent variables Welch and Leege considered, including political ideology, prayer in school, defense issues, traditional parenting and gender roles, abortion, and cohabitation (Welch and Leege 1988).

Clearly, then, religious imagery is an important and consistent predictor of political attitudes among Catholic parishioners. Parish priests, as religious leaders, might reasonably be expected to help shape the images of God held by their parishioners, and thus indirectly shape their parishioners' political attitudes. To test this proposition (hypothesis 7), I specified four, new hierarchical linear models, where the dependent variables are additive scales that measure the extent to which parishioners view God as judge, God as father, God as companion, and God as savior.[11] The Notre Dame Study survey of pastors included the same battery of questions regarding religious imagery as did the survey of parishioners. Thus, the key independent variables for these models are pastors' (centered) positions, coded in the same way as the dependent variables described above, on each of the respective religious imagery scales.[12] Additionally, the new models include a number of familiar control variables. The results of the religious imagery models are reported in table 2.9.

Table 2.9 indicates that pastor's opinion is a statistically significant predictor of parishioners' acceptance of religious imagery in one of the four models specified here. That is, the results show that parishioners who belong to parishes where the pastor accepts the image of God as judge are more likely to view God as judge than are parishioners in parishes where the pastor largely rejects the image of God as judge. However, pastors do not appear to influence their parishioners' acceptance or rejection of images of God as father, companion, or savior.

At first glance, these results may appear underwhelming. The pastor's opinion variable attains statistical significance in only one of four religious imagery models. Furthermore, the models, when considered as a whole, are not as powerful in accounting for parish-level or individual-level variance as are many of the models presented earlier in this chapter. Recall, however, that of the four religious imagery

Table 2.9 Pastors' Influence on Parishioners' Conceptions of God

	God as Judge	God as Father	God as Companion	God as Savior
Parish-level Predictor				
Pastor's Opinion	.078**	.062	−.030	−.032
Individual-level Predictors				
Age	.007***	−.003**	.002*	.001
Male	.152***	−.128***	−.083**	−.066***
Race	−.125	−.007	−.240***	−.073*
Income	.002	.008	−.008	.002
Education	−.048***	−.034***	−.068***	−.025***
Mass Attendance	.060***	.087***	.074***	.044***
Intercept	3.658***	4.349***	4.523***	4.744***
Parish-level Variance	.01671***	.00286	.00726***	.00078
Individual-level Variance	.82156	.51900	.49360	.24110
Explained Parish Variance	39.19%	—	65.88%	58.06%
Explained Individual Variance	3.33%	3.12%	4.98%	2.25%
Observations	2115	2119	2109	2124

*$p < .1$; **$p < .05$; ***$p < .01$

variables identified by Welch and Leege to be politically important, the God as Judge variable was by far the most consistent and powerful predictor of political attitudes. Even after controlling for age, race, education, income, gender, and region, Welch and Leege showed that imagining God as a judge remains an important predictor of sociopolitical conservatism on nearly a dozen important political variables, including political ideology and abortion opinion. In short, the evidence presented here suggests that while priests may not play a major role in shaping their parishioners' willingness to accept or reject all possible images of God, they do play an important role in shaping their acceptance of certain images of God (particularly as judge). Through their influence on this politically important religious attitude, priests may play an indirect role in shaping their parishioners' approach to politics.

Discussion and Conclusions

The Notre Dame Study of Catholic Parish Life is the only existing study of its kind in that it provides publicly available data on the political attitudes of Catholic pastors and on the attitudes of their parishioners. It thus provides an opportunity to undertake an initial investigation of the potential for Catholic priests to influence the political attitudes of their parishioners. Of course, the study is not ideally suited to these purposes, and was not designed specifically with these purposes in mind, and so the analyses reported here should be interpreted with caution. Nevertheless, the results presented in this chapter suggest as a whole that priests (or, more accurately, liberal priests) may indeed possess the ability to influence the political attitudes of their parishioners. Specifically, it is possible to draw several tentative conclusions with regard to priestly influence on parishioners' ideology and partisanship, issue positions, willingness to accept guidance from the church, and images of God.

With regard to political ideology, liberal pastors seem to have a direct, liberalizing effect on their parishioners. On average, parishioners in parishes with liberal pastors are more liberal than are parishioners in parishes with moderate pastors. When it comes to partisanship, on the other hand, there appears to be no direct effect of pastor ideology on parishioners' party identification.

When it comes to parishioners' opinions regarding a variety of political issues, liberal pastors again seem to have a direct, liberalizing effect. On two issues, this effect is magnified in parishes where the pastor also delivers high-quality sermons or exerts above-average effort in preaching. Conservative pastors, on the other hand, seem not to exercise the same type or degree of influence. Although a dozen issues were examined for evidence of pastor influence, in no case did the variable for conservative pastor have a statistically significant effect. In fact, detailed analysis of one political issue (busing) revealed that parishioners in parishes with conservative pastors may actually be more liberal (with regard to busing) than parishioners in parishes with moderate pastors.

Finally, it was shown that priestly influence may operate in part through indirect routes. That is, certain characteristics of a pastor's approaches to preaching and ministering are important determinants of parishioners' willingness to accept political guidance from the church, which in turn is a consistent, highly significant predictor of Catholics' issue positions. Pastors who spend above-average effort on preaching, and who are willing to allow the parish to be highly involved in secular and political issues, seem to influence their parishioners to accept guidance from the church on a variety of sociopolitical topics. Additionally, the evidence presented here suggests that pastors play an important role in shaping their parishioners' religious imagery, which has been previously shown by other scholars to be a highly important religious predictor of political attitudes. In other words, priests appear to exercise political influence in part indirectly through their influence on their parishioners' acceptance or rejection of certain religious imagery.

Though these results clearly suggest that liberal pastors may wield substantial influence with their parishioners, they are much less clear with regard to the consequences of belonging to a parish with a conservative pastor. Why is it that conservative pastors generally appear to lack influence and may even in rare instances influence their parishioners to take liberal political positions? Based on the available data, it is impossible to answer this question conclusively, though it is possible to speculate about some plausible explanations. First, recall the discussion in chapter 1 about official Church teachings on social and political issues. On most issues—including aid to the poor, capital punishment, and national defense—the Church takes relatively liberal positions. The most important and salient political issue on which the Church takes a conservative stand is abortion. Further, remember that the analysis reported in table 2.5 reveals that in no instance do pastors influence their parishioners to hold opinions contrary to those advocated by the Church. For example, while liberal pastors may essentially persuade their constituents to oppose the death penalty, conservative pastors do not persuade their constituents to support the death penalty. This is not surprising, since priests (as discussed in chapter 1) are expected to influence their parishioners not so much through their adoption or endorsement of particular political positions as through their choice of which issues to emphasize. Since it is the preeminent political issue on which the Church takes a conservative stand, abortion is the issue on which we should be most likely to see conservative pastors exercising persuasive influence. The abortion dependent variable, however, lacks variation, as nearly all parishioners in the study find abortion unacceptable. In short, it is precisely the variable on which the influence of conservative pastors is most likely to be observed that is least susceptible to this type of analysis. The 2004 study of Catholic political attitudes, introduced in the next chapter, should provide a better opportunity to delve into the nuances of the influence of conservative pastors. Since large numbers of Catholics now express pro-choice views about abortion, it is unlikely that contemporary surveys will exhibit so little variation in abortion opinion.

A second potential explanation for the lack of observed influence of conservative pastors is that American Catholics are quite unwilling to accept Church guidance regarding the issues on which the Church takes a conservative stand. Surveys suggest, for instance, that only one-fifth of Catholics believe that the locus of authority for Catholics who advocate "free choice regarding abortion" resides with Church leaders, and only one-tenth of Catholics see Church leaders as the locus of authority with regard to "contraceptive birth control" (D'Antonio et al. 2001, 76). Similarly, the Notre Dame Study reports that only just over 40 percent of Catholic parishioners think that the Pope should speak out on birth control, and only 26 percent think that parish priests should do so. An alternative explanation for the lack of influence of conservative pastors, then, may be that Catholics have simply rejected the authority of the Church with regard to issues on which the Church espouses conservative positions.

In short, the results reported here suggest that Catholic priests may at least in certain circumstances have the potential to influence the political attitudes of their parishioners. The following chapters introduce a study explicitly designed to investigate such influence and provide a more nuanced look at the political consequences of the public messages delivered by Catholic priests.

Notes

1. The Notre Dame Study of Catholic Parish Life is freely available for download from the Association of Religion Data Archives, www.thearda.com.

2. An average of just over 69 parishioners per parish provided usable responses to the surveys, and the number of parishioners from each parish that provided usable survey responses ranged from 23 to 132.

3. Pastors were asked, "Which of the following statements comes closest to your views about abortion?" Four response options were offered, ranging from most liberal ("abortion is always acceptable") to most conservative ("abortion is never acceptable").

4. Data from both the Notre Dame Study of Catholic Parish Life (analyzed in chapter 2), and the 2004 survey of Catholic parishioners (analyzed in chapter 5), consist of survey responses from individuals who are nested within parishes. Accordingly, multilevel modeling techniques are appropriate for this initial test of priestly influence.

Historically, multilevel modeling techniques have been only rarely utilized by political scientists, though their use is becoming increasingly common. Though these techniques are only just now gaining widespread use, the analysis of data that are hierarchically structured has been common for decades. Previously, political scientists tended to ignore nested data structures in their research, and instead specified models as if the data were not hierarchically structured. Such methods, though problematic, have resulted in new findings and improved understanding of American politics, especially with regard to contextual effects on political attitudes and behavior. But treating hierarchically structured data as if they are not nested poses serious risks. Perhaps most important, when hierarchically structured data are treated as if they are not nested, the researcher fails to account for the correlation of observations that are nested within the same unit. As Steenbergen and Jones explain, "In terms of statistical models, the duplication of observations violates the assumption that the errors are independent. . . . In the context of multilevel data structures, the correlation between the errors (observations) is referred to as intra-class or cluster correlation. In most cases this correlation is positive, and this will cause the estimated standard errors to be too low and the test-statistics too high. . . . As a result, Type I errors are more frequent, i.e., predictors appear to have a significant effect when in fact they do not" (2002, 220). Multilevel modeling techniques, then, represent both a more appropriate and a more rigorous method for dealing with hierarchically structured data.

For a more detailed explication of the principles and practice of multilevel modeling, see Raudenbush and Bryk (2002). Other helpful sources include Kreft 2000; Luke 2004; Singer 1998; and Steenbergen and Jones 2002.

5. Most of the models reported in chapter 2 control for several parish-level (level two) geographic variables, including *northeast* (coded 1 for parishes located in the northeast region of the United States, and 0 for all other parishes), *south* (coded 1 for parishes located in the southern region of the United States, and 0 for all other parishes), and *city/suburb* (coded 1 for parishes located in either urban or suburban areas, and 0 for parishes located in rural areas or small towns).

At the individual level (level one), the models include controls for two important political variables: *party identification* (a three-category variable which is coded 0 for those identifying themselves as Democrats; 1 for those claiming political independence, no preference for either party, or identification with a third party; and 2 for those identifying themselves as Republicans), and *political ideology* (a five-category variable coded from 0, very liberal, to 4, very conservative).

Sociodemographic control variables include *age* (a parish-centered variable, with a score of 0 indicating that the individual is of the average age for his or her parish), *male* (coded 0 for females and 1 for males), *race* (coded 0 for blacks and 1 for all others), *income* (coded from [0] under $10,000 to [8] more than $60,000), and *education* (coded from [0] eighth grade or less to [7] post-graduate or professional degree).

Finally, the models reported here control for several important religious variables. *Talk with pastor* indicates the frequency with which the respondent reports having "longer conversations" with his or her pastor, and is coded from (0) never to (3) daily. *Volunteering in parish* describes the number of hours spent volunteering in the parish per month, coded from (0) none to (4) 16 hours or more per month. *Accept church guidance* is a twenty-one-item summated scale (alpha = .903) indicating the extent to which the individual thinks three persons or institutions (the Pope, the Catholic bishops, parish priests) may appropriately speak out on seven sociopolitical issues (aid to poor countries; eliminating poverty in the United States; birth control; equal opportunities regardless of sex; sex and violence on TV; action for world disarmament; and racial integration). *Accept church guidance* is coded from (0) none of the three institutions may appropriately speak on any of these issues to (21) every institution may appropriately speak on each of these issues. *Mass attendance* is a measure of frequency of attendance at Sunday Mass, coded from (0) never to (5) once a week.

6. When multilevel models are specified the location of the independent variables is important both for statistical reasons and for ease of interpretation. In this chapter level-one independent variables are coded in such a way as to make a value of 0 meaningful (wherever possible), or they are centered around their group-mean (e.g., parish-mean) value. Level-two variables are centered around their grand-mean values, except in the case of dummy variables. (For excellent discussions of the location of variables in multilevel models, see Raudenbush and Bryk 2002, 32–35; and Singer 1998.)

7. With the exception of *opinion on aid to the poor*, each dependent variable consists of four response categories. All dependent variables are coded such that higher

scores indicate more conservative attitudes. *Abortion opinion* is coded from (1) abortion is always acceptable to (4) abortion is never acceptable. *Death penalty opinion* measures the extent to which the respondent favors the death penalty for persons convicted of murder, coded from (1) strongly oppose to (4) strongly favor. *Defense spending opinion* is coded from (1) strongly oppose increased defense spending to (4) strongly favor.

Opinion on aid to the poor is a three-item scale (alpha = .645) consisting of responses to questions that asked parishioners the extent to which their parish should devote scarce resources to (a) helping the poor within the parish, (b) helping the poor outside the parish, and (c) working to change unjust socioeconomic conditions. Each item was reverse coded from (1) give much more attention to (5) give much less attention. Thus, the scale has a range of 3 (devote much more attention to each item) to 15 (devote much less attention to each item).

Unilateral freeze is a four-category variable measuring the extent to which the respondent favors urging a unilateral freeze by the United States on the development of nuclear weapons "regardless of what the Soviet Union does," and is coded from (1) strongly favor to (4) strongly oppose. *Joint freeze* measures the extent to which the respondent favors a joint freeze between the United States and the Soviet Union on the development of nuclear weapons, and is coded from (1) strongly favor to (4) strongly oppose.

Gun control measures the extent to which the respondent favors "registration of all firearms," and is coded from (1) strongly favor to (4) strongly oppose. *Busing* is coded from (1) for those who strongly favor "busing to achieve racial integration in the public schools" to (4) for those who strongly oppose busing. *ERA* is coded from (1) for those who strongly favor passage of the Equal Rights Amendment to (4) for those strongly opposed to the ERA.

School prayer is a measure of the extent to which the respondent favors "requiring prayer in public schools," coded from (1) strongly oppose to (4) strongly favor. *Teaching creationism* measures the extent to which the respondent favors "requiring public schools to give equal time for the teaching of creation theory and evolution theory about man's origins," and is coded from (1) strongly oppose to (4) strongly favor. Finally, *opinion on homosexual teachers* is coded from (1) for those who strongly favor "allowing homosexuals to teach in public schools" to (4) strongly oppose.

8. The question in the pastor survey measuring pastor's support for school integration is used in the *busing* model here. The question in the pastor survey asks to what extent the respondent favors "working," as opposed to "busing," "to achieve racial integration in the public schools."

9. *Homily quality* is the parish average of a four-item summated scale (alpha = .856). Parishioners were asked to indicate the extent to which the average homily at their parish is uninspiring or inspiring, dull or interesting, informative or uninformative, and useful in helping their faith to grow or not. Each item was coded from 1 (uninspiring, dull, etc.) to 5 (inspiring, interesting, etc.). The average score on this scale was calculated for each parish to develop an overall measure for the quality of each pastor's homilies; then, for the *homily quality* variable, these parish averages were centered around their group mean.

The *preaching effort* variable is constructed from a three-item scale (alpha = .711). The scale items asked each pastor (a) how important preaching is to being a parish priest (coded from 1, fifth most important or lower, to 5, most important); (b) how enjoyable preaching is (coded from 1, fifth most enjoyable activity or lower, to 5, most enjoyable activity); and (c) how much time he spends on preaching (coded from 1, fifth most time or less, to 5, most amount of time). The scale was then averaged by dividing each pastor's total score by the number of items to which a valid response was provided (only pastors providing a valid response to at least two of the three items are included here) and centered around the pastor group mean, such that a score of 0 represents average effort in preaching, positive scores indicate above-average effort in preaching, and negative scores indicate below-average effort in preaching.

10. *Political involvement* is an eight-item scale (alpha = .900), with items measuring the extent to which the pastor believes his parish should be involved in advocating for the rights of minorities, local zoning laws, handling of crime and criminals, prevention of drug and alcohol abuse, medical care issues, local elections, business/government relations, and quality of public education. Each item was coded from (1) less involved to (5) more involved. Scores ranged from 8 to 40. This scale was averaged by dividing the sum of the scores for each item by the number of items to which the pastor provided a valid response, and centered around the pastor group mean. Only those pastors who provided valid responses to at least seven of the eight items are included in these analyses.

11. Drawing on the work of Welch and Leege, each of the dependent variables are defined as follows: *God as judge* is the average of a four-item scale (alpha = .641) measuring the extent to which parishioners describe God as judge and God as master, and accept as true the description of God as strict and God as judgmental. *God as judge* ranges from 1 to 5, with higher scores indicating a conception of God as judge.

God as father is the average of a five-item scale (alpha = .865) measuring the extent to which parishioners describe God as creator, God as father, God as friend, God as protector, and God as redeemer. This scale ranges from 1 to 25, with higher scores indicating a conception of God as father.

God as companion is the average of a four-item scale (alpha = .707) measuring the extent to which parishioners accept as true the description of God as "aware of everything I think," clearly knowable, close, and a constant companion. *God as companion* ranges from 1 to 5, with higher scores indicating a conception of God as companion.

Finally, *God as savior* is the average of a three-item scale (alpha = .738) measuring the extent to which parishioners accept as true the description of God as dependable, faithful, and forgiving. This scale ranges from 1 to 5, with higher scores indicating a conception of God as savior.

12. Alphas for the pastors' scales ranged from .620 for *God as companion* to .898 for *God as savior*.

chapter three
Priestly Politics in 2004

The results presented and discussed in the previous chapter are consistent with what one would expect to find if clergy influence over parishioners' political attitudes were in fact taking place. That said, the evidence presented to this point is, for two reasons, insufficient for declaring conclusively that clergy play the politically important role hypothesized by so many scholars of religion and politics. First, the results presented in chapter 2, though suggestive, are also in some instances counterintuitive and confusing. Although liberal pastors appear to wield significant political influence with their flocks, conservative pastors, surprisingly, appear not to wield the same sort of influence. Second, the data from the Notre Dame Study of Catholic Parish Life are not ideal for investigating the question of clergy influence, primarily because they contain no information about the messages delivered by clergy to their parishioners. In order to obtain more definitive answers about the extent to which clergy wield political influence, it is necessary first to obtain data that may speak more directly to the question at hand. To that end, the next several chapters describe a new study, undertaken during the course of 2004, designed specifically for the purpose of investigating the political influence of Catholic clergy.

My investigation of the extent of political influence exercised by Catholic priests is modeled closely on the Notre Dame Study and is based on detailed case studies of nine separate Catholic parishes from the mid-Atlantic region. It is designed to obtain two separate types of information from each of the nine parishes involved in the study. At each parish I sought first to obtain a thorough understanding and accurate measurement of the types of messages delivered by priests to parishioners. Second, I administered an election survey in November 2004 to a relatively large sample of parishioners at each parish. By combining information about the messages delivered by priests at each of the parishes with the results of the parishioner surveys, and by comparing the results of the different parishioner surveys, it is possible to gain a sense of the type and extent of priestly influence taking place. The methodology, details, and results from the parishioner surveys will be discussed in chapter 5. The remainder of this chapter is devoted to a discussion of parish selection and a descriptive analysis of the messages delivered by parish priests to their parishioners.

Parish Selection and Characteristics

This study focuses on three randomly selected parishes from each of three Catholic dioceses in the mid-Atlantic region (Arlington, VA; Richmond, VA; and Washington, D.C.), for a total of nine parishes.[1] Although the parishes were randomly selected, this sample of parishes is not sufficiently large to be considered representative of parishes in the United States, the mid-Atlantic region, or even of the dioceses of Arlington, Richmond, or Washington. The random selection of these parishes, however, does provide assurance that any effects of priestly communications that are uncovered are not likely to be unique to these parishes; it is reasonable to assume that any clergy influence taking place at these parishes is likely to be occurring in similar ways in other parishes. In addition, as I hope will become clear throughout the remainder of this chapter, the process of random selection yielded a quite varied, heterogeneous group of parishes, both in terms of the demographic makeup of their parishioners and in terms of the messages conveyed by the priests at each parish. In order to protect the confidentiality of the priests who participated in the study, pseudonyms have been assigned to each of the parishes and pastors discussed here and listed in table 3.1.

Table 3.1 Parishes and Pastors: 2004 Study of Priestly Political Influence

Diocese of Arlington		Diocese of Richmond		Archdiocese of Washington	
Parish	*Pastor*	*Parish*	*Pastor*	*Parish*	*Pastor*
St. Anastasia	Fr. Alexander	St. Leon	Fr. Lewis	St. Winifred	Fr. Williams
St. Barnabas	Fr. Boyd	St. Margaret	Fr. McCormick	St. Yolanda	Fr. Yardley
St. Cyrus	Fr. Cook	St. Norbert	Fr. Nolan	St. Zachary	Fr. Zimmerman

Although it is not possible (in order to protect the confidentiality of priests) to provide explicitly detailed descriptions of each of the parishes included in this study, some general information about each of the parishes illustrates that the parishes included here are a fairly heterogeneous group. In the Diocese of Arlington, one of the parishes (St. Anastasia) is located in the inner Virginia suburbs, inside the beltway and just outside of Washington, D.C. The other two Arlington parishes, St. Barnabas and St. Cyrus, are located in the Virginia suburbs of Washington, D.C., but are outside the beltway. St. Barnabas and St. Cyrus are both medium-sized parishes (that is, they have a membership of between five hundred and fifteen hundred households), and St. Anastasia is a large parish (with membership exceeding fifteen hundred households).

In the Diocese of Richmond, St. Leon is located in a relatively small town (with a population of less than twenty-five thousand), and St. Norbert is located in a medium-size town (with a population of between twenty-five thousand and seventy-five thousand). St. Margaret is located in a small town in the eastern part of the state. St. Leon and St. Norbert are medium-sized parishes, and St. Margaret is a relatively small parish (with a membership of fewer than five hundred households).

Finally, in the Archdiocese of Washington, both St. Winifred and St. Yolanda are located in the Maryland suburbs of Washington, D.C. St. Zachary, on the other hand, is located in a rural area of southern Maryland. St. Winifred is a medium-sized parish, St. Yolanda is a large parish, and St. Zachary is a relatively small parish.

Therefore, the parishes included in this study are in several ways a diverse lot. In order to investigate and demonstrate priestly political influence, however, it is necessary to demonstrate, above all else, that there is diversity in the messages delivered by the priests to the parishioners at each of these parishes. Thus, the messages emanating from priests at each parish were measured in several ways. First, during the summer of 2004 I conducted extended interviews with the pastors at each of the parishes included in the study. Unlike the Notre Dame

Study's survey of pastors, I did not ask pastors about their own personal opinions on political matters. Indeed, in seeking the permission of the bishops of each of these dioceses to carry out this project, I assured them that I would refrain from inquiring as to priests' personal opinions. Instead, I asked the pastors about the manner in which, and the frequency with which, they publicly address political matters with their parishioners. Second, in order to verify the impressions gained during these pastor interviews, I performed detailed content analysis on parish bulletins (which are weekly parish newsletters distributed to parishioners at Mass) from a sample of Sundays during the summer of 2004, and from all of the Sundays between Labor Day and Election Day 2004. Third and finally, immediately following the 2004 presidential election, I mailed a questionnaire to each of the priests at all of the parishes in the study. (Four parishes, St. Cyrus, St. Margaret, St. Norbert, and St. Zachary, are staffed only by a pastor and have no assistant priests; the rest of the parishes have at least one assistant priest.) The questionnaire asked the priests to reflect on the sermons they delivered in the months leading up to the election, and to indicate the extent to which, and the manner in which, they addressed a variety of political topics.[2]

Before detailing my findings about the messages delivered by priests to their parishioners at these nine parishes, a few words are in order concerning the nature of the variance in priestly messages that I expected to find. As mentioned in previous chapters, the Catholic Church is a hierarchical organization with clearly delineated positions on many of the issues that will be of interest here. I did not expect to find that priests publicly express opinions (such as support for legalized abortion or opposition to efforts, governmental or otherwise, to help the poor and disadvantaged) that clearly conflict with official Church teaching. I did expect, however, to find significant variance in the extent to which priests emphasize attention to some political issues as opposed to others. Specifically, I expected to find that some priests emphasize attention to Church teaching on abortion and sexual morality, as opposed to other issues, in their preaching and public announcements. Priests who adopt this approach to preaching can be thought of as being particularly focused upon personal morality in their public statements, and thus will hereafter be referred to as "personal morality priests." I expected other priests to emphasize attention to Church teaching in areas in which the Church has taken a more liberal stand, such as economic issues and capital punishment, as opposed to abortion and sexual morality. These priests focus more on the Church's social justice teachings in their public messages, and will thus be referred to as "social justice priests." Finally, I expected some priests to pay relatively equal attention to all of these issues in their preaching. These priests will be subsequently referred to as "mixed-emphasis priests."

I have adopted terms of these sorts as a matter of convenience, and do not mean to suggest anything about individual priests' personal views on any particular political or social issue. I do not mean to imply, for instance, that personal morality priests view issues of social justice as unimportant, nor that social justice priests have less stringent moral standards than personal morality priests. Rather, these terms are used solely as shorthand descriptors of priests' various approaches to preaching. I turn, then, in the remainder of this chapter, to a discussion of the results of the pastor interviews, before considering the content analysis of the bulletins and the results of the priest surveys in the next chapter.

Pastor Interviews

The theory presented and discussed throughout the entirety of this work—that parish priests exercise considerable and noticeable influence over the political attitudes and behavior of their parishioners—is predicated on the notion that there is some variance in the public messages delivered by priests to parishioners. The pages that follow demonstrate dramatically and conclusively that this is indeed the case. It is also important to point out, however, that there are some striking and important similarities in the approaches to preaching adopted by the pastors interviewed for this study (the script used in interviewing parishioners is contained in appendix A). Although this is perhaps not entirely surprising (after all, this is a group of Catholic priests, all of whom have chosen to dedicate their lives to the service of the Catholic Church and her people), these similarities are worth discussing in some detail.

Perhaps the most obvious similarity that emerged from the pastor interviews is that each pastor reported that he enjoys the act of preaching. For instance, when asked whether or not preaching is something he enjoys, Fr. Zimmerman of St. Zachary parish in the Archdiocese of Washington responded by saying, "It's probably, other than my prayers, it's probably the thing that I enjoy the most." Similarly, Fr. Nolan of St. Norbert Parish said of preaching, "Oh, it's something I very much enjoy." Fr. Cook responded to my question as to whether or not he enjoys preaching by saying, "Yes, I love preaching." Finally, Fr. McCormick replied, "I enjoy it very much. I don't know if the listeners enjoy it that much, but I do." The rest of the pastors I interviewed expressed a similar affinity for the task of delivering homilies, making this group of pastors unanimous in their enjoyment of the task of preaching.[3]

Just as all of the pastors participating in this project indicated that they enjoy preaching, they also all indicated that they approach the general task of preaching in a very similar way. Specifically, every pastor indicated that he strives to deliver homilies that are based both on reflection on the scripture readings from that week and on a practical application of those readings to parishioners' lived experiences. Fr. Zimmerman, for instance, when asked whether his sermons focused mostly on scripture, daily life, or some combination thereof, said, "Mine is a balanced mixture. . . . What I do is I take the four readings, the psalm, and the Old Testament, and the two New Testament readings, and I show them [the parishioners] how there's a common theme in them all. And then I show through the scriptures how that common theme is in the Bible, and then how . . . we apply it to today." Fr. Alexander also indicated that his preaching style is "probably a mixture. . . . I certainly will focus and pray over the scriptures for that Sunday . . . and then, you know, I do try to apply it to what's going on." Fr. Lewis expressed a similar sentiment, and said that, in his own preaching, he strives to provide his parishioners with "a deeper understanding of God's word, and then . . . (apply) that word to the life situations that we all experience."

Fr. Yardley, when asked whether he focuses primarily on scripture or on everyday life in his sermons, said, "Obviously, my intent would be to have the readings and the liturgy apply to their [each parishioner's] life in some way." Fr. Williams of St. Winifred Parish in the Archdiocese of Washington was quite explicit in describing his approach to composing and delivering a homily. He outlined his preaching by saying, "I would say the first part of my homily is more using the gospel, mostly the gospel text, and giving some historical background and exegetical material so they can understand the context of the scriptures, and then, usually the last third of the homily I try to make some practical applications that they can think about in their own lives." Perhaps the reason behind this uniformity of approach to sermonizing is best summed up by Fr. McCormick, who said that "the [canon] law says that you're supposed to use the readings and the Mass text, and then apply them to the issues of the community today. And I've always tried that. So they [the homilies] are heavily scripture based, the three readings are mentioned somehow or other, and then, general application to people's lives" is made.

In addition to their enjoyment of and approach to preaching, most of the pastors I spoke with shared similar opinions of their effectiveness as public speakers. Specifically, I asked each pastor whether or not he considered himself to be an effective speaker, and most indicated that they did in fact think of themselves as successful and persuasive in getting their messages across. Fr. Boyd, for instance, responded to my question by saying of his parishioners, "Well, I think, from the reaction, that they find it [his preaching] convincing." Fr. Lewis's perception of his own preaching was a bit more qualified, but still positive.

He said, "I think there are a considerable number of people who take to heart what I have to say. There are those who really don't pay much attention to anything that's being said . . . but after . . . [so many] years [in the parish] I think I've had a pretty good influence." Fr. Williams indicated that his parishioners may not always pay close attention to the scriptural-exegesis portion of his homilies, but that they are more intrigued and moved by the portion dealing with everyday life. He considers that portion of his homilies to be "pretty effective, cause that's where . . . you get people's attention. And I've been here [for a number of] years so they're used to me, they know how I talk, so they know that the first part [of the homily] is where I talk about the scriptures, otherwise you can turn me off for the first five minutes. So, I think when you get into those things [the everyday life portion of the homily], I think people's ears perk up."

Fr. Zimmerman considers his own preaching to be effective, in part because of his preaching style. His perception is that his parishioners find his homilies convincing because he quotes "from a lot of sources. . . . So that people know it's not me with my soapbox." He indicated that "a lot of priests . . . just get up there [on the pulpit] and think they might as well read the newspaper to them [the parishioners]. You know, it's not the Phil Donahue show or the Oprah Winfrey talk hour. You're supposed to be expounding on the scriptures and giving what the Church teaches." Yet, while most of the pastors I interviewed consider themselves to be effective preachers, there was not unanimity on this question. One pastor, Fr. McCormick, admitted bluntly that, when it comes to preaching, "It's always a struggle." Nevertheless, the degree to which the pastors agree in their perceptions of their own preaching is remarkable.

Although the pastors are clearly similar in their approaches to preaching, I expected to find more pronounced differences in the frequency with which—and the manner in which—they address certain topics. Indeed, I found this to be the case, as will be described below, with regard to a number of important sociopolitical issues, including abortion, aid to the poor, birth control, and homosexuality, and with regard to the extent to which pastors choose to emphasize one or more issues as opposed to others. The pastors continued to exhibit remarkable consistency, however, with respect to the way they reported addressing one very important political issue. Specifically, they were quite similar in their approach to their public statements about foreign affairs, including the war on terror and the ongoing conflict in Iraq. I asked each pastor both about the context in which they address foreign affairs and about the frequency with which they publicly address these matters. There was some slight variation in the frequency with which they publicly address foreign affairs; in some parishes, the global situation is addressed at the very least in the communal prayers of the faithful on a weekly basis, while at other parishes foreign affairs arise as a topic of discussion more irregularly. But all of the pastors I interviewed indicated that when foreign affairs do arise as a topic in homilies or in public prayers, they are addressed in the dual context of expressing support and hope for the safety and well-being of American troops (and other combatants), and in expressing a desire for global peace. Fr. Cook, for instance, told me that, "When the war in Iraq was beginning, I tried to, without taking a stance for or against the war, I tried to present to people what the teaching of Pope John Paul was . . . that war is a last resort and the need to seek nonviolent solutions to the problem. Always, I have to say always I make the link . . . that we have a need to pray for the support and the safety of our troops. And that's a given." Similarly, Fr. Yardley indicated that, though he could not recall ever explicitly addressing the policies of the Bush administration, he "could say that we pray for peace, for the troops, for the protection of the troops, we pray for innocent people, I pray for the end of war." Most of the other pastors described their approach to foreign affairs in similar ways.

This similarity among pastors was somewhat surprising. I expected to find some pastors who take a "conservative" approach to foreign affairs by emphasizing support for American troops, and others who take a "liberal" approach to foreign affairs by emphasizing the need to pray and work for peace. In my own personal experience, I have observed parishes take very different approaches to issues of war and peace. During the first Gulf War, in the early 1990s, for several weeks the exit hymn at the parish I attended was "Let There Be Peace on Earth, and Let it Begin With Me." On the other hand, at the (different) parish I attended on the Sunday following the September 11 attacks on New York and Washington, D.C., the exit hymn was "The Battle Hymn of the Republic." And my intuition is that, were one able to attend Mass every Sunday at each of the nine parishes included in this study, one would recognize subtle differences in their approaches to these issues. After all, one pastor, Fr. Boyd, admitted that he does "support the war." Fr. Nolan, meanwhile, told me that in his homilies, "I don't say I think President Bush should give this [attacking Iraq] a second thought. Or I just can't stand Mr. Rumsfeld. None of that comes out in homilies." It seems clear, however, that those are the opinions held by Fr. Nolan, and I would not be surprised if both Fr. Boyd and Fr. Nolan, in subtle ways, make their differing opinions known to their parishioners. While I speculate, however, that greater differences may exist in the way these pastors approach foreign affairs than emerged in the interviews, the fact remains that all the pastors reported occupying a middle ground in their public messages, emphasizing both support for American troops and the need to work and pray for peace, and I take them at their word.

While there are therefore many similarities in the messages emanating from the pastors participating in this study, there are also many important differences that may be expected to influence the political attitudes of parishioners. Specifically, during the course of my interviews with all nine pastors, important differences emerged in their approaches to economic issues and aid to the poor, abortion, homosexuality, and birth control. In addition, the interviews revealed that there are substantial differences among pastors as to which issue or issues receive paramount attention in their preaching and public messages. I discuss each of these issue areas and the question of issue emphasis in turn.

Economic Issues

As discussed in some detail in chapter 1, one sociopolitical issue on which the Catholic Church, as an institution, has taken a strong stand is the duty for individual Catholics, citizens, and even public authorities to take steps to provide for the needs and material well-being of the poor and marginalized in society. This message is promoted not only by the Church hierarchy in the form of papal encyclicals and bishops' statements; it is also promulgated at the local level by parish priests. Indeed, of the nine pastors I spoke with, eight indicated that aid to the poor is a topic that they discuss regularly with their parishioners in their homilies and other public statements, and the ninth reported that aid to the poor is an occasional topic of discussion. While the pastors are thus united in their belief that aid to the poor is an appropriate topic for priests to address, there were some important differences that emerged about the contexts in which the pastors report discussing this issue. Specifically, four pastors indicated that they address aid to the poor primarily in the context of encouraging individual parishioners to provide assistance to the disadvantaged; four other pastors suggested that they discuss aid to the needy both in terms of encouraging individual initiative in providing assistance and in terms of governmental responsibility to the disadvantaged.

When addressing aid to the poor, Fr. Boyd, Fr. Cook, Fr. Lewis, and Fr. Zimmerman indicated that they do so primarily in the context of encouraging individuals to come to the assistance of those in need, and that they are less likely to speak of the need to support government programs that assist the poor. Fr. Boyd, for instance, when asked specifically whether he emphasizes individual responsibility, public policy, or some combination thereof, responded by saying, "It's the first [individual responsibility]." He went on to say that he is a great admirer of the work of Mother Theresa, who sought "out the poorest of the poor." He pointed out, however, that "mostly, Mother Theresa, not that she didn't believe in government programs, but she, her main pitch was we do our own, and so, subsidiarity, the lowest level possible." Fr. Zimmerman, when asked the same question, replied:

> I'm more of the bent that we should try and help those we can see. I'm not fond of the anonymous institutions that you give to [such as the government] and somehow feel gratified. See, I want you to go visit a poor person, sit in their home, eat with them, just as Jesus would. See what their problems are, and how you can assist them. It's not always money. You've got people who sometimes just need companionship. And money as the solution to problems, I think, as Paul tells Timothy, money is the root of all evil. . . . In that bent I'm more toward the individual thing.

Perhaps Fr. Lewis was the most blunt of the pastors who encourage individuals to become involved in providing assistance to those in need while refraining from encouraging parishioners to support government programs designed to do the same:

> I would say that Catholics have a moral responsibility from the very aspect of what faith is to follow out Christ's call to practice the corporal and spiritual works of mercy. These are not options, they are obligations that are placed upon us. . . . And I always emphasize that we have to be personally involved, not remotely involved. And so the individual charities that we might be involved in, these are things that have direct impact in a personal way. I also believe that because of our faith we have to have a clear and consistent voice in the political domain.

Despite this need for a clear political voice, however, Fr. Lewis claimed that, "I would also say that many times, Church-sponsored agencies do a much better job of assisting the poor than government-initiated enterprises. I would for example support the whole idea of faith-based initiatives. They have a proven track record. Government-controlled agencies are inefficient and expensive and often ineffective."

Clearly, then, this subset of pastors, while not shying away from addressing the Church's teachings about aid to the poor, does so primarily in the context of encouraging individual parishioners and citizens to become involved as private citizens.

Four other pastors, however, reported taking a markedly different approach when addressing aid to the poor in their sermons and other public statements. While they share a commitment to addressing the issue and to encouraging individuals to become involved in charity and relief work, they also indicated that it is not uncommon for them to point out the government's responsibility in providing for the disadvantaged. Fr. Williams, for instance, when asked whether he preaches about aid to the poor in primarily an individual or governmental context, responded by saying, "I think, both . . . you know, if the gospel lends it to talk about the hungry in the world, for instance, I might talk about bread for the world . . . [and] how that helps people directly financially but also through lobbying groups. And . . . talk about the government responsibility, although I think one [area] where people can be more responsive nowadays is they read the paper where the government's cutting back on programs and so the churches have to pick up the slack."

Fr. McCormick, in a similar vein, reported that his own preaching on this issue is "a combination of both [individual and governmental responsibility]. To awaken the individual parishioner, but the parish as a community, as a group working together toward these issues and alleviating those issues. . . . It would be on the occasion . . . that the Diocese itself comes out with an issue as regards the Virginia legislature, or the Bishops of the United States do as regards a national motion towards something." Two other pastors, Fr. Yardley and Fr. Alexander, initially indicated that they typically preach about aid to the poor in terms of individual responsibility, but the examples they cited suggest that they, too, frequently address governmental policy toward the poor. Fr. Yardley, for instance, first indicated that he does not think aid to the poor "has much to do with public policy." He went on, however, to say that

Every once in a while we will alert people, we have a social concerns table in our gathering space. And there may be something that comes across my desk from the social concerns committee, that will say something like this is what . . . [Walmart] is doing . . . this is how it affects the local economy. Or it has to do with living wage. So there will come things, we have a legislative network here so that people can be tied into that so that they can get announcements about how to respond to their politicians from the Maryland Catholic Conference. . . . I don't preach about it very much, but it's something that they become aware of those things.

Thus, while Fr. Yardley frequently refrains from structuring his homilies around the topic of governmental responsibility to provide aid to the poor, he clearly communicates the political dimensions of this topic to his parishioners.

Fr. Alexander takes a similar approach. When asked about the context in which he publicly discusses aid to the poor, he responded by saying "all of this stuff begins in your heart and my heart, not over there in Congress. And . . . there's so many problems with [the political system] . . . that that's not the solution to the problem." He went on to say, however, that while he does not tell his parishioners that they "should be supporting legislation, it's more that you should be sensitive, and you look for ways, and hopefully that leads to your activity in the political arena to get laws passed." Fr. Alexander also told me, in response to a different question, that in one of his homilies he "mentioned if we spent half the money that we spent already in Iraq blowing things up, put tens of billions of dollars to address some needs in a developing country that's facing disaster, not only will we accomplish more towards building the Kingdom, but . . . certainly America's image would shine a lot brighter around the world. We'd be . . . safer." This is clearly a political statement about the proper avenues for government spending. Fr. Alexander, then, along with Fr. Lewis, Fr. McCormick, and Fr. Williams, demonstrates a willingness to address public policy and politics as they relate to the need to provide assistance to the poor.

In sum, all of the pastors I spoke with express a willingness and commitment to address publicly the need to provide assistance to the poor and disadvantaged. However, there were important differences in the contexts in which they report doing so. Four pastors indicated that they address this issue primarily, and perhaps exclusively, in terms of encouraging individuals to get involved in aid to those in need, while four other pastors expressed a willingness to connect aid to the poor with politics and public policy. I turn now to a discussion of the manner in which pastors discuss abortion with their parishioners.

Abortion

The pastors who participated in this project exhibit a remarkable degree of diversity in the frequency with which (and the context in which) they publicly speak about abortion with their parishioners. Three pastors indicated that they discuss abortion in their homilies on a regular basis; two pastors say that they address abortion in their public statements occasionally; and three pastors raise the abortion issue with their parishioners only rarely. Similarly, several pastors indicated that when addressing abortion, they focus primarily on the implications of abortion for individual conscience and morality, while several other pastors said that they also focus explicitly on politics and public policy as they relate to abortion. These diverging approaches to the abortion issue are crucial in demonstrating that Catholic parishioners are exposed to very different political messages emanating from their priests depending on where they go to church.

Three pastors—Fr. Boyd, Fr. Lewis, and Fr. Zimmerman—indicated that they regularly address abortion in their public statements, and that the Church's opposition to abortion is a frequently recurring theme in their preaching. For instance, Fr. Zimmerman, when asked how often he addresses abortion in his homilies, said, "Once a month . . . once or twice a month." Similarly, Fr. Lewis stated, "I have given many homilies about the problems of our declining culture and how so many of these problems are directly connected to each other. So abortion and all those threats against the defenseless are certainly things that I raise on a regular basis." Finally, Fr. Boyd indicated that he delivers homilies that focus directly and perhaps exclusively on abortion a couple of times a year, but that "it comes up often in the course of a homily as an example of something a person could do, or a listing of evils." For these three pastors, plainly, abortion is a theme that regularly arises in their preaching.

Two pastors, Fr. Alexander and Fr. Cook, indicated that abortion is a topic that arises only occasionally in their preachings. Fr. Alexander, for instance, said that his homilies during the week of the March for Life (in January) and on Respect Life Sunday (in October) "might be totally devoted to life." Otherwise, he told me that abortion might come up "as part of" a homily "four or five times a year." Fr. Cook told me that he does not

> shy away from speaking about abortion, but it's not something that comes up that frequently, but I would suppose it comes up, maybe, four to six times a year, in a special way I would say at least once a year at the March for Life in January. And in October, which is a special month that the Church designates as a month for respecting life. And then on other occasions, when it seems to be appropriate based on [the scripture] readings, or I try to be aware of what is . . . in people's attention, especially media attention to issues. So I wouldn't come up on a particular Sunday and think I haven't talked about abortion in three months, maybe I should remind people about that. I would be more looking at the fact that, since I read the newspaper everyday and I watch the news every night, . . . and if the issue is in the forefront of what the media is addressing, . . . then I would think the Church needs to share its vision or its message.

Fr. Alexander and Fr. Cook, then, do speak about abortion with their parishioners, but perhaps not as regularly as Fr. Boyd, Fr. Lewis, and Fr. Zimmerman.

At the other end of the spectrum from Fr. Boyd, Fr. Lewis, and Fr. Zimmerman are Fr. McCormick, Fr. Yardley, and Fr. Williams, who indicated that they publicly address the abortion issue only on rare occasions, most typically on special Sundays (such as the weekend of the March for Life, in January, or on Respect Life Sunday, in October) set aside by the Church as days on which to focus on abortion, or life issues in general. When asked how often the subject of abortion arises in his homilies, Fr. Yardley told me, "It comes up maybe, I think I might talk about it twice a year. At the anniversary of Roe v. Wade, and October is Respect Life month. I know that I have, yeah, it's probably only those things that prompt me to bring it up. Otherwise it doesn't come up very often." For Fr. Williams, abortion may arise even less frequently. When asked how often he speaks about abortion in his homilies, he replied, "Usually in the month of January, we're encouraged to talk about this issue, so usually I do once a year." He explained that "it's hard to bring a new slant to it [the abortion issue], and I find the people in front of you have not had abortions, so you have to treat it in a sense of education but not indict the people that are sitting in front of you, because the people who have abortions don't go to Church, so by talking about people who don't go to Church on Sunday, the people in front of you are there, so why talk about those who aren't there?" Similarly, Fr. McCormick indicated that he, too, publicly addresses abortion on only a couple of occasions throughout the year. He told me, "I preach on it on the anniversary of the Supreme Court decision. . . . And then I'll have a special Mass during the week of whenever March 25 occurs, which is the Catholic Feast of the Annunciation. So when Jesus' life began in the womb of Mary. . . . And so, it would be the occasion of the Roe decision and then March 25, so they'd be deliberate times when the thing would be on abortion."

Just as there are important differences among pastors in how frequently they discuss abortion with their parishioners, so are there important differences in the contexts in which these discussions take place. Several priests, including Fr. Zimmerman, Fr. Nolan, and Fr. Williams, suggested that they speak about the implications of abortion only as they affect individual morality and private conscience, and that they do not specifically address public policy pertaining to abortion.

Fr. Nolan made this point emphatically, stating, "I have never once said from the pulpit the words 'Roe v. Wade.' Never." He went on to explain that he thinks it is the duty of the Catholic and Christian communities to hold their members accountable on these types of issues, and that relying on politicians or public officials for moral guidance is futile. He said that he has "more trust and faith in them [his parishioners], and they should in me, because we both are trying to follow the Lord Jesus in all that we do, and I don't sit down there looking at eleven people on that dais in city council and think that any of them are trying to follow Jesus necessarily. Or Mohammed, or any of the rest of the guys." Father Williams was more concise. When asked whether he focuses on individual morality or politics and public policy with regard to abortion, he said, "Usually that issue is more individual responsibility." Fr. Zimmerman explained, "I do not ever speak explicitly about what would be appropriate public policy, but more about our individual morality. In fact I will have said at times you can't legislate morality. If this country . . . didn't want abortion, it wouldn't matter if it was legal or illegal. If our morals were in the correct place, we wouldn't be contemplating . . . should it be legal or not."

Other priests, however, including Fr. Yardley, Fr. Cook, Fr. Boyd, and Fr. Lewis, indicated that they are more willing to publicly address their parishioners about the intersection of abortion and public policy. Fr. Yardley said that he talks about abortion with regard to both individual morality and public policy. He told me that in his congregation, "there are not many people who are out having abortions. There are a number of people out there I'm aware who believe that it should be legalized. And so when I speak about it, I speak about . . . how can it be that we even can come to a conclusion that . . . having an abortion is something that we can choose to do. Because it's the taking of a life, and it's denying a fact, a reality, a person." Fr. Cook also indicated that abortion is addressed in a dual context:

> I think what I mostly try to do when it comes to the abortion issue is do two things. And that is one, give people a sense of how I, hopefully being

faithful to the Church, evaluate what is happening or has happened on a level of legislation or court decision. And secondly, remind people that we do what we can in the public policy arena but, ultimately, I think the abortion issue, like many issues, is an issue that requires a change of heart on the part of the people.

Fr. Boyd refrains from giving his parishioners specific instructions, and he hasn't "given a sermon on passing a constitutional amendment, but you could surmise" from his homilies that he would support such an amendment. Perhaps Fr. Lewis was most blunt in emphasizing his attention to public policy as it relates to abortion: "I try to express the idea that we're dealing with human life here, we're not dealing with potential human life, we're dealing with authentic human life. And I would say that our goal should be to work at minimizing the possibility of having abortions done under the mantle of law." These four pastors, then, do not hesitate to address politics as it relates to the abortion issue.

Finally, it is important to point out that Fr. McCormick takes a truly unique approach in his public discussion of this issue, at least when compared with the other pastors participating in this study. Fr. McCormick (who, you will recall, only discusses abortion on a couple of occasions each year) explained to me that, under canon law, fetuses are not considered people. Abortion, therefore, despite the claims made by so many priests and other pro-life activists, is not, under canon law, murder. He makes this point clear to his parishioners whenever he discusses abortion, telling them that "you cannot ever say it's murder." None of this is to imply that Fr. McCormick is not as pro-life as the other pastors, for he is clearly opposed to abortion. Nevertheless, it seems safe to conclude that parishioners who hear Fr. McCormick claim explicitly that abortion is not murder are hearing a message that is quite different (and so may be influenced differently) from parishioners at St. Leon parish, who hear Fr. Lewis argue that in questions about abortion, "we're dealing with authentic human life."

Clearly, then, important differences exist among pastors in both the frequency of their public remarks on abortion and the context of those remarks. Similar differences exist in the approaches adopted by pastors toward another controversial sociopolitical topic, homosexuality.

Homosexuality

The morality of homosexuality has long been an issue of concern to many politically active individuals, and some of the issues surrounding homosexuality, most notably the debate over gay marriage, were particularly prominent during the 2004 election cycle. The Catholic Church considers homosexual behavior (along with all extramarital sexual behavior) to be sinful, and it is opposed to official recognition of homosexual unions. Despite these official positions, the messages that Catholic parishioners hear regarding homosexuality from their parish priests vary considerably, primarily in terms of the frequency with which the issue is addressed, but also in terms of the contexts in which the issue is addressed.

Of the nine pastors I spoke with, six indicated that homosexuality is a topic that they never address from the pulpit, or that it is a topic that comes up only rarely. Fr. Zimmerman, for instance, told me that "I never have said anything in my homily about homosexual relations or same-sex marriages . . . the problem being that you don't know who's hearing, or what they're hearing. You know what you're saying, but in a homily sometimes you don't have time to completely express the whole point of view, you don't know who you're going to hurt, who you're going to maim by your words." Similarly, Fr. Williams, when asked whether or not he speaks about homosexuality and related issues in his sermons, responded by saying, "I've never touched that topic . . . I don't even know where I stand on that issue at the moment. . . . I don't think it's in the top ten of people's concerns." Fr. Yardley indicated that he had addressed the issue of homosexual marriage in the parish bulletin, but that it had not come up in his homilies. He said, "It has not come up, I have not spoken about homosexuality, I haven't spoken about what that is. . . . And I don't think any of the other [priests at the parish] have mentioned it either."

Fr. Alexander said that he thought that the Church was "going to have to come up with a way to talk about this [homosexuality] focusing on marriage," but in his own case, he said, "I can't remember when I gave a homily on homosexuality." Clearly, for most of the pastors I spoke with, homosexuality is not a frequent focus of public discussions.

However, there are three important exceptions. Fr. McCormick, Fr. Boyd, and Fr. Lewis all indicated that they touch on homosexuality and related topics occasionally in their homilies. Fr. McCormick, for instance, when asked about the frequency with which he publicly addresses homosexuality, responded by saying, "Not very often, but at times. And it will come into prayers of the faithful at certain times." Fr. Lewis indicated that he had spoken specifically about homosexual marriage "on several occasions," and indicated that when (in the spring and early summer of 2004) various localities in California, New York, and Massachusetts experimented with permitting gay marriages, the topic arose in his homilies "as things began to percolate on the west coast and also up north." Finally, Fr. Boyd, when asked how often homosexuality is discussed in his sermons, said that it comes up "in passing," and that when "listing . . . sins and problems today, homosexuality" comes up. He also mentioned that at times he attempts to discuss the issue in a way that gets a message across to adults in a format suitable for discussion in front of children. For instance, he has occasionally recounted the stories of famous individuals who (as the adults in the congregation know) were homosexuals, but who eventually repented and renounced that lifestyle.

While Fr. McCormick, Fr. Lewis, and Fr. Boyd thus share a willingness to talk about homosexuality and related issues in their sermons, the contexts in which they do so are quite varied. Fr. McCormick indicated that he strives to balance the Church's condemnation of the sin of homosexual behavior with a message of compassion, concern, and tolerance for those of homosexual orientation. When I asked him whether he tended to emphasize the sinfulness of homosexual behavior or the need to be compassionate toward those of homosexual orientation, he said, "I would think it's a combined thrust." Fr. Boyd and Fr. Lewis, however, both indicated that they are more straightforward in concentrating on the sinfulness of homosexual behavior and the impermissibility of gay marriage. Fr. Boyd, for instance, while reiterating the mercy of Jesus and the possibility for active homosexuals to repent and reform, said that in his own preaching he focuses primarily on "the need to repent of it [homosexuality]," as opposed to the need to have compassion for those of homosexual orientation. He also said, "I mention [in homilies] same-sex marriage as one of the problems today. I did talk on it one Sunday. That it was a danger and that, I did say we must do everything we can to support marriage, and that means opposing homosexual marriage." Similarly, Fr. Lewis said:

> I have on several occasions deplored how the court system is trying to legislate on a very clearly understood, historically defined meaning of marriage. It's one thing to recognize that in our society today there are people who are living in what they call a union of members between the same sex. We've also mentioned that people have rights to be respected though we disagree with how they're living. We recognize that they're still human beings made in the image and likeness of God. But I have very clearly denounced the idea that the institution of marriage should be compromised by any kind of recognition.

The context in which Fr. McCormick discusses homosexuality and related issues, then, appears to be quite different than the context in which Fr. Boyd and Fr. Lewis discuss these same topics.

Clearly, the messages Catholic parishioners receive (or do not receive, as the case may be) from their pastors regarding homosexuality vary widely from parish to parish. Two-thirds of the pastors in this study report speaking about homosexuality only rarely or not at all. Although the other three priests are comparatively more willing to discuss the issue, their approaches are diverse. I turn now to a discussion of another sociopolitical issue, birth control.

Birth Control

The Catholic Church teaches that it is sinful to employ the use of artificial contraceptives in order to avoid becoming pregnant. Admittedly, birth control is not a particularly controversial issue in American politics; no political party or mainstream political candidate advocates outlawing contraceptives. Nevertheless, it is reasonable to suppose that the frequency with which a priest addresses birth control in his preaching might be an accurate reflection of his sociopolitical and moral conservatism, and that Catholics who regularly hear about Church teachings on this issue might similarly be swayed in a conservative sociopolitical direction. Additionally, several scholars (Jelen 1984; Welch, Leege, and Cavendish 1995) have demonstrated a link between attitudes regarding birth control and attitudes toward other important political issues. It is, then, appropriate to consider the ways in which contraception is publicly discussed by the pastors participating in this project.

Interviews with Fr. Nolan and Fr. Alexander failed to provide a clear picture of the frequency with which they address birth control, but interviews with the other pastors were more revealing. Four pastors— Fr. Cook, Fr. McCormick, Fr. Williams, and Fr. Yardley—said that contraception is a topic that they rarely or never address in their homilies. Fr. Cook indicated that he does not discuss birth control in his homilies because there are other, much more appropriate, arenas for doing so. He said, "At this point I would say [birth control comes up] very infrequently, for this reason. First of all I feel like we address it with the people who need to hear it, first and foremost, in marriage preparation. And secondly as time goes on I really have some serious questions about the appropriateness of that in a Sunday homily." Similarly, Fr. Yardley explained, "I guess I haven't publicly said anything about it [birth control]. . . . I mean I totally accept and agree with everything the Church teaches. But I also don't feel like these are issues that I'm trying to force on people." Fr. Williams was even more explicit and forceful when asked whether or not he addresses contraception in his homilies. He said, "I think that's something that's been decided by the people. I think that issue . . . that's a nonissue. That issue's over. . . . I don't see a need to [discuss contraception] because I don't think it's an issue."[4] Finally, Fr. McCormick suggested that this is a topic that rarely arises in his homilies, but hinted that when it does, he implies that the prohibition on birth control may not be so clear cut. He explained, "I don't use the term birth control . . . or contraception. . . . When this does come up, I say people have the responsibility to plan their families reasonably. And they should do so according to how the Church teaches. But I said there's a lot of things that aren't clear in this area. It doesn't come up." For this group of pastors, then, contraception is not a key or even peripheral focus of their preaching.

On the other hand, Fr. Lewis, Fr. Zimmerman, and Fr. Boyd give birth control more prominent attention in their homilies. Fr. Zimmerman, for instance, stated:

Oh yeah, I'll bring that [birth control] up. Because it's a form of abortion, you're aborting the natural process God has. You may not be aborting a baby, but you're aborting a possible conception. Or, you may be aborting a conceived child, you don't know. Some of these artificial contraceptions abort a conceived child rather than prevent conception. But those would be . . . in that context, we may not like to hear what the Church teaches, that artificial contraception is not the way, that responsible parenthood requires natural family planning. That sort of thing.

Fr. Boyd also indicated that contraception arises sometimes as a topic in his homilies. When asked how often he speaks about it, he replied, "Whenever I talk on marriage. When I talk on slavery, I give a sermon on slavery, I connect it with birth control. Because the Church's teaching on slavery has been consistent despite what the media says," as has the Church's teaching on birth control. Finally, Fr. Lewis explained:

I have brought that [contraception] up, I have heard one of the [assistant parish] priests talk about it too. That the widespread acceptance of this has contributed to a host of social problems and that it is certainly a direct, has a direct impact on the instability of marriage and family life. Those who practice contraception have a much higher probability of having problems in their marriage, and also of having their marriage come to an end. I promote natural family planning in this parish. And I also encourage people who have formed the habit of contraception to have the courage to deal with that in the confessional.

In the homilies of Fr. Boyd, Fr. Zimmerman, and Fr. Lewis, the Church's teaching regarding artificial contraception is regularly reinforced, in stark contrast with the homilies of some of the other pastors.

When it comes to aid to the poor, abortion, homosexuality, and birth control, the preceding discussions illustrate that the approaches adopted by pastors in their public speaking vary widely. It is important to conclude this discussion of the pastor interviews with a consideration of the extent to which pastors emphasize some sociopolitical issues as opposed to others in their preaching.

Issue Emphasis

In addition to asking the nine pastors about their approaches to specific issues, I also asked them whether or not, in their preaching and public announcements, they tend to emphasize one issue (or one subset of issues) as opposed to others. Their answers were revealing, and provide further evidence that the messages to which Catholic parishioners are exposed vary widely from parish to parish. One pastor indicated that he emphasizes aid to the poor more than he does the other issues. Five pastors reported giving equal emphasis to all of the sociopolitical issues I asked about. Finally, three pastors reported placing paramount emphasis on abortion and related topics as opposed to the other issues.

Fr. Yardley was the lone pastor who claimed to emphasize aid to the poor above all other issues in his preaching and public statements. When I asked him which issues he tends to emphasize, he replied:

I mention abortion, or life issues, that happens twice a year, January and October. Unless there's something else that happens that it's right in our faces that we should bring something up. . . . But I think that, of those, the fact that we do talk about helping others does come up probably more than anything else . . . through Haiti, through other projects that we do, the Cardinal's appeal, and saying to people and talking to them about stewardship and tithing, where are they putting their treasure.

It is my experience and understanding that there are many pastors who share Fr. Yardley's tendency to emphasize these types of issues in their preaching. Nevertheless, Fr. Yardley was the only pastor participating in this study who explicitly acknowledged this pattern.

Five pastors—Fr. Alexander, Fr. Nolan, Fr. Cook, Fr. McCormick, and Fr. Williams—indicated that they attempt to place equal emphasis on all of these important sociopolitical concerns. Fr. McCormick, for instance, reports paying equal attention to all of these issues "because you can't have one without the others. Now what other people think in the pews is a completely different ballgame. . . . Put it this way. I see my job, rather than on these specific issues, whichever one you want to take as your pet, my responsibility as a priest and pastor and preacher is to tell you that you can't have any of these as pets. It's all of them or none of them. And that's my responsibility."

Fr. Cook explicitly invoked the example of Cardinal Bernardin, who developed the consistent ethic of life as an approach to a variety of political questions. Fr. Cook's statement is worth quoting at some length:

I guess I would have to say, what guides me is, in my own personal preaching and spiritual life and pastoral leadership, I think I have a pretty strong conviction that Cardinal Bernardin had a point with his consistent ethic of life. So if I had one theme that's important to me, it's that all human life is sacred. And that means one thing, that principle means one thing when it's applied to war and peace, when it's applied to abortion and euthanasia and capital punishment, when it's applied to issues of poverty, health care, housing. I guess that's what I try to do. I don't have a hierarchy. . . . If I'm pro-life, that means I'm against abortion, against capital punishment, I'm for providing healthcare to the greatest number of people, and adequate housing, and food and clothing to the greatest number of people. And I'm against war. You know, that war should be a last resort, a real last resort. So that's how I would look at it. That's the value to me that's paramount. Are we consistently pro-life?

Fr. Williams expressed a similar sentiment, albeit a bit differently. He claimed that, especially during the run-up to an election, "I think what I'll do is encourage them to look closely at what each candidate stands for, and to weigh, who do you think will be the best person for the next four years, not because they're pro-abortion, or anti-abortion, or pro-this or pro-that, but I'll ask them to look at all of the [issues], and to educate themselves about what the candidates stand for." For this subset of pastors, then, it is important that parishioners be instructed to consider political issues and concerns not in isolation, but as parts of a whole, and to formulate opinions and make decisions accordingly.

Three pastors, however—Fr. Boyd, Fr. Lewis, and Fr. Zimmerman—stated clearly and rather emphatically that, in the political arena, abortion (and closely related issues) is of paramount concern; therefore, they give special emphasis to abortion and related issues in their preaching. Fr. Boyd, for instance, said that he addresses all of these issues, but added, "The intensity of course would be abortion." Fr. Lewis was perhaps even more direct and explicit during the course of our conversation. When asked whether he preaches about abortion, he replied, "Absolutely. To me, it is the preeminent issue that we cannot ignore. Because we're dealing with the fundamental right to life here. If you cannot uphold the rights of the unborn, then you have begun to challenge if not destroy the foundation for everyone else's rights." When I asked Fr. Lewis whether or not he places particular emphasis on one issue in his sermons, he said, "Well . . . the most foundational issue is whether or not we're going to protect the young who've been brought forth into creation. If we're not going to do that, then all the other things aren't going to be able to work out. So in other words there is a bottom line that I believe we have to deal with." Finally, Fr. Zimmerman indicated that he shares the general approach adopted by Fr. Boyd and Fr. Lewis. When asked which issues he emphasizes, he responded, "I would say if I stress things more often than other things it would be premarital sex and abortion. Again I think they're becoming so commonplace."

There is, then, considerable variety among the nine pastors in their choice of which sociopolitical issues to emphasize in their preaching. One pastor emphasizes aid to the poor, while several other pastors attempt to emphasize all of these issues equally, and three pastors acknowledge attaching special importance to the abortion issue. This discussion of pastors' varying approaches to preaching about political issues makes it clear that Catholic parishioners hear very different messages depending on where they attend Mass. I realize, however, that it has been difficult for the reader to discern and maintain an overall profile of the messages delivered by each pastor to their parishioners. Accordingly, it is appropriate to conclude this chapter with a brief recap and summary of the preaching tactics of each pastor, before proceeding in the next chapter to analyses of parish bulletins and priest survey results.

Pastor Preaching Profiles

At the conclusion of the first interview I conducted, which happened to be with Fr. Williams, he conveyed a word of advice that proved quite prescient. He said, "As you talk to more and more people [pastors], I think just one thing to keep in mind [is] you're going to get a *very* big diversity of answers. And it depends what diocese you're in and what priest you're talking to. So what I say today may be totally contradicted by what you hear tomorrow. . . . You cannot categorize priests, they're uncontrollable and unorganizable." Fr. Williams' statement supports, at a fundamental level, the theory espoused and investigated in this project. Despite the hierarchical nature and clearly established teachings of the institutional Church, parish priests retain and exercise considerable autonomy in their preaching.

At the same time, however, Fr. Williams' statement represents something of a warning regarding the task undertaken here. Despite his admonition, and with awareness of the pitfalls involved, it is my intent to categorize and organize this group of pastors into distinct groups. Specifically, and with considerable trepidation, I propose that the nine pastors participating in this study can be categorized into three groups. The interviews described here suggest that, based on their preaching tendencies, three pastors can be described as social justice priests (since they preach often about the responsibility to come to the aid of the poor and disadvantaged, and less often about issues such as abortion, birth control, and homosexuality); three can be described as personal morality priests (since they place more emphasis on issues such as abortion and homosexuality, and less emphasis on issues like poverty); and three can be described as mixed-emphasis priests. By these criteria, Fr. McCormick, Fr. Lewis, and Fr. Yardley qualify as social justice priests; Fr. Alexander, Fr. Cook, and Fr. Nolan qualify as mixed-emphasis priests; while Fr. Boyd, Fr. Lewis, and Fr. Zimmerman qualify as personal morality priests. This categorization is extremely important for subsequent chapters, where I formulate and test various specific hypotheses to discern whether social justice priests have a liberalizing influence on the political attitudes and voting decisions of their parishioners, and whether personal morality pastors have a similar conservatizing influence. Of course, it is worth restating that these terms are not meant to imply that social justice priests are unconcerned with personal morality, or that personal morality priests are unconcerned about the plight of the poor; these are simply shorthand descriptors used to classify and describe the sociopolitical nature of each pastor's approach to preaching.

Pastors with a Social Justice Approach to Preaching

Fr. Williams, St. Winifred Parish

In my interview with Fr. Williams, he indicated that he frequently addresses aid to the poor in his homilies, and that he does so both in the context of encouraging individuals to provide assistance to those in need and in the context of reflecting on the role of public policy in providing relief services. When it comes to sexual issues, however, Fr. Williams is more circumspect. He stated that he never preaches about birth control and never addresses homosexuality in his sermons. Furthermore, his sermons rarely focus on abortion; when he does address abortion, he does so primarily in the context of individual morality, and he refrains from discussing public policy and politics as they relate to the abortion issue.

Fr. McCormick, St. Margaret Parish

Father McCormick frequently preaches about aid to the poor, and he considers both individual and government responsibility when doing so. Like Fr. Williams, he never preaches about contraception; however, he hinted during an interview that the Church's ban on birth control might not be as clear as some make it out to be. Fr. McCormick rarely addresses abortion, and when he does, he takes care to emphasize to his parishioners that abortion is not murder. Finally, although Fr. McCormick occasionally addresses homosexuality and related issues, he emphasizes the need to have compassion and understanding for those of homosexual orientation.

Fr. Yardley, St. Yolanda Parish

Fr. Yardley reported that he speaks frequently about aid to the poor, and he indicated that of all the sociopolitical issues discussed here, poor aid was the single issue on which he placed the most emphasis. He addresses abortion only rarely, and never preaches on homosexuality or on birth control.

Pastors with a Mixed-Emphasis Preaching Style

Fr. Alexander, St. Anastasia Parish

Fr. Alexander occasionally addresses both aid to the poor and abortion in his sermons. Although it is unclear how often he publicly discusses birth control, he did indicate that he never discusses homosexuality. Finally, he reported placing equal emphasis on all of the sociopolitical issues considered here.

Fr. Cook, St. Cyrus Parish

Fr. Cook claimed that he frequently addresses aid to the poor in his homilies, and that he addresses abortion occasionally, but not frequently. He speaks only rarely about homosexuality and birth control, and he attempts to place equal emphasis on each of the sociopolitical issues discussed here.

Fr. Nolan, St. Norbert Parish

Fr. Nolan indicated that he talks frequently about aid to the poor in his homilies. It was not clear how often abortion arises as a topic in his preaching, but he did indicate that when speaking about abortion, he does so primarily in the context of individual morality, and that he avoids discussion of public policy as it relates to abortion. It is unclear how often Fr. Nolan addresses birth control, and though homosexuality does arise as a topic in the course of his homilies, it does so only rarely. Finally, Fr. Nolan indicated that he attempts to emphasize each of these political issues equally in his preaching.

Pastors with a Personal Morality Approach to Preaching

Fr. Boyd, St. Barnabas Parish

Fr. Boyd, like most of the other pastors, reported preaching frequently about aid to the poor. Unlike most, however, he also reported preaching frequently about abortion. In addition, he speaks relatively frequently about homosexuality, emphasizing the sinfulness of homosexual behavior and opposition to gay marriage. He also addresses contraception in his homilies, and places more emphasis on abortion in his preaching than he does on the other sociopolitical issues.

Fr. Lewis, St. Leon Parish

Fr. Lewis's preaching style appears to be quite similar to that of Fr. Boyd. Fr. Lewis speaks frequently about aid to the poor, and also frequently addresses abortion in his homilies. Furthermore, Fr. Lewis pays particular attention to the public-policy aspect of the abortion issue. He preaches occasionally about homosexuality and birth control, and he stresses that abortion is the preeminent issue of concern to Catholics.

Fr. Zimmerman, St. Zachary Parish

Fr. Zimmerman frequently addresses aid to the poor in his homilies, and he also speaks often about abortion. Although he does not address homosexuality in his sermons, he does occasionally speak about birth control with his parishioners. When asked which issues he emphasizes most vigorously, he indicated that he pays maximum attention to abortion and sexual promiscuity.

Of course, it is possible that the interviews described here may not provide a complete or sufficiently accurate picture of the messages delivered by these priests to parishioners at their parishes. Accordingly, the next chapter supplements this discussion of pastor interviews with an analysis of parish bulletins and a survey of the priests at each parish, in an effort to establish a more nuanced and detailed depiction of the political messages parishioners receive from their parish priests.

Notes

1. The Diocese of Arlington encompasses 67 parishes located in the northern portion of Virginia, including those parishes located in the Virginia suburbs of Washington, D.C. The Diocese of Richmond encompasses 153 parishes, and its diocesan boundaries extend throughout the entire state of Virginia, not including

those areas within the Diocese of Arlington. Finally, the Archdiocese of Washington includes 140 parishes, and its boundaries encompass Washington, D.C., and Montgomery, Prince George's, Calvert, Charles, and St. Mary's counties in Maryland, which are either suburbs of Washington, D.C., or located in southern Maryland. I focused on these three dioceses because the territory they encompass includes a variety of regional characteristics (that is, urban, suburban, small town, and rural parishes) and political cultures, yet all of the parishes in these dioceses are within relatively easy driving distance of Charlottesville, Virginia, making it possible for me to visit all of the parishes in the three dioceses.

In several instances, pastors of parishes that were randomly selected for this study refused the invitation to participate. The most typical reason given for such refusals was an inability to commit to the time necessary for participation. In these instances, alternative parishes were randomly selected to participate in the project.

The leadership of the Diocese of Arlington expressed concern about which of their parishes would be participating in this project. Due to institutional review board constraints and the desire to preserve the integrity of the project by protecting the anonymity of the participating priests, I was unable to inform the diocesan leadership of the identity of the parishes I randomly selected. Instead, I randomly selected three parishes, plus seventeen others. I gave the resulting list of twenty parishes to the diocese. I informed them that the three parishes that were randomly selected for participation were included in the list, and asked which, if any, of the twenty parishes they desired for me to refrain from including in the study. They indicated that I should avoid seven of the twenty parishes, though none of the three parishes I originally selected were among the parishes I was told to avoid. However, one of the original three parishes I selected declined to participate, necessitating the selection of a new parish. I randomly selected this new parish from the reduced list that had been approved by the Diocese. In one instance, the pastor of an Arlington parish that had been randomly selected to be included in this study was transferred to a different parish while this study was under way. As a result, the pastor's new parish was included in the study, and his previous parish was dropped from the study. I do not expect these developments to have any implications for the interpretation of the analyses that follow.

2. Of course, the best way to obtain a sense of the messages delivered by any given priest to his parishioners would be to attend Mass at that priest's parish. For several reasons, however, this was not a feasible option in this study. Since sermons are typically based, at least in part, on the scripture readings for a particular Sunday, it would be important to attend Mass at each parish being studied on the same Sunday. Obviously, with the parishes studied here spread out over such a wide geographic area, this would be a physical impossibility for a single person. In addition, if one were to attend Mass in order to gain a sense of the types of messages delivered by a particular priest, it would be necessary to attend Mass at his parish over repeated Sundays. Once again, due to the geographic area included in this study, this was not feasible. Ideally, these difficulties would have been overcome by employing a number of highly qualified research assistants to attend Mass regularly at each of

these different parishes. Financial constraints prohibited this approach, requiring the development of alternative strategies for measuring messages emanating from Catholic priests that, when considered in sum, provide a reasonable substitute for attending Mass.

3. This is consistent with findings from national surveys of priests. Hoge and Wegner's 2001 survey of priests, for instance, found that 80 percent said that "the satisfaction of preaching the Word" is of great importance as a source of satisfaction to them (Hoge and Wenger 2003, 26).

4. This statement, along with Fr. Williams's earlier indication that he only rarely addresses abortion (in part, because those who attend Mass at his parish are not directly confronted with abortion), suggests that priests may tailor their public messages based on their perceptions of the attitudes and beliefs of their congregants. This, in turn, suggests that caution is in order in interpreting correlations between priests' public messages and beliefs and parishioners' political attitudes as evidence of priestly influence, since any such correlations may be a function of priests tailoring their public statements in this way. In other words, even though Catholic parishioners do not choose their priests, the potential that priestly messages are being influenced by parishioners must be taken seriously.

chapter four
Priestly Politics
Confirmed

 Chapter 3 concluded with a categorization of the preaching characteristics of the pastors at each of the nine parishes participating in this project. There is no reason to suspect that any of the pastors I spoke with were less than forthright in their descriptions of the way they address various sociopolitical topics. Indeed, the fact that there is a wide variety of approaches to preaching even among pastors in the same diocese provides reassurance that pastors were speaking frankly, and not simply trying to toe a line established by the diocesan hierarchy. (Recall that of the three Arlington pastors, two are mixed-emphasis priests and one is a personal morality priest; that of the three Richmond pastors, one is a social justice priest, one is a mixed-emphasis priest, and one is a personal morality priest; and that of the Washington pastors, two are oriented toward social justice issues and one is focused on personal morality.)

Nevertheless, since I was not able to attend Mass and observe homilies at each of these parishes, it is helpful to supplement the information gathered from the pastor interviews with additional information gleaned from other sources. Specifically, in order to verify the information presented in chapter 3, I performed a content analysis of a sample of the parish bulletins from each parish. In addition, I mailed a post-election survey to every priest (including pastors and assistant priests) at each parish; the survey requested that they reflect and report on the homilies they delivered in the months leading up to the election. The results of the content analysis and priest surveys are presented here.

Content Analysis of Parish Bulletins

Most Catholic parishes (and all of the parishes participating in this study) print a weekly bulletin, or short newsletter, that is typically distributed to parishioners as they leave Mass. These bulletins alert parishioners to various activities happening at the parish, provide a schedule of upcoming events, and keep parishioners abreast of the general goings on in the parish. Even though most of the material in parish bulletins is apolitical, it is possible to review these bulletins for evidence of the type, frequency, and tenor of messages delivered by priests at each parish. This is so for two reasons. First, most parish bulletins (including bulletins at seven of the nine parishes discussed here) include a brief, weekly statement by the pastor. Second, though pastors are not typically responsible for compiling the weekly bulletin, they do have final authority over what material goes into the bulletin—and what material does not. It is feasible, then, to look to parish bulletins for evidence of the types of messages emanating from priests at each parish.

In order to obtain a systematic overview of the messages contained in parish bulletins, I performed a content analysis of a sample of each parish's bulletins. Specifically, I randomly selected two Sundays from each of the summer months (the second and fourth Sundays of June and July, and the first and third Sundays of August), and analyzed bulletins printed for those Sundays. In addition, I conducted a content analysis of every parish bulletin for the period between Labor Day and Election Day, 2004.[1]

For each parish bulletin I analyzed and coded both the weekly pastor's column (which appears in bulletins at seven of the nine parishes), as well as every item in the bulletin. "Items" include all announcements and statements, and they are typically easy to recognize; for the most part, each separate item is distinguishable from other items, as items typically begin with a bold headline or are separated by text boxes and other devices. For the purposes of this analysis I did not consider listings of schedules, Mass times, and parish office hours, or information regarding weekly scripture readings; accordingly, I did not code these aspects of parish bulletins.

Each pastor's column and each analyzed bulletin item was coded on thirty-three separate variables: four variables for each of eight sociopolitical issues (abortion, aid to the poor, contraception, sexual morality, homosexuality, capital punishment, international aid, and foreign affairs), and one variable that measures whether the item in question encourages parishioners to register to vote. For each sociopolitical issue, each item was coded so as to indicate whether the item was about the issue of interest, whether the item expressed agreement with Church teaching on the issue of interest, whether politics or public policy was mentioned in connection with the issue of interest, and whether the item expressed support for public policies more in line with Church teaching. For illustrative purposes, consider the following four-variable coding strategy for abortion, as the other issues were coded in a nearly identical fashion.

First, each item was coded so as to reflect whether, and to what extent, it was about abortion (and other abortion-related issues, such as embryonic stem cell research). For this variable, each item was coded on a scale of 0 to 3. Items that contained no mention of abortion were coded 0. If abortion was mentioned in an item, but was not a key feature of the item, then it received a code of 1. More specifically, items were coded 1 on abortion if Church teaching on abortion was addressed in a clause, and even if Church teaching on abortion rose to the level of being the subject of several clauses or a sentence within the item, but only if Church teaching on abortion did not rise to the level of being the primary focus of several sentences. Items for which abortion was a key subcomponent were coded 2. Abortion was considered a "key subcomponent" of an item if it was the primary focus of at least one sentence or of a substantial portion of the item, but only if the item also addressed other or broader issues as well. Finally, those items that focused primarily on abortion received a code of 3.

Items received a 3 on this variable if and only if Church teaching on abortion was mentioned throughout the item and was the subject, at least indirectly, of many of the clauses or sentences within the item. An item may touch on subjects other than abortion and still receive a 3 on the abortion variable, but only if the item is substantially and primarily about Church teaching on abortion.

Next, each item was coded on a scale of 0 to 3 to describe whether it expressed agreement with Church teaching on abortion. Items that did not address abortion at all (i.e., those items that received a 0 on the variable described above), received a 0. Items in which it was unclear whether the viewpoint being expressed was supportive of or opposed to Church teaching on abortion were coded 1. Those items that expressed support for the Church's teaching on abortion (i.e., that were pro-life) were coded 2; and those items that expressed disagreement with the Church's teaching on abortion (i.e., were pro-choice) were coded 3.

Third, items were coded as to whether they mentioned politics or public policy in connection with abortion. Items that did not mention politics or public policy with regard to abortion were coded 0. Conversely, items that mentioned politics with regard to abortion, including those articles that identified pro-choice or pro-life politicians or candidates, were coded 1.

Finally, each item was coded on a 0 to 2 scale to indicate whether it expressed support for politicians or public policies that would work to enforce Church teaching on abortion. If the item did not address politics or public policy with regard to abortion, or if the public policy preference of the item was unclear, it received a 0. Those items that reflected political support for Church teachings on abortion (such as those that indicated that politicians and public policy should do more to limit abortion, or that praised policies or politicians that work to limit abortion, or that criticized pro-abortion politicians and policies) were coded 1. Conversely, those items that expressed political opposition to Church teaching on abortion (for instance, by opposing politicians or policies that would restrict abortion) were coded 2.

To better illustrate this coding scheme, it is useful to consider the coding of a few sample bulletin items. One bulletin from mid-summer of 2004 contained the following item:

> The [name omitted] Pregnancy Center is seeking a person with strong secretarial skills . . . to work closely with the director. Knowledge of Microsoft Office and Windows is necessary. Work environment warm and friendly. Personnel team supportive. *We are a nonprofit organization focused on helping women choose life for their unborn baby.* Salary is based on nonprofit standards. This position is part time, W, TH, F, 9:00 a.m.– 5:00 p.m. If interested contact [name and phone number omitted].

This item is primarily about an employment opportunity. In one sentence, however, abortion is mentioned (i.e., via reference to "helping women choose life"), and opposition to abortion is implied. Accordingly, this item received a 1 on the variable measuring the extent to which the item is about abortion, and a 2 on the variable measuring whether or not the item is in agreement with Church teaching on abortion (since it expresses agreement with Church teaching). This item does not mention politics or public policy, and so it received a 0 on each of the final two abortion variables (those that measure whether or not politics is mentioned, and the political thrust of the item).

Consider another item found in a bulletin from late September in another parish:

> The 12th Annual International Week of Prayer and Fasting, October 3–11, 2004—A benefit dinner sponsored by the IWPF Committee to *honor several pro-life speakers including Norma McCorvey—the "Roe" of the Roe v. Wade decisions,* will be held on Sunday, October 10, St. Joseph Parish Hall, Herndon, VA. Wine reception at 5 pm, Dinner at 6 pm, followed by a concert by Irish singer Dana. For tickets call [phone number omitted]. On Monday, October 11, an all-day Eucharistic

Rosary Prayer Vigil for the conversion of nations, world peace and an *end to abortion* will be held from 9 am to 5 pm at the Basilica of the National Shrine of the Immaculate Conception in Washington, D.C. Mass will be celebrated at noon by Bishop Michael Sheridan, Colorado Springs. Featured speakers include *Norma McCorvey*, and Leonardo DeFilippis of LUKE Filmes, director of *Therese*. See www.sign.org or call [phone number omitted].

Though this item is primarily about a dinner and other special events, it mentions abortion several times (see the italicized portions), and so it received a code of 2 on the abortion variable. (Incidentally, since the item also mentions world peace once, it also received a 1 on the foreign affairs variable). The item is clearly pro-life in tone, and so it received a 2 on the variable designed to measure support or opposition to Church teaching. Finally, since politics and public policy are not mentioned here, this item received a 0 on the two variables that measure whether politics as it relates to abortion is addressed in the item.

One parish bulletin from mid-June provided an obvious example of an abortion-related item:

Respect LIFE: *I am sure that all people know deep down inside that the little child in the mother's womb is a human being from the moment of conception, created in the image of God to love and to be loved. Let us pray that nobody will be afraid to protect that little child, to help that little child be born. Jesus said, "If you receive a little child in my name you receive me."*

— Mother Teresa

THE RESPECT LIFE COMMITTEE invites you to come to their meeting this Monday, June 14, at 7:00 PM in the [location omitted]

Pray Daily for Respect Life Intentions!

This item, clearly, focuses primarily and substantially on abortion, and so received a code of 3 on the abortion variable, along with a code of 2 on the variable measuring the item's tone, since it clearly expresses opposition to abortion. It does not mention politics or public policy, however, and so received a 0 on each of the final two abortion variables.

Finally, consider an item that appeared in a parish bulletin in mid-September. The item (which is too lengthy to quote in its entirety) addressed a recent letter written by the former Cardinal Ratzinger, a prominent Vatican official (and now Pope Benedict XVI). Cardinal Ratzinger's letter stated in part that though Catholics are not permitted to vote for pro-choice political candidates as an expression of their support for the candidate's stand on the abortion issue, Catholics may vote for a pro-choice candidate if there are other compelling, proportionate reasons for doing so. This particular bulletin item sought to clarify Cardinal Ratzinger's position; it read in part:

> Cardinal Ratzinger meant that a faithful Catholic might vote for a candidate who supports abortion *if there were another moral issue as grave and as clear as the abortion issue* [italics and bold in the original]. In the text of his letter the Cardinal made it quite clear that *there is no such commensurate issue* [italics added].

This item is clearly primarily focused on abortion and is in agreement with Church teaching, and so it received a 3 on the abortion variable, and a 2 on the variable measuring the tone of the article. In addition, the item clearly has a political component, and so received a 1 on the variable designed to measure whether the item mentions politics or public policy with regard to abortion. Finally, the item encourages opposition to pro-choice political candidates, and so it received a score of 1 on the variable designed to measure whether the item expresses political support or opposition for Church teaching with regard to abortion.

As mentioned above, in addition to being coded in this fashion with regard to abortion, each item analyzed was coded in identical fashion in relation to seven other sociopolitical issues of interest (aid to the poor, contraception, sexual morality, homosexuality, capital punishment, international aid, and foreign affairs). Complete details on the coding scheme employed here are available in appendix B.

For the most part, the results of the content analysis of parish bulletins confirm the description of pastors' preaching habits outlined in the previous chapter. Just as the pastors' self-described preaching habits were, in many respects, quite similar, so too was the content of the parish bulletins. Most obviously, the consensus exhibited in the parish bulletins on all of the issues discussed here was striking. In total, 3,335 separate bulletin items (including pastor columns), consisting of 23,525 lines of text, were coded. Of these, there were only four items, consisting of a total of thirty-one lines of text, that expressed any sentiment (theological, political, or otherwise) that could be interpreted as opposed to Church teaching. (They largely discussed homosexuality and stressed the need to be supportive and compassionate towards homosexuals without mentioning Church teaching about the sinfulness of homosexual behavior.) In no instance did any parish bulletin express support for legalized abortion, opposition to efforts (including governmental efforts) to help the poor, opposition to Church teaching on contraception, or support for capital punishment. Of course, as mentioned previously, I did not expect this project to uncover evidence of priests who publicly contradict Church teaching on any important sociopolitical issue. Nevertheless, this unanimity of approach and tone is remarkable.

In addition, just as there was a high degree of similarity in the frequency with which pastors reported preaching about certain topics, so was there a high degree of similarity in the frequency with which most political topics were addressed in parish bulletins. Table 4.1 reports the proportion of bulletin items (including pastors' columns)—and the proportion of lines of text contained within those items—that address contraception, homosexuality, capital punishment, international aid, and foreign affairs. A glance at table 4.1 reveals that, for the most part, bulletins from each of the parishes lacked significant

Table 4.1 Bulletin Discussion of Birth Control, Homosexuality, Capital Punishment, International Aid, and Foreign Affairs (Proportions)

	Parish	Birth Control		Homosexuality		Capital Punishment		International Aid		Foreign Affairs	
		Items	Lines	Items	Lines	Items	Lines	Items	Lines	Items	Lines
Social justice pastors	St. Margaret	0	0	.01	0	.01	.01	.03	.04	.03	.04
	St. Winifred	.01	.03	0	0	0	.01	.02	.02	0	0
	St. Yolanda	.01	0	0	0	.01	.01	.03	.06	.01	.01
Mixed-emphasis pastors	St. Norbert	0	0	0	0	0	.01	0	.01	0	0
	St. Anastasia	0	0	0	0	0	0	.01	.02	.03	.04
	St. Cyrus	0	0	0	0	0	0	.01	.01	.01	.03
Personal morality pastors	St. Zachary	0	0	0	0	0	0	0	0	0	.01
	St. Leon	.01	.01	0	0	0	0	.04	.06	.01	.02
	St. Barnabas	0	0	.03	.05	0	.02	.04	.02	.02	.04

Note: "Items" columns report the proportion of bulletin items that address the corresponding issue. "Lines" columns report the proportion of bulletin lines that are included in items that address the corresponding issue; the "Lines" columns *do not report* the proportion of bulletin lines that address the corresponding issue, as bulletins were coded on an item-by-item, and not on a line-by-line, basis.

discussion of contraception, homosexuality, and capital punishment. With regard to contraception, for instance, bulletins from six of the nine parishes had no discussion of this topic, while the proportion of items in the other three parish bulletins that addressed contraception was .01. Similarly, though the proportion of bulletin items addressing homosexuality was .03 at St. Barnabas parish (which has a personal morality pastor), the rest of the parish bulletins contained almost no discussion of homosexuality. Capital punishment, as well, was rarely discussed in any of the parish bulletins. International aid and foreign affairs were discussed somewhat more frequently than contraception, homosexuality, and capital punishment, but there was not a high degree of variation in the extent to which bulletins from different parishes discussed this issue. St. Zachary devoted the least amount of bulletin space to international aid, but in no parish did the proportion of bulletin items that addressed international aid exceed .04, and the parish bulletins devoted a similar amount of attention to foreign affairs.

While parish bulletins displayed a remarkably high degree of similarity in the extent to which they addressed contraception, homosexuality, capital punishment, international aid, and foreign affairs, there was much more variation in the extent to which bulletins included discussion of abortion and aid to the poor. Table 4.2 reports the extent to which these two highly important political issues were addressed in parish bulletins. For the most part, the results reported in table 4.2 confirm the categorization of pastors made in the previous chapter. With regard to abortion, for instance, the bulletins from parishes with social justice pastors were similar in their lack of attention to this issue. In no instance did the proportion of bulletin items that addressed abortion in social justice parishes exceed .02; similarly, in no instance did the proportion of bulletin lines that addressed abortion in social justice parishes exceed .04. The bulletins from parishes with personal morality pastors, however, devoted relatively more attention to abortion. The proportion of bulletin items that

Table 4.2 Bulletin Discussion of Abortion and Aid to the Poor (Proportions)

	Parish	Abortion		Poor Aid	
		Items	Lines	Items	Lines
Social	St. Margaret	.01	.03	.15	.19
justice	St. Winifred	.01	.04	.11	.14
pastors	St. Yolanda	.02	.04	.07	.09
Mixed-	St. Norbert	.01	.02	.08	.13
emphasis	St. Anastasia	.01	.03	.05	.11
pastors	St. Cyrus	.07	.08	.09	.15
Personal	St. Zachary	.04	.22	.06	.07
morality	St. Leon	.05	.07	.09	.08
pastors	St. Barnabas	.12	.18	.04	.04

Note: "Items" columns report the proportion of bulletin items that address the corresponding issue. "Lines" columns report the proportion of bulletin lines that are included in items that address the corresponding issue; the "Lines" columns *do not report* the proportion of bulletin lines that address the corresponding issue, as bulletins were coded on an item-by-item, and not on a line-by-line, basis.

addressed abortion in these parishes ranged from a low of .04 to a whopping .12, and the proportion of bulletin lines contained in items that addressed abortion ranged from .07 to .22. With regard to aid to the poor, parishes with social justice pastors and parishes with personal morality pastors exhibited the opposite pattern. Poor aid received a relatively high degree of attention in bulletins from social justice parishes (where the proportion of items that addressed poor aid ranged from .07 to .15, and the proportion of lines that addressed poor aid ranged from .09 to .19). In parishes with personal morality pastors, however, there was relatively less attention devoted to poor aid. The proportion of bulletin items in these parishes that addressed aid to the poor ranged from a low of .04 to a high of .09, and the proportion of lines that addressed aid to the poor ranged from .04 to .08.

Although table 4.2 exhibits precisely the pattern one would expect to find with regard to both parishes with social justice pastors and those with personal morality pastors (and thus helps to verify the categorization of these parishes made in the preceding chapter), the results reported with regard to parishes with mixed-emphasis pastors are somewhat less clear. If the categorization of pastors' preaching styles outlined in chapter 4 is to be verified through this content analysis of parish bulletins, one would expect to find more attention paid to poor aid in bulletins in parishes with mixed-emphasis pastors than in bulletins from parishes with personal morality pastors, and less attention to poor aid than in parishes with social justice pastors (which, for the most part, was found to be the case). One would also expect to find more attention paid to abortion in bulletins in mixed-emphasis parishes than in bulletins from parishes with social justice pastors, and less attention to abortion than in personal morality parishes (which, for the most part, was not found to be the case). The significance of these findings with regard to mixed-emphasis parishes will be discussed in more detail below.

The information reported in table 4.2 is important for providing a comparison among the different parishes. It may be even more important to obtain a sense of the internal parish dynamics by considering the emphasis each parish places on abortion as opposed to aid to the poor. Accordingly, table 4.3 reports the ratio of poor aid to abortion coverage contained in the bulletins for each parish. If the parish categorizations set forth previously are correct, I would expect to find the ratio of poor aid coverage to abortion coverage to be much greater in bulletins from parishes with social justice pastors than in bulletins from parishes with personal morality pastors.

The results reported in table 4.3 provide even more striking evidence than the results reported in table 4.2 of the correctness of the classification of both social justice and personal morality parishes. In parishes with social justice pastors, the ratio of the proportion of items that address poor aid to the proportion of items that address abortion ranges from 3.5:1 to 15:1. In other words, in the least social justice–oriented of the social justice parishes, there are 3.5 times more items that discuss poor aid in parish bulletins than there are items that address abortion; in the most social justice–oriented of the social justice parishes, there are 15 times more items that address poor

Table 4.3 Discussion of Aid to the Poor Compared with Discussion of Abortion in Parish Bulletins

	Parish	Items Poor Aid : Abortion	Lines Poor Aid : Abortion
Social justice pastors	St. Margaret	15:1	6.33:1
	St. Winifred	11:1	3.5:1
	St. Yolanda	3.5:1	2.25:1
Mixed-emphasis pastors	St. Norbert	8:1	6.5:1
	St. Anastasia	5:1	3.66:1
	St. Cyrus	1.29:1	1.88:1
Personal morality pastors	St. Zachary	1.5:1	1:3.1
	St. Leon	1.8:1	1.14:1
	St. Barnabas	1:3	1:4.5

Note: The "Items" column reports the ratio of the proportion of items that address aid to the poor to the proportion of items that address abortion. The "Lines" column reports the ratio of the number of lines in those items that address aid to the poor to the number of lines in those items that address abortion.

aid in parish bulletins than there are items that discuss abortion. This pattern is reversed, as expected, in the parishes with personal morality pastors. In the bulletins from St. Zachary and St. Leon, for instance, the ratio of poor aid coverage to abortion coverage is much closer to 1 to 1; in St. Barnabas, coverage of abortion actually exceeds coverage of poor aid in terms of both the number of items and the number of lines devoted to these subjects. Table 4.3, however, much like table 4.2, offers less clear-cut results for parishes with mixed-emphasis pastors; the bulletins of such parishes do not fall neatly into either of the two main patterns discussed above with respect to the attention they devote to poor aid and abortion.

What, then, should be concluded from this analysis of parish bulletins? First, and most importantly, the analysis revealed no information that would cast doubt on the appropriateness of categorizing St. Margaret, St. Winifred, and St. Yolanda as social justice parishes, or on the appropriateness of categorizing St. Zachary, St. Leon, and St. Barnabas as personal morality parishes. Parishes with personal morality pastors, as expected, tended to devote more attention in their bulletins to abortion than did the social justice parishes, while the parishes with social justice pastors devoted more attention to poor aid in their bulletins than did the personal morality parishes. In addition, bulletins from social justice parishes devoted much more attention to poor aid in their bulletins than they did to abortion, while the personal morality parishes were more balanced in their coverage of these issues; in fact, St. Barnabas devoted substantially more attention to abortion than to poor aid.

With regard to parishes with mixed-emphasis pastors, however, the results of this analysis are somewhat less straightforward. On the one hand, the content of bulletins from these parishes does not fall neatly between the extremes of the social justice and personal morality parishes. In fact, if one were attempting to categorize the parishes based solely on this content analysis of the bulletins, one would likely classify St. Norbert and St. Anastasia as social justice parishes, and St. Cyrus as a personal morality parish. Recall, however, that the purpose of this content analysis is not to categorize parishes, but rather to verify (or revise, as the case may be) the categorization made previously on the basis of detailed interviews with pastors. From this perspective, though the bulletins from mixed-emphasis parishes appear not to represent a middle ground between the social justice and personal morality parishes, the question of real interest is whether or not the results of the content analysis are sufficiently inconsistent with the pastor interviews to significantly decrease confidence in the correctness of the categorization of St. Norbert, St. Anastasia, and St. Cyrus as mixed-emphasis parishes. A consideration of the results of the survey of priests at each parish will help resolve this question.

2004 Survey of Priests

The final step necessary to sufficiently describe and categorize the political messages emanating from priests was the administration of a postelection (2004) survey to each of the priests at all of the parishes involved in this project. This survey of priests was necessary for several reasons. First, like the content analysis of parish bulletins, the surveys should serve as an effective check of the information gathered during the pastor interviews. Additionally, the surveys (which were administered immediately following the 2004 national elections) provided the opportunity to ask priests specifically about the homilies they delivered in the months preceding the election; the pastor interviews, on the other hand, which were conducted during the summer of 2004, were most useful in obtaining a sense of each pastor's general speaking style. Finally, and most importantly, the survey of priests afforded an opportunity to ask the assistant priests (in addition to the pastors) at each parish about the characteristics of their homilies. This is of vital importance, since parishioners at parishes with one or more assistant priests will regularly be exposed to messages delivered by priests other than their pastor.

At the time of the 2004 elections, there were twenty priests serving at the nine parishes that participated in this study. Four parishes were served by only one pastor, while the other five parishes had at least one—and as many as five—assistant priests. In order to maximize the response rate to the priest surveys, each priest was contacted four times (Dillman 2000). Priests were mailed a notification letter in late October, received the survey in early November, were mailed a follow-up reminder letter in mid-November, and were mailed a second copy of the survey (if they had not already returned it) in late November. I received completed surveys from sixteen of the twenty priests, including responses from at least one priest at eight of the nine parishes participating in the study (all except St. Zachary). Of course, a sample size of sixteen makes quantitative analyses of the priest surveys inadvisable. Instead, the surveys are best conceptualized as a qualitative check of the parish preaching profiles from chapter 3.

The survey of priests contained questions designed to measure the extent to which important political issues—including abortion, homosexuality, poor aid, capital punishment, and foreign affairs—were discussed in homilies in the months immediately preceding the election. In addition, priests were asked about the frequency with which they explicitly encouraged their parishioners to consider each of the aforementioned issues when deciding how to vote. Priests were also asked about the extent to which, and the context in which, they discussed the communion controversy that received extensive media attention in 2004 (i.e., the controversy about how the Church should respond to openly pro-choice politicians who wish to receive communion). Finally, priests were asked whether or not their parishes distributed voter guides or other political pamphlets to parishioners. The discussion of each of these components of the survey (frequency of discussion of issues, frequency with which issues were explicitly linked to voting decisions, discussion of the communion controversy, and voter guides) will make clear that the categorization of priestly political messages set forth previously is quite accurate. (The complete survey can be found in appendix C.)

Priestly Discussion of Political Issues

Some of the most informative questions contained in the priest surveys asked priests about the frequency with which they discussed abortion, homosexuality, poor aid, capital punishment, and foreign affairs in their homilies prior to the election. The survey results were generally consistent with what one would expect to find if the categorizations presented earlier of the priestly messages at each parish are correct. Generally, priests in parishes with personal morality pastors reported preaching more frequently in the months preceding the election about issues on which the Church takes a conservative stand (abortion and homosexuality and related issues) than did priests in parishes with social justice pastors. Priests in personal morality parishes also indicated that they "extensively addressed" abortion and homosexuality in their preaching, and that they did so as often as they addressed aid to the poor. Similarly, priests in parishes with social justice pastors indicated, for the most part, that they "extensively addressed" aid to the poor more frequently than they addressed abortion or homosexuality. Priests in social justice parishes also tended to preach more regularly than did priests in parishes with personal morality pastors about issues on which the Church takes a liberal position. Furthermore, the results from the priest surveys with regard to the mixed-emphasis parishes are also more consistent with the pastor interviews than were the results of the content analysis of bulletins, in that there is considerable similarity in the frequency with which the priests at these parishes report addressing each issue. That is, though the surveys of mixed-emphasis priests do not necessarily indicate that they discuss conservative issues less frequently than personal morality priests and liberal issues less frequently than social justice priests, they did tend to be more balanced in their preaching than either personal morality or social justice priests. Priests in mixed-emphasis parishes apparently do strive to emphasize Church teachings across the spectrum of political issues, including those on which the Church takes a liberal position and those on which the Church takes a conservative position. This result is consistent with the results of the pastor interviews, in which each mixed-emphasis pastor reported placing essentially equal emphasis on each political issue of interest here.

The survey of priests, then, provides support for the categorization of priestly messages presented earlier. In the months just prior to the 2004 elections, priests in personal morality parishes tended to discuss abortion and homosexuality more frequently than their counterparts in social justice parishes, while priests in social justice parishes discussed other issues, especially poor aid, more regularly than did priests in personal morality parishes. In addition, priests in personal morality parishes generally placed relatively more emphasis on abortion and homosexuality as compared to poor aid than did priests in social justice parishes. Priests in mixed-emphasis parishes, as expected, reported relative equality in the frequency with which they addressed various political issues.

Priestly Advice on Voting Considerations

In addition to questions designed to gauge the extent to which they discussed various issues in their sermons and other public announcements, the postelection survey administered to priests also included questions that asked priests about the frequency with which they encouraged their parishioners to consider each political issue when deciding how to vote. Responses to these questions were highly consistent with the categorization of parish preaching. In two of the three parishes with social justice pastors, no priest ever encouraged parishioners to consider abortion or homosexuality when deciding how to vote. By contrast, in both of the parishes with personal morality parishes from which surveys were returned, priests did report encouraging their parishioners to consider these issues in making their voting decisions. With regard to poor aid, capital punishment, and foreign affairs—issues on which the Church takes a liberal position—priests in social justice parishes were less reticent; in two of these three parishes, at least one priest indicated that he had explicitly encouraged his parishioners to consider one or more of these issues when deciding how to vote. On the other hand, in the two parishes with personal morality pastors from which completed surveys were obtained, no priest ever encouraged parishioners to consider any issue other than abortion or homosexuality when deciding how to vote. Priests in mixed emphasis parishes, once again, were much more balanced when urging their parishioners to remember certain considerations in casting their votes, urging their parishioners to consider abortion along with aid to the poor and capital punishment.

Priestly Statements on the Communion Controversy

During the course of the 2004 presidential election campaign, the question of how Catholic priests should respond when openly pro-choice politicians and candidates for public office present themselves to receive communion received widespread media attention. This issue was not new in 2004. According to the *Washington Post*, Gray Davis, then the governor of California, was instructed in 2003 by

Bishop William Weigand of Sacramento either to change his pro-choice stance on abortion or to refrain from receiving communion (Allen 2004). Similarly, then Senate Minority Leader Tom Daschle of South Dakota, another openly pro-choice Catholic politician, had been warned by his own bishop about presenting himself in campaign literature as a Catholic (Allen 2004).

But the issue of how Church leaders should publicly deal with openly pro-choice politicians was the focus of an unprecedented level of media attention in 2004, since for the first time one of the major party presidential candidates—John Kerry—was both pro-choice on abortion and a Catholic. This prompted several high-profile Catholic bishops, and even Church officials in the Vatican, to weigh in on the matter of whether pro-choice politicians should receive communion. During a Kerry campaign trip to Missouri, Raymond Burke, the Archbishop of St. Louis, publicly and explicitly warned the candidate "not to present himself for communion" (Tumulty and Bacon 2004). Other Church leaders, including Archbishop Sean O'Malley of Boston, refused to name Kerry explicitly but nonetheless indicated that Catholic politicians should refrain from receiving communion if their "political views," as reported by the *Washington Post*, "contradict Catholic teaching" (Allen 2004; see also Goodstein 2004). Other Church leaders were more circumspect and refused to suggest that pro-choice politicians should be denied communion or excommunicated.

One of the questions in the survey asked each priest whether he had discussed the communion controversy in his homilies; if so, the survey asked about the context in which it had been discussed. In four of the eight parishes from which completed surveys were returned (including all three parishes with mixed-emphasis pastors), the communion controversy was not discussed at all. In four other parishes, however, the controversy was addressed, and in starkly different terms. At St. Winifred, Fr. Williams (a social justice pastor) discussed the controversy with his parishioners and told them that communion should not be denied to those who request it. An assistant priest at St. Yolanda (which also has a social justice pastor) raised the issue as well, though the context in which he addressed the issue is not entirely clear.

On the other hand, at St. Leon and St. Barnabas, both of which have personal morality pastors, priests publicly expressed their support for denying communion to pro-choice politicians like John Kerry. Fr. Lewis, for instance, the pastor of St. Leon Parish, told his parishioners that "pro-abortion politicians have no business presenting themselves for communion." Similarly, the priests of St. Barnabas Parish informed their parishioners that "priests should not provide communion to pro-abortion politicians." These different approaches to addressing the communion controversy by priests at social justice and personal morality parishes are just what one would expect if the categorization of parishes presented previously is correct.

Parish Voter Guides

At many Catholic parishes voter guides or similar political pamphlets are distributed to parishioners prior to elections. These guides are typically nonpartisan and refrain from endorsing particular candidates or political parties, so as not to endanger the tax exempt status of the parish involved. Although these voter guides are therefore not particularly explicit, it is true that some provide more straightforward guidance to parishioners than others. It is worthwhile, then, to consider the voter guides distributed by the parishes in some detail.

At the parishes with social justice and mixed-emphasis pastors, the voter guides distributed by the parishes were relatively noncontroversial. All three social justice parishes (St. Margaret, St. Winifred, and St. Yolanda) and two of the mixed-emphasis parishes (St. Norbert and St. Cyrus) distributed the U.S. Catholic Bishops' statement titled *Faithful Citizenship: A Catholic Call to Political Responsibility* (United States Conference of Catholic Bishops 2003). *Faithful Citizenship* is a truly nonpartisan document. It encourages Catholics to consider a number of issues (including abortion, poverty, foreign affairs, euthanasia, marriage, and family life) when deciding how to vote, but it does not prioritize these issues or provide guidance on how to select among candidates who fail to adopt Church teaching on every issue of concern.

St. Yolanda and St. Cyrus supplemented *Faithful Citizenship* by providing their parishioners with additional informational pamphlets. St. Yolanda, for instance, which has a social justice pastor, distributed a pamphlet printed by Our Sunday Visitor, a Catholic nonprofit organization that publishes periodicals and books. It identified five "nonnegotiable" issues (abortion, euthanasia, embryonic stem cell research, human cloning, and gay marriage) that Catholics must consider when deciding how to vote (Thigpen 2004). In addition to this relatively conservative pamphlet, St. Yolanda also distributed a "St. Yolanda Parish Voting Guide." This parish voting guide was considerably more "liberal" in that it devoted much more attention to issues like poverty, health insurance, affordable housing, living wage, capital punishment, and gun control than to issues like abortion and gay marriage. Parishioners of St. Cyrus (which has a mixed-emphasis pastor) also received *Faithful Citizenship*, as well as a letter written by Arlington Bishop Paul Loverde. Without endorsing a candidate, this letter emphasized abortion more prominently than other political issues (Loverde 2004). Finally, parishioners of St. Anastasia (which also has a mixed-emphasis pastor) received a flyer prepared by the parish priests that was unexpectedly conservative in tone. The flyer was similar to the Our Sunday Visitor guide described above in that it identified five issues that are "nonnegotiable" for Catholic voters. The flyer, however, was short and not sufficiently conservative (given the rest of the evidence presented in the discussion of pastor interviews, bulletin analysis, and priest surveys) as to cast doubt on the classification of St. Anastasia as a mixed-emphasis parish.

At the two parishes with personal morality priests from which completed surveys were returned (St. Leon and St. Barnabas), voter guides with much more conservative overtones were distributed to parishioners. St. Leon's parishioners received *Faithful Citizenship*, but they also were provided access to at least two additional pamphlets:

Voter's Guide for Serious Catholics (2004) and *A Brief Catechism for Catholic Voters* (Torraco 2003). The *Voter's Guide for Serious Catholics* is quite similar to the Our Sunday Visitor guide, in that it once again identifies five issues (abortion, euthanasia, embryonic stem cell research, human cloning, and homosexual unions) as "nonnegotiable," but the *Voter's Guide* is more explicit in its directive to vote according to these criteria. Whereas the Our Sunday Visitor's guide states that these nonnegotiable issues are "by no means" the only important ones to consider in voting, the *Voter's Guide* instructs Catholics to "first determine how each candidate stands on each of the five nonnegotiable issues" (2004, 8). Then, voters are to "eliminate from consideration candidates who are wrong on any of the nonnegotiable issues. No matter how right they may be on other issues, they should be considered disqualified if they are wrong on even one of the nonnegotiables" (2004, 8). Thus, the *Voter's Guide* distributed at St. Leon is more strident in its conservative tone and more explicit in its direction than is the Our Sunday Visitor guide distributed at St. Yolanda. In addition, the *Brief Catechism* distributed by St. Leon explicitly addresses the question of whether a Catholic may vote for a pro-choice candidate for political office. The *Brief Catechism* considers whether it is a mortal sin (punishable by eternal damnation) "to vote for a pro-abortion candidate"; it concludes:

> Except in the case in which a voter is faced with all pro-abortion candidates . . . a candidate that is pro-abortion disqualifies himself from receiving a Catholic's vote. This is because being pro-abortion cannot simply be placed alongside the candidate's other positions on Medicare and unemployment, for example; and this is because abortion is intrinsically evil and cannot be morally justified for any reason or set of circumstances. To vote for such a candidate simply with the knowledge that the candidate is pro-abortion is to become an accomplice in the moral evil of abortion. If the voter knowingly and freely assents to his or her status as such an accomplice, then the voter sins mortally (Torraco 2003, 16).

Clearly, the messages conveyed by the voter guides distributed at St. Leon Parish are more politically conservative than those found in the voter guides distributed at the parishes with social justice and mixed-emphasis pastors.

St. Barnabas parish distributed similarly conservative materials to parishioners in the weeks preceding the 2004 election. Just as at St. Leon, parishioners of St. Barnabas received the *Voter's Guide for Serious Catholics*. In addition, a booklet titled *"Gay Marriage:" A Catholic Answers Special Report* (2004) was made available to St. Barnabas parishioners. This lengthy report urged Catholics to oppose providing legal recognition of homosexual relationships. Clearly, then, the nature and tone of the voter guides distributed at St. Leon and St. Barnabas provide further support for the categorization of these as personal morality parishes.

In sum, the results of the survey of priests confirm that the political messages delivered by priests at St. Margaret, St. Winifred, and St. Yolanda parish can accurately be characterized as oriented toward social justice issues; that the political messages delivered by priests at St. Norbert, St. Anastasia, and St. Cyrus are mixed in their emphases; and that the messages delivered by priests at St. Leon and St. Barnabas are oriented toward personal morality. Priests at personal morality parishes place more emphasis on issues like abortion and homosexuality than do priests at social justice parishes, and more emphasis on abortion and homosexuality than on economic issues. Priests at social justice parishes place more emphasis on poor aid than do priests at personal morality parishes, and more emphasis on economic issues than on abortion and homosexuality. Priests at mixed-emphasis parishes are relatively evenhanded in the frequency with which they address the political issues considered here.

Summary of Priestly Politics

The findings presented in chapter 3 and here in chapter 4 clearly demonstrate that the political messages emanating from parish priests vary widely from parish to parish. Of the nine randomly selected parishes participating in this study, three are staffed by social justice priests whose political preaching focuses primarily on aid to the poor and other issues on which the Church takes a "liberal" stand, three are staffed by mixed-emphasis priests whose political preaching is equally focused across the spectrum of political issues, and three are headed by personal morality priests who place paramount emphasis on abortion and homosexuality—issues on which the Church espouses conservative teachings.

These findings are noteworthy in and of themselves. The Church and its teachings are too often portrayed in monolithic and simplistic terms in academic and journalistic publications when in reality the messages that Catholic citizens are actually exposed to from Church leaders are remarkably diverse in tenor and content. The final task of this project, undertaken in subsequent chapters, is to attempt to isolate and understand the effect of these different priestly messages on the political attitudes and voting behavior of Catholic parishioners.

Note

1. For four of the nine parishes I was able to obtain every bulletin from this time period for inclusion in the content analysis. For five parishes, however, I was unable to obtain every bulletin. Specifically, I was unable to obtain the July 25 bulletin from St. Barnabas Parish; the October 10 bulletin from St. Leon Parish; the June 13, June 27, October 24, and October 31 bulletins from St. Margaret Parish; the September 19, October 10, and October 17 bulletins from St. Zachary Parish; and the June 13 and June 27 bulletins from St. Cyrus Parish. Despite these missing bulletins, I have a sufficient number of bulletins from each parish and do not believe that the missing bulletins would differ systematically from the analyzed bulletins.

chapter five
The Influence of Priests on Parishioners' Politics

 The preceding chapters demonstrate conclusively that the political messages that Catholic parishioners hear from their parish priests vary dramatically depending on where they attend Church. It remains to be seen, however, whether or not (and in what ways) these varying messages have any influence on the political behavior or attitudes of parishioners. To investigate this question I administered a postelection survey to a large sample of parishioners at each of the nine parishes that participated in this study (see appendices D and E for more details on the administration and content of the survey of parishioners). By comparing the opinions and electoral decisions of parishioners across parishes while controlling for a host of demographic, political, and religious variables, it is possible to isolate the likely influence of priestly messages on parishioners' political attitudes. I turn now to a description of this survey of parishioners and a discussion of the demographic and political attributes of the sample of parishioners, followed by an analysis of the effects of priestly messages on Catholic politics.

2004 Survey of Parishioners

To obtain a sense of the sociopolitical attitudes of the parishioners at each of the nine parishes included in this study, I designed and administered a postelection survey, via U.S. mail, to a sample of parishioners (drawn from the parish directory) at each parish. The survey contained questions that asked parishioners about their electoral behavior, their political attitudes on a variety of salient political topics, their opinions toward a number of political and religious leaders, some of their religious behaviors and beliefs, and their demographic characteristics.

In total, surveys were mailed to 1,309 parishioners, and 533 usable responses were returned, including 512 paper questionnaires that were returned via U.S. mail and 21 surveys that were completed online, for a healthy final response rate of 40.7 percent. This may, however, be overstating things a bit, since 51 respondents are excluded from most of the statistical analyses that follow because they indicated either that they regularly attend Mass at some parish not included in this study, or that they attend a parish included in this study, even though they live outside the parish's boundaries, precisely because of some characteristic or trait of the priests at the parish. This suggests that even though Catholic parishioners do not have the power to hire or fire their parish priests, a sizeable subset of practicing Catholics may base their decision as to where to attend Mass in part on specific characteristics of parish priests. In other words (as was suggested in chapter 1) some caution must be exercised, even when considering Catholics, in interpreting any observed correlation between priestly messages and parishioners' political attitudes as conclusive evidence of priestly influence. While this concern must be born in mind when considering the results presented below, the important point here is that the number of responses received proved sufficiently large to support quantitative analysis of potential priestly effects on Catholic politics.

Table 5.1 reports some of the important demographic characteristics of the survey respondents. There were many more female than male respondents (by approximately a two to one margin), and many more older respondents than younger respondents, with 30 percent of the sample older than fifty-nine years of age, and only 15 percent of the sample younger than thirty-eight years of age. Moreover, the respondents to this survey are an extremely well-educated, high-earning group. Nearly seven in ten respondents (68 percent) had at

Table 5.1 Demographic Characteristics of Respondents (%)

	1999 National Survey of Catholics[a]	Notre Dame Study of Catholic Parish Life (1983/1984)	2004 Survey of Catholics
Gender[b]			
Male	49	37	35
Female	51	63	65
Age[c]			
18–38	46	32	15
39–58	34	38	55
59 or older	20	30	30
Race[d]			
White	82	88	90
Nonwhite	18	12	10
Education			
High School or Less	39	40	10
Some Coll./Tech. School	34	31	22
Finished Coll. or More	27	29	68
Income[e]			
Less than $20,000	21	—	5
$20,000–$50,000	42	—	16
$50,000–$75,000	19	—	19
$75,000–$100,000	11	—	18
$100,000 or more	7	—	42

[a] *Sourco*: D'Antonio et al. 2001, 20, 24.

[b] There is a large discrepancy between the 2004 study and the 1999 national survey of Catholics. The results of the 2004 study, however, are consistent with the Notre Dame Study of Catholic Parish Life, which found that approximately 63 percent of parish-connected Catholics are women.

[c] Respondents in the 2004 study are clearly much older than respondents to the 1999 national survey of Catholics, and are even somewhat older than the respondents to the Notre Dame Study.

[d] The Notre Dame Study asked respondents, "Besides being an American, what is your main nationality background?" Those who responded black, Asian, Hispanic, American Indian, or Middle Eastern are included in the nonwhite category. Those who provided any other response (such as English, Irish, Italian, etc.) are included in the white category.

[e] In the 2004 study, the low-income categories are less than $25,000 and $25,000–$50,000. Income figures from the Notre Dame Study are not reported here because they are not comparable due to inflation. The highest income category from the Notre Dame Study was for individuals from households with yearly income in excess of $45,000.

least a college degree, and 60 percent of respondents had an annual household income in excess of $75,000.

Table 5.1 also indicates that the Catholics that participated in this study are different in many important ways from nationally representative samples of Catholics. Specifically, the respondents in this study are substantially older, more female, more likely to be white, better educated, and more affluent than are American Catholics as a whole. Although this should be kept in mind, it is not at all surprising. The Notre Dame Study, for instance, found that parish-connected Catholics (which is the population from which this sample is drawn) are indeed significantly older and more female than are American Catholics generally. Furthermore, the highly educated and affluent status of the sample discussed here is undoubtedly due to the fact that the sample is drawn in large part from parishes located in the highly educated and affluent Washington, D.C., area. In short, while the Catholics sampled for this study are not a microcosm of American Catholics, their demographic characteristics are not particularly unusual given the population from which the sample was drawn.

Table 5.2 reports on some of the salient political characteristics of the sample, and table 5.3 disaggregates these political characteristics by parish. Considered as a whole, Catholics who participated in this study were more inclined to vote for George W. Bush, who received votes from nearly 60 percent of this sample, than for John Kerry. Furthermore, a slim majority of the sample reported identifying with the Republican Party, while less than 40 percent reported Democratic party affiliation. Finally, 44 percent of the sample consider themselves to be ideologically conservative, while a mere 17 percent identify themselves as ideologically liberal.

Table 5.3 suggests that there are important differences in the political atmosphere from parish to parish. Three parishes—St. Margaret, St. Leon, and St. Barnabas—were overwhelmingly supportive of George W. Bush in the 2004 election, while the other parishes, though typically supportive of Bush, were more muted in their support. Parishioners from St. Margaret, St. Leon, and St. Barnabas are also

Table 5.2 Political Characteristics of Respondents

	Notre Dame Study of Catholic Parish Life (%)	2004 Survey of Catholics (%)
Vote Choice		
Bush	—	59
Kerry	—	36
Other	—	1
Did Not Vote	—	4
Partisanship		
Republican[a]	19	51
Democratic[b]	48	38
Independent/Other	12	11
Ideology		
Conservative	32	44
Liberal	16	17
Moderate	52	40

[a] In the 2004 survey, Republicans include those who identified themselves as strong Republicans, weak Republicans, and independents who lean Republican.

[b] In the 2004 survey, Democrats include those who identified themselves as strong Democrats, weak Democrats, and independents who lean Democratic.

Table 5.3 Political Characteristics of Respondents by Parish

	Parish	Percent Bush Vote (%)	Partisanship (Parish Mean)[a]	Ideology (Parish Mean)[b]
Social	St. Margaret	82	5.00	3.50
justice	St. Winifred	50	3.97	3.21
priests	St. Yolanda	49	4.02	3.12
Mixed-	St. Norbert	58	4.37	3.50
emphasis	St. Anastasia	56	4.11	3.09
priests	St. Cyrus	46	4.06	3.06
Personal	St. Zachary	21	2.04	3.21
morality	St. Leon	75	5.27	3.72
priests	St. Barnabas	83	5.40	3.81

[a] Respondents were coded on a scale ranging from (1) Strong Democrat to (7) Strong Republican.

[b] Respondents were coded on a scale ranging from (1) Very liberal to (5) Very conservative.

substantially more likely to identify themselves as Republicans and ideological conservatives than are parishioners from other parishes. Of course, it is risky and ill-advised to make inferences about priestly influence after simply disaggregating political characteristics by parish, as table 5.3 does. Drawing conclusions about priestly influence requires more sophisticated analysis that controls for variables other than priestly influence that might play a role in shaping parishioners' political attitudes. I turn now to that analysis.

Analysis and Results

The survey of parishioners permits analysis both of the degree to which priests may play a role in directly shaping their parishioners' political attitudes and, to a lesser extent, of the degree to which priests may exercise political influence indirectly through their influence on their parishioners' religious attitudes. The survey was designed primarily for the purpose of investigating direct clergy influence for two reasons. First, the results of the analysis of the Notre Dame Study (from chapter 2) suggest that priests do exercise a substantial degree of direct influence in shaping their parishioners' general orientation toward politics as well as their opinions on a number of important political issues. These results suggested, in short, the potential fruitfulness of continuing to explore the nature and extent of direct clergy political influence. Second, since the question of clergy influence is as yet an underexplored and undeveloped topic in the religion and politics literature, establishing the degree to which priests are a source of direct (as opposed to indirect) political influence is a logical first-step in the broader investigation of clergy influence.

Because the survey was designed primarily with the intent of investigating direct priestly political influence, it consisted mainly of questions designed to measure parishioners' political attitudes. But in addition to wielding direct political influence, Catholic priests might also possess the capacity to exercise indirect political influence. Recall from chapter 1 that political scientists and other scholars have, over the years, documented a number of ways in which individuals' political attitudes are partly shaped by their religious attitudes (Leege and Kellstedt 1993; Leege and Welch 1989; Wald et al. 1988; Welch and Leege 1988, 1991; Welch et al. 1995). It is highly plausible to suspect that clergy, whether or not they directly shape individuals' political attitudes, may influence their congregants' religious views, which in turn are important in shaping political attitudes. Indeed, it is perhaps even more plausible to expect clergy to wield influence indirectly, via their influence on individuals' religious beliefs and attitudes, than directly: as religious authority figures, it is likely that clergy are looked to as sources of religious—rather than explicitly political—guidance and instruction.

In addition to the items measuring political attitudes and behaviors, the survey also contained two items that make it possible to consider the extent to which clergy political influence is wielded through influence on parishioners' religious beliefs. First, the survey included a number of questions that gauged the extent to which parishioners think it proper for various Church authorities to speak out on political topics, and thus provides a measure of parishioners' willingness to accept guidance from the Church. Given the findings reported in chapter 2, it is reasonable to expect that increased willingness to accept Church guidance leads to increased support for the Church's position on a variety of political topics. The parishioner surveys make it possible to investigate this hypothesis and to consider whether priests may exercise indirect political influence through their ability to shape this important religious variable.

Second, the survey included a battery of questions that asked parishioners whether or not individuals who engage in certain behaviors (including rarely attending Mass, living together outside of marriage, getting married outside the Church, urging or undergoing abortion, practicing homosexuality, and using artificial birth control) should be considered "true Catholics." These items can be combined to form a scale of religious particularism, which provides a measure of Catholics' level of commitment to some of the core moral teachings of the Church; it is also an indicator of the extent to which Catholics regard adherence to these teachings as truly central to the practice of the faith. In this way, the religious particularism scale might be thought of as tapping into roughly similar constructs as do the measures of religious commitment and orthodoxy developed by Green and others (Green et al. 1996; Guth et al. 2005; Layman and Green 2006). For these reasons—and since the measure of religious particularism is also a basic indicator of one's degree of intolerance, and even abhorrence, for certain behaviors such as abortion and homosexuality—high levels of religious particularism might plausibly be expected to be related to conservative opinions on certain political issues (such as abortion and gay marriage) and to a generally conservative political outlook.

Respected scholars have previously posited a link between religious particularism and Catholic political attitudes. Specifically, Welch, Leege, and Cavendish, using data from the Notre Dame Study of Catholic Parish Life, hypothesized that Catholics' attitudes toward abortion could be significantly predicted by what they call "boundary maintenance mechanisms," which are represented by a scale (highly similar to the particularism scale described above) that measures whether individuals who engage in various activities "should be considered 'true' Catholics" (Welch et al. 1995, 148). Of course, Welch and his colleagues found that the role of religious particularism in shaping abortion attitudes was unimportant after controlling for respondents' degree of sexual restrictiveness and views of women's autonomy.[1] Nevertheless, the potential political importance of religious particularism, and the role of priests in shaping this religious attitude among their congregants, have yet to be fully explored. Data from the survey can be analyzed both to consider the extent of the political importance of religious particularism during the 2004 election season and to investigate the extent of clergy influence on parishioners' level of religious particularism. To the extent that religious particularism differentiates the religiously orthodox from the religiously heterodox—and to the extent to which such differences are politically consequential (Hunter 1991; Wuthnow 1988) and attributable in part to variance in priestly messages—priests may be said to exercise political influence indirectly through their influence on their parishioners' religious beliefs.

Much of the rest of this chapter is devoted to a consideration of the extent to which Catholic priests were a source of political influence—both direct and indirect—in the 2004 election. First, a series of models that attempt to predict parishioners' political choices and attitudes using the preaching profiles of parish priests as well as the individual-level religious beliefs described previously (willingness to accept guidance from the Church and religious particularism) are specified and discussed. More specifically, the models that follow examine the correlates of parishioners' vote choice, partisanship, ideology, presidential approval, candidate evaluations, and opinions on social, economic, and foreign policy issues. Additionally, the analysis also considers whether (and how) Catholic priests might perform an agenda-setting function, shaping their parishioners' views of which political issues are most important. These models provide little evidence to suggest that priests in this study played an important, direct role in shaping their parishioners' electoral choices in 2004. Willingness to accept guidance from the Church and religious particularism, however, do emerge as significant predictors of a variety of political and social attitudes. The chapter thus concludes with an examination of whether these religious attitudes are related to the preaching profiles of the priests at each parish; these final models suggest that priests may well play an important indirect role in shaping their parishioners' political attitudes via their influence on parishioners' religious orientations.

Priestly Influence on Presidential Vote Choice

The notion that clergy wield significant political influence would be most obviously demonstrated by documenting a direct link between clergy political speech and the voting behavior of parishioners.

Accordingly, to begin this investigation of the influence of Catholic priests in the 2004 presidential election, I hypothesize that parishioners in parishes with personal morality priests (defined and described in chapters 3 and 4 as those priests who, in their preaching, emphasize abortion and other issues on which the Church takes a conservative stand) would be more likely to vote for the Republican candidate, George W. Bush, than would parishioners in parishes with mixed-emphasis priests. In addition, I hypothesize that parishioners in parishes with social justice priests (defined and described in chapters 3 and 4 as those priests who, in their preaching, emphasize aid to the poor and other issues on which the Church takes a liberal stand) would be less likely to vote for Bush than would parishioners from parishes with mixed-emphasis priests. To test these hypotheses, I specify a hierarchical generalized linear model with logit link function, where the dependent variable—the probability of voting for Bush—is coded 1 for respondents who reported voting for Bush in the presidential election, and coded 0 for all other respondents.[2] The key independent variables—*social justice priests* and *personal morality priests*— relate to the political messages delivered by priests at the respondent's parish.

Based on the analysis presented in chapters 3 and 4, those respondents who belong to the parishes of St. Margaret, St. Winifred, or St. Yolanda are coded 1 on social justice priests (that is, they belong to parishes with social justice priests), whereas all other respondents are coded 0 on this variable. Those respondents who belong to the parishes of St. Zachary, St. Leon, or St. Barnabas are coded 1 on personal morality priests, and all other respondents are coded 0. The baseline group for this model—and for the rest of the models presented in this chapter—are respondents who belong to one of the parishes with mixed-emphasis priests: St. Norbert, St. Anastasia, or St. Cyrus. I expect the coefficient for *social justice priests* to be statistically significant and negative, which would indicate that parishioners in parishes with social justice priests were significantly less likely to vote for Bush than were parishioners in parishes with mixed-emphasis priests. In addition, I expect the coefficient for *personal morality priests* to be statistically significant and positive, which would indicate that parishioners in parishes with personal morality priests were significantly more likely to vote for Bush than were parishioners in parishes with mixed-emphasis priests.

Even if there is no direct link between priestly preaching characteristics and vote choice, it may be the case that parishioners' voting decisions are shaped by their own, individual religious beliefs. Accordingly, the model also includes the religious particularism variable described above. More specifically, *religious particularism* is a six-item scale (alpha = .860) constructed from responses to questions as to whether or not individuals who engage in each of six behaviors (rarely attending Mass, living together outside of marriage, getting married outside the Church, urging or undergoing abortion, practicing homosexuality, and using artificial birth control) should be considered "true" Catholics or not. For each of the six behaviors in question, parishioners who indicated that individuals who engage in the behavior should not be considered true Catholics are coded 1, and parishioners who indicated that individuals who engage in the behavior should be considered true Catholics (or who refused to judge) were coded 0. The particularism scale ranges from 0, for those parishioners who said that individuals who engage in each of the six behaviors should be considered true Catholics (or who refused to judge), to 6, for those parishioners who indicated that no one who engages in any of the six behaviors should be considered a true Catholic. I hypothesize that religious particularism, generally speaking, will be correlated with political conservatism; thus, in this instance, I expect the coefficient for *religious particularism* to be statistically significant and positive, indicating that individuals who score high on the particularism scale were more likely than others to vote for Bush over Kerry. In addition to these independent variables, the models also include a number of political, religious, and demographic control variables.[3] The results are reported in table 5.4.

A glance at table 5.4 indicates that there is no evidence in these data to suggest that Catholic priests directly influence the voting

Table 5.4 Religious Influences on Vote Choice (Hierarchical Generalized Linear Model with Logit Link Function)

	Probability of Bush Vote
Parish-level Predictors	
Social Justice Priests	.106
Personal Morality Priests	.379
Rural/Small Town	−.049
Individual-level Predictors	
Party	1.047^
Ideology	1.120^
Mass Attendance	.122
Education	−.146
Gender	−.196
Race	.415
Income	−.043
Age	.021**
Religious Particularism	−.101
Intercept	−5.321***
Remaining Parish-level Variance	.30857**
Explained Parish-level Variance	60.44%
Observations	426

*p < .15; **p < .1; ***p < .05; ^p < .01

decisions of their parishioners. Perhaps not surprisingly, the strongest predictors of vote choice included in the model are party identification and political ideology, which are both highly significant and in the expected direction. The coefficient for *age* is positive and statistically significant, indicating that older parishioners in this sample were more likely to cast a vote for Bush than younger parishioners. Most importantly, the coefficients for both *social justice priests* and *personal morality priests* fail to attain statistical significance, indicating that parishioners in parishes with social justice priests were no less likely to vote for Bush than were parishioners in parishes with mixed-emphasis priests, and that parishioners in parishes with personal morality priests were no more likely to vote for Bush than were parishioners in parishes with mixed-emphasis priests. In short, the results presented in table 5.4 fail to support the hypothesis that parishioners' voting decisions will be directly influenced by their parish priests. Additionally, religious particularism fails to attain statistical significance; though it was hypothesized that the most religiously particularistic parishioners would be more likely than others to vote for Bush over Kerry, this turns out not to be the case after controlling for alternative explanations of vote choice.

Religious Influence on Partisanship and Political Ideology

Even if priests apparently do not shape their parishioners' voting decisions, it is important to consider whether priests might influence a number of their parishioners' political attitudes and predispositions. I begin this consideration by hypothesizing that parish priests will influence both the partisanship and political ideology of their parishioners. Specifically, I hypothesize that parishioners in parishes with social justice priests will be more Democratic and more politically liberal than will parishioners from parishes with mixed-emphasis priests. Similarly, I hypothesize that parishioners in parishes with personal morality priests will be more Republican and politically conservative than their counterparts who belong to parishes with mixed-emphasis priests.

At the individual level, I also hypothesize that religious particularism, to the extent that it taps religious traditionalism, should be positively correlated with Republicanism and political conservatism. Thus, I expect the coefficient for *religious particularism* to be statistically significant and positive in both the party identification and political ideology models.

To test these hypotheses, I specify two new hierarchical linear models, where the dependent variables are *party identification* (coded from 1, strong Democrat, to 7, strong Republican) and *ideology* (coded from 1, very liberal, to 5, very conservative). The independent and control variables in these new models are identical to those contained in table 5.4. The results of these models are reported in table 5.5.

Table 5.5 Religious Influences on Partisanship and Ideology (Hierarchical Linear Models)

	Party Identification	Ideology
Parish-level Predictors		
Social Justice Priests	.198	−.042
Personal Morality Priests	−.325	.099
Rural/Small Town	−.239	.134
Individual-level Predictors		
Party	—	.257^
Ideology	1.579^	—
Mass Attendance	−.040	.032
Education	−.084**	−.005
Gender	.181	.027
Race	.584***	−.181**
Income	.171^	−.011
Age	−.012***	−.004*
Religious Particularism	.061*	.077^
Intercept	−.032	2.302^
Remaining Parish-level Variance	.55994^	.00739**
Remaining Individual-level Variance	2.18174	.36490
Explained Parish-level Variance	44.59%	89.40%
Explained Individual-level Variance	48.74%	50.26%
Observations	431	431

*p<.15; **p<.1; ***p<.05; ^p<.01

Just as there was no evidence to indicate the existence of direct priestly influence on parishioners' vote choice, so table 5.5 suggests that priests do not directly shape their parishioners' partisanship or ideological leanings. In no case, in either model, did the coefficients for *social justice priests* or *personal morality priests* attain statistical significance, indicating that, after controlling for the other variables included in the model, parishioners in parishes with social justice priests are not, on average, more Democratic or politically liberal than are parishioners in parishes with mixed-emphasis priests. Similarly, parishioners in parishes with personal morality priests are not, on average, different from their counterparts in parishes with mixed-emphasis priests in terms of their partisanship or political ideology.

This is not to suggest, however, that religious traits are unimportant for explaining political outcomes. For instance, table 5.5 reports that religious particularism is significantly and positively correlated with political conservatism, indicating that the most religiously particularistic parishioners are also the most politically conservative. If it can be shown in subsequent analyses that priests play a role in shaping their parishioners' level of religious particularism, then it might also be inferred that priests play an indirect role in shaping their parishioners' political ideology. Religious particularism is a less powerful predictor of partisan affiliation than of political ideology, though even in the party identification model the coefficient is in the expected direction and has a fairly low p-value (.129).

Religious Influence on Presidential Approval and Candidate Evaluations

The survey of parishioners also makes it possible to consider the extent to which priests affect their parishioners' evaluations of President George W. Bush and his 2004 opponent, John Kerry. I hypothesize that parishioners in parishes with social justice priests, who often hear about Church teachings on aid to the poor, for instance, will have a more positive impression of Kerry (who, presumably, would be more generous in outreach to the poor than would Bush) than parishioners from parishes with mixed-emphasis priests, and that they will have a more negative impression of Bush. On the other hand, it is reasonable to suspect that parishioners from parishes with personal morality priests, who hear often about Church teachings on abortion and gay marriage, will have a more negative impression of the (pro-choice, pro-civil unions) Kerry than will parishioners from parishes with mixed-emphasis priests, and a more positive impression of the (pro-life, antigay marriage) Bush. Religious particularism, to the extent that it is a reflection of moral traditionalism, should be correlated with a favorable impression of Bush (the conservative candidate) and with an unfavorable impression of Kerry (the liberal candidate).

Table 5.6 Religious Influences on Presidential Approval Rating and Candidate Evaluations (Hierarchical Linear Models)

	Presidential Approval	Bush Evaluation	Kerry Evaluation
Parish-level Predictors			
Social Justice Priests	.088	.020	−.015
Personal Morality Priests	.021	−.041	−.047
Rural/Small Town	.110	.010	−.036
Individual-level Predictors			
Party	.260^	.117^	−.093^
Ideology	.205^	.066^	−.101^
Mass Attendance	.020	.013	−.028^
Education	−.024	−.013**	.018***
Gender	−.076	−.056***	.043**
Race	.092	.022	.031
Income	−.044**	−.000	.013*
Age	.001	.001	−.000
Religious Particularism	.044***	.011**	−.005
Intercept	1.123^	−.035	.942^
Remaining Parish-level Variance	.01563***	.00012	.00061
Remaining Individual-level Variance	.44875	.05551	.05296
Explained Parish-level Variance	80.08%	99.40%	95.44%
Explained Individual-level Variance	53.07%	60.18%	58.38%
Observations	430	428	424

*p<.15; **p<.1; ***p<.05; ^p<.01

To test these hypotheses, I specify a series of three new hierarchical linear models, the results of which are reported in table 5.6. The dependent variables in these three models are *presidential approval* (which ranges from 1, strongly disapprove, to 4, strongly approve) and normalized thermometer ratings for both Bush and Kerry.[4] In table 5.6, support for the hypotheses outlined above would be demonstrated by significant, negatively signed coefficients for *social justice priests* in the presidential approval and Bush evaluation models, and a significant, positively signed coefficient for *social justice priests* in the Kerry evaluation model (since in this model higher scores on the dependent variable indicate a more positive evaluation of Kerry). I expect, on the other hand, the coefficients for *personal morality priests* in the presidential approval and Bush evaluation models to be statistically significant and positively signed, and to be significant and negatively signed in the Kerry evaluation model. *Religious particularism* should be significant and positive in the Bush evaluation models, but negative in the Kerry evaluation model.

In keeping with the results presented in tables 5.4 and 5.5, table 5.6 indicates that Catholic priests do not play a direct role in shaping their parishioners' impressions of Bush or Kerry. In no instance is any coefficient for *social justice priests* or *personal morality priests* statistically significant, which suggests that, after controlling for other theoretically important variables, the average impressions of Bush and Kerry held by parishioners do not vary from parish to parish based on the messages emanating from parish priests.

Religious particularism, by contrast, behaves largely as expected, at least with respect to views of Bush. Parishioners who are the most religiously particularistic are significantly more likely than other parishioners to approve of Bush's performance in office, and to feel warmly towards Bush as compared with other political figures. The religiously particularistic are not, however, more likely than others to have a negative impression of Kerry.

Religious Influence on Parishioners' Issue Positions

Parish priests apparently do not directly influence their parishioners' voting decisions, partisanship, political ideology, or evaluations of the presidential candidates. This does not imply, however, that religious considerations are unimportant in shaping Catholics' political predilections. Religious particularism, for instance, was a significant predictor both of political ideology and of attitudes toward Bush in the 2004 election. The survey of parishioners also makes it possible to explore the religious basis of parishioners' opinions on political topics in three issue domains: social issues, economic issues, and foreign affairs.

I began the investigation of clergy influence on parishioners' issue positions by considering the effects of priestly messages on parishioners' opinions regarding five different social issues: abortion, stem cell research, birth control, gay marriage, and capital punishment. By 2004 several of these issues had figured prominently on the American political agenda for decades. Abortion, for instance, remained one of the core lines of demarcation in the American "culture wars." The issue of homosexual rights took on renewed urgency in the early part of the twenty-first century as the question of whether gay and lesbian couples should be afforded the ability to enter marriage-like arrangements was debated in courtrooms in several states and in the court of public opinion nationwide. Stem cell research had been the focus of George W. Bush's first televised address to the nation as president. In the 2004 election the national exit poll revealed that more than one in five voters (22 percent) cited moral values as the most important issue in the campaign (Pomper 2005, 56). Although these initial findings turned out to have overstated the importance of moral values and cultural issues in the campaign—more detailed analyses showed that the interpretation of the electoral importance of moral values in general (see, for instance, Pomper 2005, 59; Pew Research Center 2004) and gay marriage in particular (Freedman 2004; but also see Campbell and Monson 2005) was less straightforward than initially thought—there is no question that social and moral issues figured prominently in American politics during the 2004 election season.

I specified five new hierarchical linear models to test for clergy influence on these dependent variables, each of which is coded such that higher scores indicate a more conservative opinion on the issue.[5] For each model I hypothesized that parishioners in parishes with personal morality priests will be more conservative on the issue at hand (that is, score higher on the dependent variable) than will parishioners in parishes with mixed-emphasis priests, and that parishioners in parishes with social justice priests will be more liberal on the issue at hand (that is, score lower on the dependent variable) than will parishioners in parishes with mixed-emphasis priests. Accordingly, I expected the coefficients for *social justice priests* to be statistically significant and negatively signed, and the coefficients for *personal morality priests* to be statistically significant and positively signed. Such findings would constitute evidence that priests may play a direct role in shaping their parishioners' approaches to social issues. In addition, I expected religious particularism, which reflects parishioners' moral traditionalism on a variety of topics, to be correlated with political conservatism on social issues. Thus, the coefficients for *religious particularism* should be statistically significant and positive.

Finally, there is solid theoretical reason to suspect that a second religious attitude—willingness to accept political guidance from the church—is significantly related to attitudes about social issues. The survey asked parishioners twenty-four questions as to whether or not each of three sources (the pope, the U.S. bishops, and parish priests) should speak out on each of eight sociopolitical issues (aid to poor countries, fighting poverty in the United States, birth control, the war on terror, capital punishment, abortion, foreign affairs/war, and gay marriage/civil unions).

Responses to each question were coded 0 if the respondent indicated that the source in question should not speak on the issue (or if the respondent declined to answer the question), and 1 if the respondent indicated that the source in question should speak on the issue in question. Responses were summed for each individual to create a scale (alpha = .926) measuring the extent to which respondents are willing to accept political guidance from the Church. Scores on this scale ranged from 0 (for respondents who indicated that no source of Church authority should speak on any of the eight political issues) to 24 (for parishioners who indicated that every source of Church authority should speak on every one of the eight political issues). Recall from chapter 2 that the analysis of the Notre Dame Study data found the direction of influence of this particular variable to be contingent upon the issue at hand. On issues where Church teachings are clearly conservative, increased willingness to accept Church guidance exercised a conservatizing influence. On issues on which Church teachings are clearly liberal, this variable exerted a liberalizing influence.[6] Thus, in the abortion, birth control, stem cell research, and gay marriage models, *accept church guidance* should be associated with political conservatism, with positively signed, statistically significant coefficients. With respect to capital punishment, by contrast, the church takes a much more liberal position. Thus, the coefficient for *accept church guidance* on the death penalty model should be significant and negative.

The independent and control variables included in these five models are identical to those included in the models previously reported in this chapter. The results of the models investigating parishioners' opinions on social issues are reported in table 5.7.

The results reported in table 5.7, like those reported previously, continue to suggest that priests do not play a role in directly shaping their parishioners' politics. Though the coefficient for *personal morality priests* is in the expected direction and approaches statistical significance in the death penalty model, these models indicate that parishioners' opinions on social issues do not vary from parish to parish based on the messages emanating from parish priests.

The coefficients for *religious particularism* and *accept church guidance*, by contrast, conform quite closely with the hypotheses outlined above. In four of the five models (abortion, birth control, gay marriage, and stem cell research), the coefficient for *religious particularism* is statistically significant and positive; on these issues, the most religiously particularistic parishioners are also the most socially and politically conservative. *Accept church guidance* also behaves just as expected. On those issues on which the Church takes a conservative position, those parishioners who are most willing to accept political guidance from the Church are also the most politically conservative. On the issue on which the Church espouses a more liberal point of view (capital punishment), by contrast, those parishioners who are most willing to accept guidance from the Church are also the most politically liberal.

Table 5.7 Religious Influences on Parishioners' Opinions on Social Issues (Hierarchical Linear Models)

	Abortion	Stem Cell Research	Birth Control	Gay Marriage	Death Penalty
Parish-level Predictors					
Social Justice Priests	-.010	-.036	-.112	.055	.044
Personal Morality Priests	-.206	.140	.081	-.088	.183*
Rural/Small Town	.076	-.016	-.039	.097	.093
Individual-level Predictors					
Party	.022	.075^	.008	.022	.102^
Ideology	.396^	.205^	.260^	.218^	.016
Mass Attendance	.221^	.211^	.162^	.021	-.133^
Education	-.035	-.049**	-.022	-.047***	-.030
Gender	.110	.021	.235^	.033	.222^
Race	-.062	.107	-.105	-.221^	-.085
Income	.013	-.029	-.081^	-.016	-.007
Age	-.001	-.010^	-.005**	0	.001
Religious Particularism	.138^	.099^	.101^	.081^	-.006
Accept Church Guidance	.033^	.019^	.022^	.007**	-.045^
Intercept	-.147	.361	.341	1.715^	3.556^
Remaining Parish-level Variance	.03951^	.00003	.00957**	.00017	.00030
Remaining Individual-level Variance	.68967	.56541	.57780	.26085	.62655
Explained Parish-level Variance	51.41%	99.95%	88.33%	99.23%	95.26%
Explained Individual-level Variance	43.57%	38.40%	31.98%	33.04%	17.34%
Observations	418	413	418	422	417

*p<.15; ** p<.1; *** p<.05; ^ p<.01

Figure 5.1 Effect of Religious Particularism on Catholics' Opinions on Social Issues

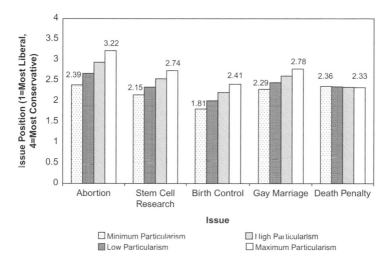

Figures 5.1 and 5.2 illustrate the impact of these religious variables on parishioners' attitudes on social issues, while holding all other variables at 0 (for dummy variables) or at their mean value. Figure 5.1 shows that the most religiously particularistic parishioners score nearly one full point higher in the (four-point) abortion model than do parishioners who score lowest on the religious particularism scale. And in the stem cell, birth control, and gay marriage models, the difference between the most- and least-religiously particularistic parishioners approaches or exceeds one-half point. Figure 5.2 paints a similar picture for the effects of willingness to accept Church guidance; parishioners who are most willing to accept guidance from the Church are substantially more conservative, holding all else equal, on the issues on which the Church takes a conservative stand, but much more liberal in their views of capital punishment. If, in subsequent analyses, these two religious variables can be shown to be shaped in part by characteristics of priests, then priests might be said to play an indirect role in shaping their parishioners' political views.

Figure 5.2 Effect of Willingness to Accept Church Guidance on Catholics' Opinions on Social Issues

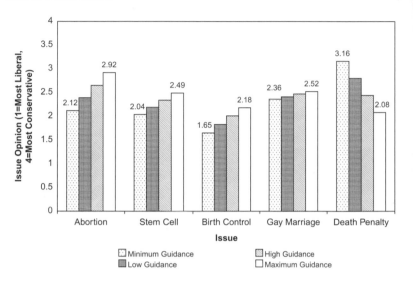

I next investigate whether parishioners' opinions on a number of economic issues are contingent in part on priestly messages. Just as social issues are of longstanding importance in American politics, so the question of the extent to which government should be involved in providing for the material needs and well-being of citizens is of perennial political concern. Indeed, in 2004, even in an atmosphere in which concern about moral values and questions about foreign policy (inspired by the events of September 11 and the debate over the appropriate response to the terrorist attacks) figured so prominently, fully 20 percent of voters cited the economy and jobs as being the most important issue in the election, and another 8 percent indicated that health care was their overriding electoral concern (Pomper 2005).

To examine the religious correlates of parishioners' attitudes on economic issues, I specify five new hierarchical linear models to determine the sources of parishioners' views on the appropriate level of government services, government-sponsored health care, government's role in guaranteeing a minimum standard of living, welfare, and homelessness. In each of these models, higher scores on the dependent variable reflect more conservative opinions (i.e., opposition to government efforts to provide for the material well-being of the disadvantaged).[7] I hypothesize that there will be a significant, negative relationship between belonging to a parish with social justice priests (because parishioners in these parishes hear often about the need to reach out to the poor) and conservatism on these poor-aid issues, and a significant, positive relationship between belonging to a parish with personal morality priests (because priests in these parishes emphasize attention to other political issues) and conservatism on poor-aid issues. I also expect religious particularism, to the extent that it is a measure of moral traditionalism and thus associated with political conservatism, to be associated with conservative positions on these issues (and thus positively signed and statistically significant). *Accept church guidance*, by contrast, should be negatively correlated with conservatism on these issues, since the institutional Church is a strong advocate of governmental efforts to help the poor. The results of the economic issues models are reported in table 5.8.

Considered as a whole, the results reported in table 5.8 indicate that religious factors are less important in shaping attitudes on economic issues as compared to social issues. As in all of the previous analyses, there is no evidence here to suggest that priests directly influence their parishioners' opinions on these five issues. More precisely, in no instance do the data indicate that parishioners in parishes with social justice priests are more liberal on average in their opinions toward economic issues than are their counterparts in parishes with mixed-emphasis priests; nor are parishioners in parishes with personal morality priests more conservative on average in their opinions toward poor-aid issues than are parishioners in parishes with mixed-emphasis priests. Priests appear, then, not to shape directly their parishioners' attitudes on these political issues.

Neither does religious particularism appear to play a role in shaping Catholics' opinions with regard to economic issues. In only one

Table 5.8 Religious Influences on Parishioners' Opinions on Economic Issues (Hierarchical Linear Models)

	Government Services	Health care	Standard of Living	Welfare	Homeless
Parish-level Predictors					
Social Justice Priests	-.046	.006	.035	.058	.092
Personal Morality Priests	-.004	.053	.007	.001	.081
Rural/Small Town	.072	-.067	.084	.204***	.064
Individual-level Predictors					
Party	.089^	.030**	.036***	.041***	.038***
Ideology	.305^	.170***	.091***	.193^	.237^
Mass Attendance	-.038	-.057***	.010	-.021	-.015
Education	.023	-.018	-.023*	-.030*	.007
Gender	.223^	.030	.094***	.025	.172^
Race	.382^	.085	.055	.238***	.259^
Income	.003	.038***	.043^	-.012	.005
Age	-.003	-.000	-.003***	-.006^	.002
Religious Particularism	-.009	-.009	-.002	-.009	-.027**
Accept Church Guidance	-.007	.001	-.004	-.021^	-.016^
Intercept	.649***	1.677^	1.684^	1.689^	.969^
Remaining Parish-level Variance	.00380	.00027	.00006	.00008	.00499
Remaining Individual-level Variance	.40427	.26351	.19628	.36374	.34798
Explained Parish-level Variance	87.96%	88.75%	97.68%	99.73%	70.47%
Explained Individual-level Variance	31.37%	13.18%	12.06%	15.19%	16.13%
Observations	421	426	426	424	425

* $p < .15$; ** $p < .1$; *** $p < .05$; ^ $p < .01$

instance does the coefficient for *religious particularism* attain statistical significance (in the homelessness model), and there it is not in the expected direction.[8] But willingness to accept Church guidance is a statistically significant predictor of parishioners' attitudes with regard to government spending on welfare programs and homelessness. Specifically, increased willingness to accept guidance from the Church leads, as hypothesized, to increased liberalism on these political issues. In short, though the willingness to accept Church guidance variable is not a significant source of influence across the spectrum of poor-aid issues, it is an important predictor of Catholics' attitudes toward welfare and homelessness.

The last issue domain in which it is possible to consider the role of priestly influence in shaping parishioners' attitudes is the domain of foreign affairs. Questions about foreign policy figured very prominently in the 2004 presidential election. In response to the terrorist attacks of September 11, 2001, the United States had become involved in a military effort to displace the ruling Taliban regime and combat terrorism in Afghanistan. In 2003 the United States initiated military action—on an even larger scale than that seen in Afghanistan—against Iraq. While the use of military force in Iraq was initially applauded by large swaths of the public, support for the war gradually declined in the months preceding the 2004 election. Exit polls revealed that concern over both foreign policy issues—how best to combat terrorism and how best to handle the war in Iraq—were highly important to voters in the presidential election. Indeed, 19 percent cited terrorism as the most important issue in the election, and another 15 percent cited Iraq as their paramount concern (Pomper 2005). Pomper argues that foreign policy was the central topic at issue in 2004, and that this worked to the advantage of President Bush (despite the decline in support for the war since the invasion of Iraq). As Pomper notes, "the election of 2004 was fought primarily on Bush's agenda: foreign policy and terrorism. The Republican campaign focused on those questions, both as substantive policy questions and as choices about which candidate would be the better commander in chief. Kerry could not avoid the centrality of these issues, given the trauma of 9/11 and the subsequent war in Iraq" (Pomper 2005, 58).

The survey of parishioners makes it possible to investigate whether or not priests influence their parishioners' views on a variety of foreign policy topics, including defense spending, the use of force in foreign affairs generally, the use of force in combating terrorism specifically, and the war in Iraq.[9] Once again, I expected parishioners in parishes with personal morality priests to be more conservative in their opinions toward these issues than parishioners from parishes with moderate priests, and parishioners in parishes with social justice priests to be more liberal. These hypothesized relationships would be supported by significant, negatively signed coefficients for *social justice priests*, and significant, positive coefficients for *personal morality priests*. In addition, I hypothesized that religious particularism would be positively related to conservative positions on foreign policy issues, and that willingness to accept Church guidance would be negatively related to conservatism in the foreign policy arena. The results of the foreign affairs models are reported in table 5.9.

The results reported in table 5.9 suggest once again that priests do not directly influence their parishioners' issue positions. That is, parishioners in parishes with social justice priests are not more liberal (or dovish) in their approach to foreign policy than are parishioners in parishes with mixed-emphasis priests, nor are parishioners in parishes with personal morality priests more conservative (or hawkish) in their approach to foreign policy.

In addition, table 5.9 indicates that there is only modest influence of individual-level religious variables on Catholics' attitudes toward foreign affairs. *Accept church guidance* fails to attain statistical significance in all four models, while *religious particularism* approaches significance only in the use-of-force-on-terror model and in the defense-spending model (p = .155). In short, though religious influences on foreign policy attitudes can be detected, they are limited in scope.

Table 5.9 Religious Influences on Parishioners' Opinions on Foreign Affairs Issues (Hierarchical Linear Models)

	Deferse Spending	Use of Force—Generally	Use of Force—Against Terror	Iraq
Parish-level Predictors				
Social Justice Priests	-.112	-.020	.024	-.020
Personal Morality Priests	.061	.110	.111	.003
Rural/Small Town	.065	-.089	-.102	.023
Individual-level Predictors				
Party	.029*	.071^	.043***	.200^
Ideology	.217^	.116***	.148^	.180^
Mass Attendance	-.055***	-.026	-.048**	.040
Education	-.069^	-.026	-.038***	-.093^
Gender	-.245^	-.000	.040	.027
Race	.144	-.044	-.015	.011
Income	.032	.017	.025	-.008
Age	.003	-.001	.003	-.001
Religious Particularism	.024	.004	.024*	.001
Accept Church Guidance	.002	-.000	.004	-.008
Intercept	1.825^	2.452^	3.265^	1.228^
Remaining Parish-level Variance	.00507*	.00688*	.00004	.00004
Remaining Individual-level Variance	.37110	.38730	.34253	.50275
Explained Parish-level Variance	79.38%	4.44%	99.22%	99.93%
Explained Individual-level Variance	18.63%	11.68%	13.08%	37.63%
Observations	426	425	429	430

* p < .15; ** p < .1; *** p < .05; ^ p < .01

Priestly Agenda Setting

Even if priests apparently do not directly shape the political opinions of their parishioners, they may help to shape their parishioners' conception of the political agenda. That is, messages emanating from parish priests may shape the extent to which parishioners consider some issues to be politically important and other issues to be less so. The data from the survey of parishioners permit an investigation into whether or not priests help to form the political agenda of their parishioners in this way.

The survey of parishioners asked each respondent to report which political issues were most important, second most important, and third most important in the presidential election campaign. Respondents could choose from eight political issues: the economy, national security/war in Iraq/war on terror, taxes, abortion, welfare, health care, the values and integrity of the candidates, and gay marriage/civil unions. To investigate the potential agenda setting influence of Catholic priests, parishioners' responses regarding the importance of various political issues were recoded into dummy variables. For each of the eight issues mentioned above, parishioners were coded 1 if they indicated that they considered the issue to be among the top three most important in the presidential election, and 0 otherwise.

To investigate the extent of priestly agenda-setting influence, I specified a series of eight new hierarchically generalized linear models with logit link function. The dependent variables (economy, national security, taxes, abortion, welfare, health care, values, gay marriage) indicate the probability that a respondent identified that issue as one of the top three on the political agenda. I hypothesized that parishioners in parishes with personal morality priests will be more likely than parishioners in parishes with mixed-emphasis priests to identify social issues such as abortion, the values of the candidates, and gay marriage as politically important, since personal morality priests emphasize these and related issues in their preaching. In addition, I hypothesize that parishioners in parishes with social justice priests will be more likely than their counterparts in parishes with mixed-emphasis priests to place importance on issues such as the economy, taxes, welfare, and health care, since social justice priests emphasize the need to reach out to the less fortunate. These hypotheses would be supported by significant, positive coefficients for *social justice priests* in the economy, taxes, welfare, and health care models, and by significant, positive coefficients for *personal morality priests* in the abortion, values, and gay marriage models. In addition, since religious particularism is an indicator of religious traditionalism primarily with respect to social issues, I hypothesize that religious particularism will be positively related to the probability of identifying social issues (including abortion, the values and integrity of the candidates, and gay marriage) as politically important, and negatively related to the probability of identifying other issues (such as the economy, national security, taxes, welfare, and health care) as politically important. As noted previously, while the institutional Church provides a great deal of guidance to Catholics with respect to an authentic Catholic approach to a number of specific political issues, there is relatively less explicit guidance provided as to how to establish priorities among political issues. Thus, there is no theoretical reason to suspect that a general willingness to accept Church guidance will lead parishioners to prioritize certain issues over others; thus *accept church guidance* is not included in these models. The results of the agenda setting models are reported in table 5.10.

The results reported in table 5.10 are not consistent with what one would expect to find if Catholic priests are performing a direct agenda-setting function for their parishioners. With the exceptions of the coefficient for *personal morality priests* in the economy model (which indicates that parishioners in parishes with personal morality priests are significantly less likely than are parishioners in parishes with mixed-emphasis priests to identify the economy as an important political issue) and the coefficient for *social justice priests* in the gay marriage model (which indicates that parishioners in parishes with social justice priests may be more likely to consider gay marriage a politically

Table 5.10 Religious Influences on Parishioners' Political Priorities (Hierarchical Generalized Linear Models with Logit Link Function)

	Economy	National Security	Taxes	Abortion	Welfare	Health Care	Values	Gay Marriage
Parish-level Predictors								
Social Justice Priests	-.295	.071	.238	-.165	.145	.024	.139	1.114*
Personal Morality Priests	-.523*	.241	-.396	.237	-.657	-.066	.031	.098
Rural/Small Town	.034	-.407	-.008	.134	.767	.441	.060	-.740
Individual-level Predictors								
Party	.102	.054	.172**	.116	-.193	-.186***	.070	-.198
Ideology	-.764^	.210	-.076	.653^	-.100	-.467***	.327**	1.471^
Mass Attendance	-.249***	-.049	.158	1.109^	.384	-.263***	-.082	.379
Education	-.076	-.006	-.105	.064	-.022	.022	.005	-.173
Gender	-.007	-.403*	.598***	.060	-.278	-.121	-.048	-.116
Race	-.898***	.335	.412	.460	-1.048	-.678***	.767***	.226
Income	.108	.140	.168*	-.073	.332	-.240^	.089	-.337***
Age	.017***	.007	-.000	-.052^	.033	.018***	-.013**	-.024*
Religious Particularism	-.039	-.071	-.246^	.285^	-.087	-.047	.084*	.196**
Intercept	4.497^	.904	-3.032***	-10.592^	-4.997**	3.279***	-1.618**	-7.200***
Remaining Parish-level Variance	.00002	.08752	.00006	.00003	.00068	.01990	.00002	.00062
Explained Parish-level Variance	99.98%	—	99.88%	99.99%	—	61.25%	—	99.64%
Observations	431	431	431	431	431	431	431	431

*p<.15; **p<.1; ***p<.05; ^p<.01

important issue than are parishioners in parishes with mixed-emphasis priests), none of the coefficients for *social justice priests* or *personal morality priests* are statistically significant. This indicates that there are no differences in the extent to which parishioners attach (or fail to attach) importance to certain political issues traceable to differences in messages emanating from parish priests. In short, parish priests appear not to directly influence the political agendas of their parishioners.

Religious particularism, by contrast, is a more consistent predictor of parishioners' issue priorities. Notice, first, that the coefficient for *religious particularism* is correctly signed in each of the eight models. That is, particularism is negatively related to the probability of identifying the economy, national security, taxes, welfare, and health care as among the three most important political issues, and it is positively related to identifying abortion, the values of the candidates, and gay marriage as politically important. Notice as well that in two of the eight models (taxes and abortion), the coefficient for *religious particularism* is highly significant (p < .01), and in two other models (gay marriage and values) the coefficients attain or approach significance at the .1 level. More religiously particularistic parishioners, then, are more likely than others to view social issues like abortion, the values and integrity of candidates, and gay marriage as politically important, and less likely to view economic issues (like taxes) as high priorities.

Influence of Priests on Parishioners' Religious Attitudes

The analyses presented thus far clearly indicate that in 2004 the priests at the parishes participating in this study did not appear to have exercised direct influence on the politics of their parishioners. There is no evidence to suggest that parishioners' voting decisions, evaluations of candidates, partisanship, or ideological leanings were directly influenced by priestly messages. Nor does the evidence suggest that parishioners' opinions on a variety of political issues were directly affected by messages emanating from parish priests. Nor, finally, is there evidence to suggest that priests wield direct political influence through their ability to set the political agenda.

This is not to suggest, however, that religion is unimportant in shaping the political views of this sample of parishioners. Indeed, just the opposite is true; the analyses presented here show that for Catholics, political attitudes are clearly shaped in part by religious attitudes, including religious particularism and willingness to accept political guidance from the Church. Specifically, religious particularism plays an important conservatizing influence with respect to Catholics' partisanship, political ideology, presidential approval ratings, evaluations of Bush, and opinions on abortion, stem cell research, birth control, gay marriage, and the appropriateness of using military force in combating terrorism. Additionally, religious particularism appears to serve an important political agenda-setting function. Willingness to accept Church guidance is, as expected, a statistically significant predictor of conservative views on abortion, stem cell research, birth control, and gay marriage, and a statistically significant predictor of liberal views on capital punishment, welfare, and homelessness. Demonstrating that these two politically important religious variables may be shaped in part by parish priests suggests that priests play an important, albeit indirect, role in shaping their parishioners' politics.

I begin the consideration of the indirect political influence of Catholic priests by hypothesizing that personal morality priests (as defined in preceding chapters) would inspire in their parishioners increased religious particularism. I test this hypothesis by specifying a new hierarchical linear model where the dependent variable is *religious particularism*. The independent variables of interest are *social justice priests*, which I expect to be statistically significant and negatively signed, and *personal morality priests*, which I expect to be significant and positive. In addition, the model controls for frequency of Mass attendance, education, gender, race, income, and age.

Before turning to a discussion of the results of this model, a few words are in order as to the appropriateness of asserting that parishioners' religious particularism—which is a religious attitude—will be influenced by political messages emanating from parish priests. It would be ideal to investigate priestly influence on parishioners' religious particularism by measuring the extent to which priests publicly address the question of who constitutes a true Catholic, rather than by relying on the classification of the extent to which (and the manner in which) priests discuss a variety of political issues, as I do here. Nevertheless, because personal morality priests are classified as such because of the degree to which they concentrate on urging their parishioners to oppose permissiveness towards behaviors like abortion and gay marriage, and because social justice priests are classified as such because of their public attention to the need to reach out to those in need (of financial and material assistance but also, presumably, to those in need of forgiveness, welcome, or tolerance), it is plausible to hypothesize that priestly messages, operationalized in this way, will have an effect on parishioners' level of religious particularism. It is also true that the Church's teachings on many political issues, including abortion, marriage, sexual morality, and aid to the poor, are not merely political. Opposition to abortion, belief in the sanctity of marriage, and the obligation to help those in need are all components of the Catholic faith and are not simply political positions of the institutional Catholic Church. In short, since priestly political messages, as I define them here, might plausibly be expected to influence parishioners' religious particularism, and since no alternative measure of the religious aspects of priests' preaching is available, I rely on the measures of the political nature of priestly messages as the key independent variables in the model designed to investigate priestly influence on parishioners' religious particularism, the results of which are reported in table 5.11.

The results reported in table 5.11 suggest that priests do play an important role in shaping their parishioners' religious particularism. Specifically, the coefficient for *personal morality priests* is highly significant ($p < .05$) and positive, which indicates that on average (and even after controlling for all of the other control variables in the model) parishioners in parishes with personal morality priests score significantly higher on the religious particularism scale than do their

Table 5.11 Effects of Priestly Messages on Religious Particularism (Hierarchical Linear Model)

	Religious Particularism
Parish-level Predictors	
Social Justice Priests	.219
Personal Morality Priests	1.173***
Individual-level Predictors	
Mass Attendance	.503^
Education	−.022
Gender	.127
Race	−.286
Income	−.109*
Age	.017***
Intercept	.221
Remaining Parish-level Variance	.06332*
Remaining Individual-level Variance	3.80121
Explained Parish-level Variance	83.85%
Explained Individual-level Variance	11.28%
Observations	437

*p < .15; **p < .1; ***p < .05; ^p < .01

counterparts in parishes with mixed-emphasis pastors. While the coefficient for *social justice priests*, by contrast, fails to attain statistical significance, the model suggests that personal morality priests may exercise substantial influence in shaping their parishioners' religious particularism.

This point is presented graphically in figure 5.3, which reports differences in parishioners' predicted values on the religious particularism scale attributable to variations in priestly messages. Figure 5.3 indicates that, with the values of all control variables held constant, members of parishes with personal morality priests are predicted to score more than one point higher on the six-point religious particularism scale than are parishioners in parishes with mixed-emphasis priests, and nearly one point higher than parishioners in parishes with social justice priests. This figure illustrates, then, the apparently

Figure 5.3 Effect of Priestly Messages on Parishioners' Religious Particularism

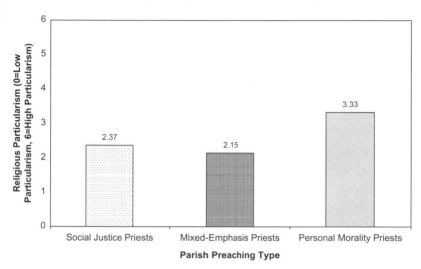

substantial impact of priestly messages on Catholics' level of religious particularism.

Finally, I continue the investigation of indirect priestly influence by considering the extent to which Catholic priests may influence their parishioners' willingness to accept guidance from the Church. For this model, a new predictor variable is in order, since there is no theoretical reason to expect personal morality and social justice priests to have different effects on their parishioners' willingness to accept Church guidance. Instead, rather than looking to the content of priestly messages as influences on parishioners' willingness to accept Church guidance, it is more plausible to look to the types of messages, or the style of homilies that priests deliver, as determinants of parishioners' willingness to accept Church guidance. Specifically, I hypothesize that parishioners' willingness to accept Church guidance will be predicated, in part, on the quality of the homilies they hear. In other words, parishioners who are regularly exposed to high-quality homilies from their local representative of the institutional Church should be more likely to be willing to accept guidance from the

Church than should parishioners regularly exposed to lower-quality homilies.

Recall that a phenomenon similar to that described and hypothesized here was reported in chapter 2, where it was determined that the effort expended by pastors in preaching, combined with the level of political involvement of pastors, was an important determinant of parishioners' willingness to accept Church guidance. Although no measure of pastors' preaching effort or overall level of political involvement is available here, it is possible to measure priests' homily quality, and to utilize this measure as an alternative to preaching effort and priestly political involvement. Respondents were asked to rate the typical homily at their parish in terms of three characteristics: whether or not homilies are interesting, informative, and inspiring. Responses to these three questions were summed and averaged to form a homily-quality scale (alpha = .850), where higher scores indicate better (that is, more interesting, informative, and inspiring) homilies. Scale scores were then averaged for each parish, so as to be able to compare homily quality for each parish, and centered around the parish grand mean. This new homily-quality variable is the key explanatory variable in table 5.12, which reports the results of a new hierarchical linear model specified to test the hypothesis that parishioners in parishes where priests deliver above-average homilies will be more willing to accept Church guidance than parishioners in parishes where priests deliver average or below-average homilies. This new model, like the religious particularism model, controls for frequency of Mass attendance, education, gender, race, income, and age.

Table 5.12 suggests that parishioners' willingness to accept Church guidance is predicated, in part, on the quality of the homilies delivered at their local parish. The coefficient for *homily quality* approaches statistical significance at the .1 level (p = .119). And the positive coefficient for *homily quality* indicates that parishioners in parishes where priests deliver above-average homilies are, on average,

Table 5.12 Effects of Priestly Messages on Willingness to Accept Church Guidance
(Hierarchical Linear Model)

	Accept Church Guidance
Parish-level Predictors	
Homily Quality	2.091*
Individual-level Predictors	
Mass Attendance	1.064^
Education	.163
Gender	1.580***
Race	.725
Income	−.049
Age	−.062^
Intercept	11.338^
Remaining Parish-level Variance	.30347
Remaining Individual-level Variance	35.12094
Explained Parish-level Variance	41.57%
Explained Individual-level Variance	5.73%
Observations	437

*p<.15; **p<.1; ***p<.05; ^p<.01

more willing to accept Church guidance than are parishioners in other parishes. It appears, then, that parishioners' willingness to accept Church guidance, which is an important predictor of several political attitudes among Catholics, may be influenced by the quality of homilies emanating from parish priests.

To further demonstrate this point, figure 5.4 illustrates the extent to which differences in parishioners' willingness to accept Church guidance may be attributable to the quality of the homilies delivered at their parishes. Even after controlling for the other variables in the model, parishioners in parishes where priests deliver the best homilies are predicted to have a value on the twenty-four-point willingness-to-accept-Church-guidance scale that is more than a point higher than the predicted value on this variable for parishioners in parishes where priests deliver homilies of average quality, and to have a value

Figure 5.4 Effect of Homily Quality on Parishioners' Willingness to Accept Church Guidance

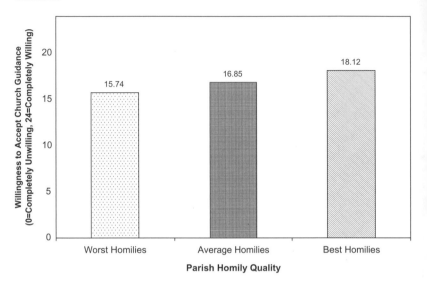

on this variable that is more than two points higher than the predicted value for parishioners in parishes where priests deliver the worst homilies.

Discussion and Conclusion

The results presented here paint a clear picture. In 2004 the priests at the parishes participating in this study did not appear to have exercised direct influence on the politics of their parishioners. There is no evidence to suggest that parishioners' voting decisions, evaluations of candidates, partisanship, or ideological leanings were influenced by priestly messages. Nor does the evidence suggest that parishioners' opinions on a variety of political issues were affected by messages emanating from parish priests. Nor is there evidence to suggest that priests wield direct political influence through their ability to set the political priorities held by their parishioners.

It is also important to point out that, in addition to the models presented here, hundreds of additional, alternative models (which are not presented here) were investigated in this search for direct priestly political influence. Recall, for instance, that many of the models presented here indicate that frequency of Mass attendance is a significant predictor of a number of political attitudes for Catholics. Accordingly, to test the hypothesis that the effect of Mass attendance will vary depending on the messages delivered by priests at the respondent's parish, each of the models reported here was run with a priestly message/ Mass attendance interaction. No pattern emerged, however, to suggest that the political effects of Mass attendance vary from parish to parish. In addition, dozens of models that included interactions between homily quality (as rated by parishioners) and priestly messages were examined to determine whether direct priestly influence is contingent upon the quality of the homilies delivered at a particular parish. Here again, no pattern emerged that suggested direct priestly influence. Drawing on Zaller's work, I separated the sample of parishioners by political awareness levels to determine whether or not priestly influence is present but only operating among individuals of a certain level of political awareness (Zaller 1992). Again, in no subsample did evidence of direct priestly influence emerge. Finally, I ran analyses similar to those described here that included interactions between the content of priestly messages and the length of pastors' tenure, as well as other analyses that included interactions between priestly messages and the length of time that individual parishioners reported attending their parish, in order to investigate whether clergy influence is contingent upon the length of time during which parishioners have been exposed to a given preaching style. These analyses again uncovered no evidence of direct priestly political influence. In short, the survey of parishioners reported here uncovers no evidence of direct priestly influence on the voting behavior or political attitudes of Catholic parishioners during the 2004 election season.

The analyses presented here do show, however, that for Catholics, political attitudes are clearly shaped in part by religious attitudes, including religious particularism and willingness to accept political guidance from the Church. Specifically, religious particularism plays an important conservatizing influence with respect to Catholics' political ideology, presidential approval ratings, evaluations of Bush, and opinions on abortion, stem cell research, birth control, gay marriage, and the appropriateness of using military force in combating terrorism. Additionally, religious particularism appears to serve an important political agenda-setting function, and is very nearly a significant predictor of Republicanism and of opinions on spending on national defense. Willingness to accept Church guidance is, as expected, a statistically significant predictor of conservative views on abortion, stem cell research, birth control, and gay marriage, and a statistically significant predictor of liberal views on capital punishment, welfare, and homelessness.

Even more important, the evidence presented here indicates that priests play an important role in shaping their parishioners' level of religious particularism and willingness to accept Church guidance. Specifically, personal morality priests may inspire in their parishioners increased religious particularism, and priests who give high-quality homilies may inspire in their parishioners an increased willingness to accept political guidance from the Church. The implication of these findings is that Catholic priests—through their ability to influence their parishioners' attitudes on these two religious variables that are, in turn, highly important predictors of a variety of political attitudes—may indirectly influence Catholic politics. In short, the analyses presented here suggest that priestly political influence may be subtle and indirect, but that priests may nevertheless be an important source of political influence for American Catholics.

Notes

1. Similarly, my own analysis of the Notre Dame Study of Catholic Parish Life did not reveal sufficiently consistent patterns to suggest that priests wield indirect political influence through their ability to shape their parishioners' degree of religious particularism.

2. Of course, a sample of only nine level-two cases (i.e., nine parishes) is, potentially, problematically small for the estimation of multilevel models. Multilevel modeling remains, however, a more rigorous method of testing the hypotheses of interest here compared to alternative modeling techniques. The analyses reported here were replicated using OLS and logistic regression models (as appropriate), and the results were very similar to those obtained through the multilevel modeling approaches described in the text.

3. *Rural/small town* is a parish-level dummy variable coded 1 for parishes located in rural areas or small towns, and 0 for parishes located in cities or suburbs. *Party* is a seven-category variable coded in the following manner: (0) strong Democrat, (1) weak Democrat, (2) Independent, but lean Democratic, (3) Independent/Other, (4) Independent, but lean Republican, (5) weak Republican, (6) strong Republican. *Ideology* is a five-category variable coded in the following manner: (0) very liberal, (1) liberal, (2) moderate, (3) conservative, (4) very conservative. *Mass attendance* is an eight-category variable ranging from (0) for those who never or rarely attend Mass, to (7) for those who attend Mass every day. *Education* is a seven-category variable ranging from (0) some high school or less, to (6) advanced degree. *Gender* is coded 1 for men and 0 for women. *Race* is coded 1 for whites and 0 for nonwhites. *Income* is a six-category variable ranging from (0) less than $25,000, to (5) more than $125,000. Finally, *age* is a parish centered variable, where a score of 0 indicates that a respondent is of average age for his or her parish; scores above 0 indicate that a respondent is older than average for his or her parish, while scores below 0 indicate that a respondent is younger than average.

4. Normalized thermometer ratings are essentially continuous variables that range from 0 to 1. Respondents were asked to provide a thermometer rating of eleven public figures (Bush, Kerry, Dick Cheney, John Edwards, Dennis Hastert, Nancy Pelosi, Bill Frist, Tom Daschle, Pope John Paul II, their diocesan bishop, and their pastor). Thermometer ratings were normalized by subtracting the respondent's lowest thermometer rating from the rating of the figure in question, and then dividing by the range of the respondent's thermometer ratings. See Abramson et al. 1992.

5. *Abortion* is a four-category variable ranging from (1) by law, a woman should always be able to obtain an abortion as a matter of personal choice, to (4) by law, abortion should never be permitted. *Stem cell research* is a four-category variable ranging from (1) strongly favor allowing research on embryonic stem cells, to (4) strongly oppose allowing research on embryonic stem cells. *Birth control* is also a four-category variable ranging from (1) strongly disagree that the Church should remain firm in its opposition to the use of contraceptives, to (4) strongly agree that the Church should remain firm in its opposition to the use of contraceptives. *Gay marriage* is a three-category variable ranging from (1) gays and lesbians should be allowed to get legally married, to (3) there should be no legal recognition of gay and lesbian relationships. Finally, *death penalty* is another four-category variable ranging from (1) strongly oppose the death penalty, to (4) strongly favor the death penalty.

6. By contrast, on issues where the institutional Church does not take a clear stand, the expected direction of influence of this variable is less straightforward; that

is, though the Church clearly urges faithful Catholics to oppose abortion and to support aid to the poor, the Church takes no clear position on whether Catholics should support Republicans or Democrats, or on which political issues are of paramount importance. This is why *accept church guidance* is not included in the previous vote choice or candidate approval models or in the subsequent models of political priorities.

7. *Government services* is a three-category variable ranging from (1) government should provide more services even if it has to increase spending, to (3) government should provide fewer services to reduce spending. *Health care* is also a three-category variable ranging from (1) favor government insurance plan, to (3) favor private insurance plans only. *Standard of living* ranges from (1) government should see to it that every person has a good standard of living, to (3) government should let each person get ahead on their own. *Welfare* is a three-category variable ranging from (1) government spending on welfare programs should be increased, to (3) government spending on welfare programs should be decreased. Finally, *homeless* is a three-category variable ranging from (1) government spending on the problem of the homeless should be increased, to (3) government spending on the problem of the homeless should be decreased.

8. This may suggest that religious particularism, in addition to measuring moral traditionalism, also taps into Catholic orthodoxy more broadly; thus, much like a willingness to accept church guidance, religious particularism may make Catholics more likely to accept the Church's position on political issues.

9. *Defense spending* is a three-category variable ranging from (1) decrease defense spending, to (3) increase defense spending. *Use of force—general* is a four-category variable measuring the extent to which respondents think the United States should be willing to use military force to solve international problems, ranging from (1) never willing, to (4) very willing. *Use of force—against terror* is a four-category variable measuring the extent to which respondents think the United States should be willing to use military force to fight terrorism, ranging from (1) never willing, to (4) very willing. Finally, *Iraq* is a three-category variable coded from (1) the United States made the wrong decision in using military force against Iraq, to (3) the United States made the right decision in using military force against Iraq.

Conclusion

 The question of the extent to which American clergy wield significant political influence is an important one. Burgeoning research in the subfield of religion and politics consistently demonstrates that religious factors play an important role in shaping the way Americans approach politics, and research in political communications makes clear that clergy represent an entirely plausible source of influence. Until recently, however, the nature and extent of clergy political influence has been underexplored, and the ability of clergy to exercise influence with their flocks has largely been assumed but not empirically documented. The research presented here has attempted to address this shortcoming of the existing literature by looking specifically at whether or not Catholic priests exercise political influence with their own parishioners.

Key Findings

The weight of the evidence presented in the preceding chapters suggests two key findings. First, Catholic priests are a diverse lot, and it seems clear that the political messages emanating from parish priests to which Catholics are exposed are quite different depending on where one attends church. Recall from chapter 2, for instance, that the pastors surveyed in the Notre Dame Study expressed a wide range of opinions on a number of political issues. Most pastors eschewed membership in either of the two major political parties, but roughly 10 percent identified themselves as Republicans, and 29 percent described themselves as Democrats. Similarly, though most priests described themselves as ideological moderates, one in five said that they were politically liberal and a comparable number described themselves as politically conservative. In addition, while the pastors surveyed in the Notre Dame Study were unanimous in their opposition to abortion and nearly unanimous in their support for a joint freeze on the development of nuclear weapons, opinions were much more varied on most other political issues. Indeed, despite the Church's clear opposition to capital punishment and dovish approach to foreign affairs, roughly one-in-three pastors expressed support for the death penalty, with a comparable number expressing support for increased defense spending.

Similarly, the interviews with pastors, surveys of priests, and content analyses of parish bulletins conducted during the summer and fall of 2004 (and described in chapters 3 and 4) conclusively document that the political messages that Catholic parishioners are exposed to from religious authorities vary considerably, even radically, from parish to parish. Specifically, priests in some parishes are primarily concerned with abortion and other issues related to respect for life or sexual morality. These personal morality priests speak often on these topics and more irregularly on other political issues, and they leave no doubt that they consider abortion to be the preeminent issue on the political agenda. In one case, a parish even made available a voter's guide that claimed that voting for a political candidate who supports legal abortion is a mortal sin punishable by eternal damnation. Priests at other parishes, however, take a radically different approach by concentrating in their homilies and other public statements on the Church's teachings about aid to the poor, capital punishment, and related social justice issues. These social justice priests speak only rarely about abortion and may never publicly address Church teachings on issues like birth control. And when abortion is addressed by priests at these parishes, it may be done with a different tone than that observed in the parishes where priests focus especially on abortion and related issues; one priest, for instance, made clear that on the (rare) occasions that he publicly addresses abortion, he is careful to make clear to his parishioners that abortion is not, under canon law, synonymous with murder. Finally, there are still other parishes staffed by mixed-emphasis priests, where clergy attempt to adopt a somewhat more evenhanded approach and to emphasize all of these sociopolitical issues equally. Clearly, American Catholics hear a wide variety of political points of view emanating from their local parish priests.

What, then, are the consequences of these varied priestly messages for Catholic politics? The second key finding suggested by the weight of the evidence presented here is that clergy political influence may indeed be a common occurrence in American politics. The analysis of the Notre Dame Study in chapter 2 is built upon the theoretical foundations laid by prominent scholars of religion and politics, and upon the empirical findings of Bjarnason and Welch, whose research demonstrates that, at least with regard to capital punishment, Catholics' political opinions seem to be influenced by their parish priests. The results reported in chapter 2 indicate that priests may exercise direct influence on Catholics' opinions on many political issues. More specifically, parishioners who belonged to parishes with liberal pastors were shown to be much more politically liberal in their opinions with regard to a number of political issues than were parishioners in parishes with moderate or conservative pastors.

Furthermore, in addition to exercising direct political influence, the findings reported in chapter 2 indicate that priests may also exercise political influence indirectly, through their ability to shape some of their parishioners' politically important religious beliefs and attitudes. Specifically, the analysis of the Notre Dame Study revealed Catholics' willingness to accept political guidance from the Church to be a consistently significant predictor of adopting Church-sanctioned positions on a variety of political issues. This religious disposition—a willingness to accept church guidance—was in turn shown to be influenced by characteristics of the preaching at local parishes; parishioners with politically involved pastors who devote time and effort to attempting to preach effectively are more likely to look to the Church for guidance than are parishioners in parishes with less involved, less attentive pastors. Finally, chapter 2 also suggests that pastors may exercise indirect political influence via the ability to shape the images of God held by parishioners. More specifically, parishioners were more likely to imagine God as similar to a judge if their pastors subscribed to this image. Previous research shows this conception of God to be a politically meaningful predictor of sociopolitical attitudes (Welch and Leege 1988).

The analysis of the 2004 survey of parishioners uncovered no evidence of direct clergy influence on vote choice in the 2004 presidential election or on partisanship, ideology, or other political attitudes. However, the 2004 survey did suggest once again that priests may exercise indirect political influence through their ability to shape their parishioners' politically important religious beliefs. Two religious variables—religious particularism (a measure of the extent to which parishioners subscribe to a strict definition of who qualifies as "Catholic") and willingness to accept political guidance from the Church—emerged as important predictors of a variety of political attitudes. Specifically, high levels of religious particularism were shown to be correlated with political conservatism. Religiously particularistic parishioners are also more likely than others to rank the abortion issue as politically important, and less likely than others to place a high political priority on tax policy. In addition, increased willingness to accept Church guidance evokes agreement with Church teachings on a variety of political issues. Most important, these politically important religious variables were shown to be correlated with characteristics of the preaching of one's local priests. That is, parishioners in parishes with personal morality priests were substantially more religiously particularistic than were their counterparts in parishes with mixed emphasis or social justice priests. And parishioners in parishes where priests deliver high-quality homilies were more willing to accept political guidance from the Church than were parishioners in parishes where priests deliver homilies of lesser quality. These findings suggest that while the priests participating in the 2004 study of Catholic parishes appear not to have exercised direct political influence with regard to their parishioners' voting decisions, they may have played an indirect role in helping to shape their parishioners' views on a variety of social and political issues.

Of course, it is worth keeping in mind that a certain amount of caution must be exercised in the interpretation of any one of these findings. Recall that the Notre Dame Study, for instance, measured pastors' political and social opinions, but it did not ask priests about the extent to which they convey these sentiments in their public statements. For the purposes of understanding contemporary American politics, the Notre Dame Study suffers also from the fact that it was conducted in the early 1980s. The 2004 study of Catholic parishes and survey of parishioners is limited in scope, both in terms of geographic coverage and sample size (since it is restricted to nine parishes from three Catholic dioceses in the mid-Atlantic region) and in terms of the topics covered in the survey of parishioners (i.e., as an early step in investigating and attempting to understand clergy political influence, the survey of parishioners consisted mainly of items designed to tap parishioners' political opinions; it contained notably fewer measures of religious beliefs and social attitudes). To be sure, the measures of the extent to which priests publicly deliver political cues to parishioners in the 2004 study are based on self-reports, survey responses, and content analyses of parish bulletins, and they are therefore more direct measures of priests' approach to preaching than those contained in the Notre Dame Study. Nonetheless, they are not based on direct observations of homilies or other public statements. In all, the Notre Dame Study remains the best publicly available dataset for investigating clergy political influence, in that it includes data pertaining both to clergy and to parishioners at a reasonably large, representative sample of parishes. What is unique (and uniquely valuable) about the 2004 survey is that it was designed for the specific purpose of investigating the political influence of priests.

In sum, despite the limitations of the data used here, the cumulative weight of the numerous models and analyses is powerfully suggestive. The conclusion to be drawn from the evidence is that the assumption that clergy exercise significant political influence may well be correct. The Notre Dame Study suggests that the nature of clergy influence may sometimes be straightforward and direct; but both the Notre Dame Study and the 2004 survey of Catholic parishioners suggest that clergy influence may also be exercised more subtly, through priests' ability to shape their parishioners' politically important religious dispositions.

Implications and Further Considerations

The findings described and elaborated upon here have a number of implications for those seeking to understand Catholic politics in the United States (and, by extension, American politics more generally). They also present several puzzles and raise questions that might be addressed by future research.

One important implication suggested by this research is that scholars, journalists, and other observers who hope to understand the political views of American Catholics would do well to consider the local religious context. Local Catholic priests are likely to play a role in helping to shape their parishioners' views, just as much previous research demonstrates that other sources of influence encountered in a religious context are also politically meaningful (Gilbert 1993; Huckfeldt et al. 1993; Wald et al. 1988). In other words, while it has long been clear that Catholic politics is less than monolithic at the individual level (e.g., Catholic voters have divided their support relatively evenly between the two major parties in recent elections), it should also be kept in mind that the political cues conveyed by representatives of the institutional Church are also less than monolithic. This has consequences of potential political importance.

The apparent importance of the political cues delivered by Catholic priests is not to suggest that the cues emanating from the hierarchy of the Church (such as from the American bishops or the Vatican) are inconsequential. Although it has gone largely unremarked thus far, it is worth recalling that in the analyses of both the Notre Dame Study and of the 2004 survey of parishioners, frequency of Mass attendance was often a significant predictor of Catholics' political attitudes. Furthermore, the direction of the relationship between Mass attendance and political attitudes was consistent with what one would expect to find were institutional influence taking place. That is, Mass attendance is correlated with conservative attitudes on issues on which the Church takes a conservative stand, and with liberal attitudes on issues on which the Church takes a liberal stand. The evidence suggests, in other words, that the Church is effective in articulating its positions to those who attend Mass, and in persuading frequent Mass attenders to adopt those positions, regardless of the messages emanating from the local priests.

This could be a product of the nature of the diversity of the preaching at local parishes; that is, the variance in priestly messages from parish to parish is attributable primarily to differences in emphasis rather than to differences in actual content. The 2004 case studies of Catholic parishes confirmed that even those priests who focus their preaching primarily on social justice issues sometimes remind parishioners of the Church's stance on abortion and other issues on which it takes a conservative stand; in much the same vein, priests who emphasize abortion and related issues in their preaching also speak occasionally about poverty and other social justice issues with their parishioners. The correlation of Mass attendance with adoption of Church-sanctioned positions could also reflect greater exposure on the part of frequent Mass attenders to religiously based political cues emanating from sources outside of Mass, such as those contained in Catholic periodicals or websites. In short, Catholic identity, political cues emanating from the Church hierarchy, and local religious context are all likely to be relevant for a complete understanding of Catholics' political preferences.

The analyses contained here document the potential influence that priests may possess with respect to their parishioners' opinions on a wide variety of social and political issues. The analyses do not uncover, however, any link between the messages emanating from local Catholic priests and parishioners' voting decisions. (Of course, the Notre Dame Study of Catholic Parish Life did not ask parishioners about their voting habits, which made it impossible to use its data to investigate possible links between priests' political inclinations and the voting decisions of their parishioners.) This raises an important question: if priests represent a meaningful source of political influence for American Catholics, why is there no apparent link between priestly messages and individual-level vote choice?

There are several potential explanations for this puzzle. Priests' apparent lack of sway over their parishioners' voting decisions in the 2004 election may be a reflection of the issues at stake in that particular election season; while there were strong indirect links between priestly messages and parishioners' views on a variety of social and moral issues, priests apparently exercised less influence with respect to parishioners' views in other important issue domains, including foreign policy. Despite early postelection analyses that suggested that concern about moral values was paramount in voters' minds on election day, it may have been the case that in the first presidential election after September 11, foreign policy and related concerns figured more prominently than did concerns about social and moral issues (e.g., see Freedman 2004; Pew Research Center 2004). This explanation is consistent with the data from the survey of parishioners, the analysis of which failed to uncover any consistent evidence to suggest that priests exercise political influence through their ability to prime certain considerations in their parishioners' minds. Although personal morality priests apparently inspire increased conservatism among their parishioners on social issues like abortion and gay marriage, the data do not suggest that parishioners in parishes with personal morality priests evaluate presidential candidates based on the candidates' positions on social issues more than do parishioners in other parishes.

Similarly, the evidence does not indicate that parishioners in parishes with social justice priests rely more on economic criteria in evaluating presidential candidates than do other parishioners. Priests' ability to shape their parishioners' voting decisions, in other words, may depend on the political dynamics of a particular election year, and it may simply have been the case that the dynamics of the 2004 presidential election did not lend themselves to a high degree of priestly political influence with respect to vote choice.

One specific, idiosyncratic element of the 2004 election that may account for priests' apparent lack of influence with respect to parishioners' vote choices may lie in the controversy over Catholic politicians' fitness (or lack thereof) to receive the sacrament of communion. John Kerry, the 2004 Democratic presidential candidate, is a pro-choice Roman Catholic. While the USCCB has been strong and consistent over the years in condemning abortion, several bishops made particularly strong statements in 2004 condemning Kerry's support for legalized abortion precisely because Kerry is Catholic (Goodstein 2004). Specifically, several bishops indicated that communion should not be administered to Kerry (or other pro-choice politicians). Other bishops indicated that denying communion to Kerry and others would be an inappropriate way of addressing the abortion issue. It is possible that this debate among the American hierarchy, which was covered widely in the media, increased the visibility and importance of bishops (as opposed to parish priests) as influential Catholic cue-givers in 2004. Direct priestly political influence may be more evident during more typical election seasons when the major-party presidential candidates do not include a Catholic.

The lack of priestly influence on vote choice may also reflect an inability on the part of political candidates to adequately recognize and capitalize upon the nuances of Catholics' opinions on issues across the political spectrum. Even Catholics who hold conservative positions (possibly attributable in part to their local priests' consistent attention to these issues) on social issues may be uneasy with Republican candidates' stances on economic and social justice issues. And Catholics who are sympathetic with the Democratic Party's positions on economic issues may be uneasy with that party's stance on abortion and related issues. Peter Steinfels, writing about the failure of conservatives and Republican strategists to move Catholic voters solidly and consistently into the Republican electoral coalition, argues that "in Ronald Reagan and his successors the born-again style more frequently (compared with Jimmy Carter) manifested itself in an ebullient certainty, and this religiously infused politics seemed to short-circuit those prudential judgments and consequent compromises that Catholicism respected" (Steinfels 2003, 94). Steinfels goes on to document the long list of issues on which the institutional Church, despite its affinity with American conservatives' position on abortion, has "butted heads with conservatives lodged predominantly in the Republican Party" (Steinfels 2003, 94–95). In other words, it may be that like the institutional Church, Catholic priests, though apparently influential with respect to their parishioners' issue positions, are constrained in their ability to exercise influence when it comes to voting decisions because of the misalignment of Catholic teaching and American politics; the fact that neither party consistently reflects Catholic principles may mean that the ultimate basis of Catholics' electoral decision making lies outside the realm of religion.

Another puzzle that emerges from the findings presented here relates to the types of priests who appear to wield the most political and social influence. Recall that the analyses of the Notre Dame Study, which was conducted in the early to mid-1980s, indicated that political influence was wielded primarily by liberal priests. That is, parishioners in parishes with a liberal pastor consistently expressed more liberal positions on social and political issues than did parishioners in parishes with moderate pastors. But the opinions of parishioners in parishes with a conservative pastor did not, for the most part, differ significantly from the opinions expressed by parishioners in parishes with moderate priests. The 2004 study of Catholic parishes, by contrast, produced just the opposite result: Personal morality priests (who might plausibly be thought of as relatively conservative, since they emphasize the Church's teachings on those issues on which the Church takes a conservative stance) appear to have been relatively influential in 2004 via their ability to help shape their parishioners' level of religious particularism, whereas social justice priests appear to have been much less influential by this measure. Why is this the case?

Here again, there are several possible explanations for this puzzle. Perhaps most obviously, these divergent findings may simply be arti- facts of the nature of the two datasets, which are based on fairly small samples of Catholic parishes (thirty-five parishes from the Notre Dame Study are analyzed here, and nine parishes were included in the 2004 study). It may simply be the case that the conservative priests from the Notre Dame Study were less influential (because of flaws in their delivery of homilies, or unpopularity with parishioners, or for any number of other reasons) than were their liberal counter- parts. In 2004, by contrast, the personal morality priests included in the sample may simply have been more effective in exercising politi- cal influence compared to their social justice counterparts. Alterna- tively, it may be that the influence of conservative priests was not observed in the 1980s because many issues, including stem cell re- search and gay marriage, on which the Church has adopted a conser- vative stance, were not yet on the political agenda (see the discussion in chapter 2).

One final (and related) puzzling finding from the 2004 study of Catholic parishes worth considering concerns the types of issues on which priests appear to have been politically influential. Recall that conservative priests appear to have been politically influential with respect to their parishioners' views on social issues, via their influence on their parishioners' religious particularism. Religious particularism proved to be a much less powerful predictor, by contrast, of parish- ioners' views on economic and foreign policy issues. Similarly, priests who delivered high-quality sermons also appear to have been influ- ential with respect to parishioners' views on social issues, via their influence on parishioners' willingness to accept political guidance from the Church. Here again, however, willingness to accept political guidance from the Church is a much less powerful predictor of economic and foreign policy views as compared to views on social issues. Why are characteristics of priests' preaching more closely associated with views on social issues than with parishioners' views on economic and foreign policy issues?

As with some of the other puzzling findings reported here, this one may be an artifact of the religious measures used in predicting the social and political items that serve as dependent variables. The analysis of religious particularism (which measures the extent to which individuals disqualify themselves from the ranks of "true" Catholics by engaging in a variety of behaviors, including urging or undergoing an abortion, practicing homosexuality, using birth control, and the like), in particular, relates parishioners' religious views on certain topics to their sociopolitical views on closely related social issues (such as the legality of abortion, gay marriage, and stem cell research).

Alternatively, to the extent that parishioners look to their religious beliefs and their religious leaders for moral (as opposed to political) guidance, priests' greater influence on social issues may reflect a greater proclivity on the part of parishioners to view social issues, more than economic or foreign policy issues, as inherently rooted in principles of morality. Of course, it is not the case that social issues are inherently moral in nature, while economic and foreign policy issues are not. Indeed, both the institutional Church and liberal political activists have sought in recent years to explicitly make the case that economic and foreign policy issues are just as morally consequential as are social issues. In parishioners' minds, however, morality may simply be more closely linked with social issues than with economic and foreign policy concerns.

These and other puzzling findings highlight the need for further research to delineate the specifics of the nature and extent of clergy influence in American politics. Such research could take several forms that might shed additional light on the findings presented here, and it could also extend the investigation of clergy influence beyond the

Catholic case. One potentially fruitful method by which such future research might be conducted is experimentation. Participants might be shown video of clergy from their own denomination or religious tradition delivering a series of sermons. The points of emphasis and the nature of the opinions expressed in these sermons (along with other variables) could vary across treatment conditions. Comparing participants' religious and political views following exposure to the various treatment conditions could shed additional light on the mechanisms through which clergy influence is exercised and better explain the conditions under which such influence is likely to occur. Such an experimental approach—no matter how well designed and executed—is likely to fall short of adequately recreating the atmosphere and dynamics of an actual religious service. But experimentation would make it possible to more decisively disentangle the extent to which the clergy influence that survey-based research suggests may be taking place is actually a product of congregations taking clergy-delivered cues to heart, and not simply an artifact of clergy adopting and echoing the views they believe are held by their congregation, or of parishioners deciding where to attend church services based on their like (or dislike) of particular clergy, or (in the case of many protestant denominations) of congregations hiring clergy of their choosing.

In addition to experimentation, further survey-based research projects also have the potential to continue exploring clergy political influence. Such efforts might be based on a model similar to that employed in the Notre Dame Study of Catholic Parish Life and the 2004 study of Catholic parishes reported here. Ideally, however, subsequent survey-based research would be broader in scope, covering a larger number and more geographically diverse sample of parishes, increasing the nuance with which the nature and consequences of clergy political speech could be investigated. Such studies might also include a longitudinal component, presenting the possibility of studying some parishes both before and after a change of pastors. A longitudinal approach, unlike the Notre Dame Study or the 2004 study of Catholic parishes, would allow researchers to go beyond answering the question of whether parishioners in parishes with liberal priests are more liberal than their counterparts in parishes with moderate or conservative priests (and vice versa). Instead, a longitudinal approach could provide an answer to a different (and perhaps even more interesting) question: Are parishioners in parishes with liberal priests more liberal than they otherwise would have been—and are parishioners in parishes with conservative priests more conservative than they otherwise would have been—had they had a different priest?

A longitudinal, survey-based approach would also be less subject to misinterpretation of findings based on the idiosyncratic conditions prevailing at the time of any single survey snapshot. Here, for instance, the question of clergy influence in the 2004 election was investigated in an atmosphere permeated by the ongoing revelations about sexual abuse of minors by Catholic priests. It is impossible to know with certainty what sort of effect these revelations may have had on the outcome of the 2004 study of Catholic parishes. It is certainly possible that the apparent political influence of priests could have been diminished in 2004 as a result of a loss of trust on the part of parishioners in the Church, its leadership, and perhaps even its local representatives, parish priests. Conversely, if those Catholics who were most disappointed and disillusioned by the revelations of sexual abuse responded by attending Mass less frequently or leaving the Church altogether, thus leaving only the most steadfast parishioners in the parishes and pews (and, by extension, in the sampling frame for the 2004 study), the apparent influence of Catholic priests might be artificially inflated here. Only a longitudinal approach could determine with certainty how changing religious and political dynamics impact the extent to which priests wield significant political influence.

Finally, a longitudinal survey-based approach has distinct advantages for pursuing a crucial next step in research on clergy influence: extending this research beyond the Catholic case. As noted previously, Catholics constitute an ideal starting point for seeking to understand clergy influence for the simple fact that Catholic parishioners do not choose their own priests. Of course, this is not to suggest that there are no concerns about the direction of the causal arrow linking priests' approaches to preaching with parishioners' attitudes and beliefs. Catholic priests are certainly not assigned to parishes in a random fashion, and priests may also seek popularity with their parishioners by avoiding controversial topics or echoing their congregations' views rather than forcefully expounding the Church's (possibly unpopular) positions on various political issues. Such concerns, and thus the interpretation of survey results and statistical analyses, are certainly even more problematic when considering the potential influence of Protestant clergy. But while the political influence of Protestant (as opposed to Catholic) clergy may be more difficult to examine, it is certainly no less important. Indeed, there is reason to suspect that Protestant clergy may be more influential than Catholic priests. Many Protestant clergy are less constrained by hierarchy and by institutional position-taking than are Catholic priests. A Protestant minister who favors legal access to abortion may well be freer to express this point of view than is a Catholic priest. On the other hand, Protestant clergy face the prospect of losing their jobs should they alienate their congregations with their sermons and other public messages, which potentially limits the inclination of Protestant clergy to play a prophetic role on controversial topics. A longitudinal design that studies Protestant congregations both prior to and following a change in clergy would be well-suited to deciphering the complicated interactions likely to come into play when considering the political influence of Protestant clergy.

Religion is likely, perhaps certain (especially given developments in the war on terror and the evolution of political Islam) to remain of paramount concern to political scientists for the foreseeable future. One of the most pressing demands on scholars of religion and politics has been to understand the consequences of political messages emanating from clergy and other religious leaders. This project, which demonstrates that different Catholic priests convey very different political messages to their parishioners—and that these varying messages may carry important, if often indirect, political sway—has been an early step on the road to understanding clergy political influence. But more work is needed to continue to improve our understanding of clergy as political leaders. Building on the research design and drawing on the findings presented here will allow scholars to pursue this understanding and, in so doing, to obtain a clearer picture of the workings of American politics.

Appendix A
Pastor Interviews

The following is the script used to structure the interviews conducted with Catholic pastors in the summer of 2004. This script was not followed verbatim but rather was used to guide the conversation with pastors.

1. When were you first ordained? How long have you been assigned to this parish?

2. What was it that made you want to become a priest?

3. How would you describe your style of preaching? For example, would you say that you mostly attempt to explain and expound upon the weekly scriptural readings, or do you attempt to provide advice to your parishioners as to how they should live their own lives? Generally speaking, do you enjoy preaching, or is it something that you don't really look forward to?

4. Now I'd like to talk a little bit about some public policy topics that are of interest to the Church, and I'd like to start by considering aid to the poor. Is this a topic that you think it is appropriate for parish priests to speak out about (for example, in their homilies, in public announcements, in the bulletin), or should discussion of this topic be left up to Church leaders like the bishops and the pope? Do you ever address issues like aid to the poor in your homilies or other public announcements? If so, how (that is, do you encourage individuals, in their capacity as private citizens, to participate in charitable projects, or do you link aid to the poor with public policy concerns)? How often would you say that you publicly address this issue with your parishioners?

5. Do you think it is appropriate for parish priests to speak out about public policy towards abortion, or should discussion of this topic be left up to Church leaders like the bishops and the pope? Do you ever speak about abortion in your homilies or other public announcements? If so, how (in other words, do you speak about abortion with regard to individual morality

only, or do you sometimes speak about what an appropriate public policy on abortion would be)? How often would you say that you publicly address this issue with your parishioners?

6. Do you think it is appropriate for parish priests to speak out about capital punishment, or is this an issue better left for Church leaders to discuss? Do you ever speak out on capital punishment in your homilies and other public announcements? If so, how? How often?

7. What about foreign affairs and the war on terror? Is this an issue that parish priests should speak out about, or should consideration of foreign affairs be left to Church leaders? Do you ever address issues of foreign affairs in your homilies and other public announcements? If so, how (that is, do you ever express support for American troops, or pray, and encourage parishioners to work for, peace)? How often would you say that you publicly address foreign affairs with your parishioners?

8. Do you think it is appropriate for parish priests to speak out about issues like homosexuality and gay marriage, or should these issues be left up to bishops and the Pope to discuss? Do you ever address homosexuality in your sermons? If so, how (in other words, when you address this issue, would you say you normally stress the need to have compassion and care for those with such inclinations, or do you reiterate the Church's teaching that such activity is sinful)? How often would you say you publicly address this issue with your parishioners?

9. Generally speaking, do you think that birth control is a subject that is appropriate for parish priests to address, or is it better left to Church leaders? Do you ever address the Church's teachings on birth control in your homilies or other announcements? If so, how? How often?

10. A lot of what I've read about what it's like to be a priest really brought home to me what a physically, spiritually, mentally, emotionally, and spiritually challenging task Catholic priests have. One challenge in particular that some priests might face is walking that fine line between instructing and leading their parishioners in their faith journey, and overstepping that line by being too forceful, which could risk alienating their parishioners. In your own leadership of the parish, and especially in your homilies and public announcements, to what extent do you tell the people what you think it is necessary for them to hear, and to what extent do you sometimes find it necessary to temper your remarks and the topics you address in order to avoid conflict with your parishioners?

11. In your homilies and public announcements, do you ever encourage your parishioners to support (or oppose) particular political candidates? Do you ever encourage them to support (or oppose) political parties?

12. Do you ever find that, at election time, you pay special attention in your homilies and public announcements to public policy concerns? If so, are there any specific issues (like aid to the poor, abortion, foreign affairs, the death penalty, etc.) to which you give special emphasis? Do you ever explicitly encourage your parishioners to consider a particular issue when voting, or do you simply mention the issue without explicitly linking it to voting? Do you ever encourage your parishioners to vote?

13. In the past year or so, has your parish organized transportation to any political events or rallies or things of that nature (such as the March for Life or candlelight vigils to oppose the death penalty, etc.)? If so, what kind of rally or event was it?

14. In the past couple of years or so, has your parish urged parishioners to contact elected officials? If so, which officials? About what issues?

15. In your homilies and public announcements, do you ever recommend reading material (such as newspaper or magazine articles, books, or websites) to your parishioners? If so, how often? What types of things do you usually recommend? Can you remember any specific examples of reading material that you have recommended in the last year or so?

16. On the other hand, are there ever times that you recommend to your parishioners that they avoid some media outlet, or news topic, etc.? For example, I remember back in the late 1990s I heard a priest, in a homily, recommend that parishioners avoid reading Kenneth Starr's report on the Monica Lewinsky investigation because it was inappropriate. Have you ever suggested anything similar?

17. Sometimes, during or after Mass, individuals or representatives of groups are allowed to make short announcements designed to solicit participation or financial contributions from parishioners. How often does this happen at this parish? What kind of groups have been invited or permitted to make these kinds of presentations?

18. How would you rate yourself as a public speaker? Generally, do you think that your homilies are effective in convincing your parishioners of the correctness of your message and in exhorting them to action or reform, or do you struggle with this?

19. About how long would you say your average homily is?

20. How did you come to be assigned to this parish? Did you request the assignment? Were you consulted about it? Did you have any reservations, or were you particularly enthusiastic, about coming here? Why?

21. About what percentage of the people who regularly attend Mass at this parish would you estimate are actually registered at this parish?

22. Are there any special characteristics or attributes of your parish that make it especially unique, or is it pretty similar to other parishes to which you've been assigned?

23. What are the three or four largest, most active and influential groups in your parish? What types of activities are they involved in? Do you play an influential or a leadership role in these groups, or not? Did you assist in founding or establishing these groups, or not? Generally speaking, do you approve of their activities and foci, or do you have reservations about them?

24. What is the most enjoyable and rewarding aspect of being a priest and a pastor?

25. What is the most difficult or least enjoyable aspect of being a priest and a pastor?

26. What do you think is the greatest challenge facing the Church in the next decade or so? Why do you think this? How serious is this challenge . . . in other words, does it constitute a full-blown crisis, or is it only a minor problem for a relatively thriving institution, or somewhere in between?

27. What do you think is the greatest challenge facing this parish in the next decade?

28. What do you think is the greatest strength or attribute of the Catholic Church today?

29. What do you think is the greatest strength or attribute of this parish?

30. Do you have a parish council? How active is the parish council in your parish? Generally speaking, would you say you have a cooperative and good working relationship with the parish council, or are you sometimes at cross purposes?

Appendix B
Analysis of Bulletins

Each bulletin item was coded on the following variables:

Abortion

In addition to obvious references to abortion, items are considered to mention or to be about abortion if they deal with issues of embryonic or fetal research.

Variable: Abortion

Code	Description
0	No mention of abortion in item
1	Church's teaching on abortion is mentioned, but is not a key feature, in item
2	Church's teaching on abortion is a key subcomponent of the item
3	Church's teaching on abortion is the primary focus of the item

Variable: Abortion/Church Direction

Code	Description
0	No mention of abortion in item
1	Whether or not item is pro-life or pro-choice is unclear
2	Item expresses support for Church teaching (i.e., pro-life viewpoint)
3	Item expresses opposition to Church teaching (i.e., pro-choice viewpoint)

Variable: Abortion/Politics

Code	Description
0	Item does not address politics/public policy with regard to abortion
1	Item addresses politics/public policy as they relate to abortion

Variable: Abortion/Politics Direction

Code	Description
0	Item does not address politics/public policy, or political viewpoint of item is unclear
1	Item indicates that politics/public policy should limit access to abortion/make abortion illegal
2	Item indicates that politics/public policy should keep abortion legal/maintain status quo

Contraception

Variable: Contraception

Code	Description
0	No mention of contraception in item
1	Church's teaching on contraception is mentioned, but is not a key feature, in item
2	Church's teaching on contraception is a key subcomponent of the item
3	Church's teaching on contraception is the primary focus of the item

Variable: Contraception/Church Direction

Code	Description
0	No mention of contraception in item
1	Whether item is supportive of or opposed to Church teaching on contraception is unclear/not explicit
2	Item expresses pro-Church viewpoint/support for Church teaching on contraception
3	Item expresses anti-Church viewpoint/questions Church teaching on contraception

Variable: Contraception/Politics

Code	Description
0	Item does not address politics/public policy with regard to contraception
1	Item addresses politics/public policy as they relate to contraception

Variable: Contraception/Politics Direction

Code	Description
0	Item does not address politics/public policy with regard to contraception, or public policy/political preference with regard to contraception is unclear
1	Item indicates that politics/public policy should do more to enforce/encourage adherence to Church teaching on contraception
2	Item indicates that politics/public policy should do less to encourage or should not address Church teaching on contraception

Pre/Extramarital Sex

Variable: Sexual Morality

Code	Description
0	No mention of sexual morality in item
1	Church's teaching on sexual morality is mentioned, but is not a key feature, in item
2	Church's teaching on sexual morality is a key subcomponent of the item
3	Church's teaching on sexual morality is the primary focus of the item

Variable: Sexual Morality/Church Direction

Code	Description
0	No mention of sexual morality in item
1	Whether or not item is supportive of or opposed to Church teaching on sexual morality is unclear/not explicit
2	Item expresses pro-Church viewpoint/support for Church teaching on sexual morality

3   Item expresses anti-Church viewpoint/questions Church teaching on sexual morality

Variable: Sexual Morality/Politics

Code   Description
0   Item does not address politics/public policy with regard to sexual morality
1   Item addresses politics/public policy as they relate to sexual morality

Variable: Sexual Morality/Politics Direction

Code   Description
0   Item does not address politics/public policy with regard to sexual morality, or public policy/political preference with regard to sexual morality is unclear
1   Item indicates that politics/public policy should do more to enforce/encourage adherence to Church teaching on sexual morality
2   Item indicates that politics/public policy should do less to encourage or should not address Church teaching on sexual morality

Homosexuality

Variable: Homosexuality

Code   Description
0   No mention of homosexuality in item
1   Church's teaching on homosexuality is mentioned, but is not a key feature, in item
2   Church's teaching on homosexuality is a key subcomponent of the item
3   Church's teaching on homosexuality is the primary focus of the item

Variable: Homosexuality/Church Direction

Code   Description
0   No mention of homosexuality in item
1   Whether or not item is supportive of or opposed to Church teaching on homosexuality is unclear/not explicit

2   Item expresses pro-Church viewpoint/support for Church teaching on homosexuality (i.e., is primarily anti-homosexual behavior in tone)

3   Item expresses anti-Church viewpoint/questions Church teaching on homosexuality (i.e., primarily expresses support/compassion for homosexuals)

Variable: Homosexuality/Politics

Code   Description

0   Item does not address politics/public policy with regard to homosexuality

1   Item addresses politics/public policy as they relate to homosexuality

Variable: Homosexuality/Politics Direction

Code   Description

0   Item does not address politics/public policy with regard to homosexuality, or public policy/political preference with regard to homosexuality is unclear

1   Item indicates that politics/public policy should do more to enforce/encourage adherence to Church teaching on homosexuality (that is, the item indicates that politics should do more to discourage homosexual behavior by, for instance, prohibiting homosexual marriage)

2   Item indicates that politics/public policy should do less to encourage or should not address Church teaching on homosexuality (that is, the item indicates that homosexuals should receive increased support from the political and legal systems)

Death Penalty

Variable: Death Penalty

Code   Description

0   No mention of death penalty in item

1   Church's teaching on death penalty is mentioned, but is not a key feature, in item

2   Church's teaching on death penalty is a key subcomponent of the item

3   Church's teaching on death penalty is the primary focus of the
         item

Variable: Death Penalty/Church Direction

Code   Description
0   No mention of capital punishment in item
1   Whether item is supportive of or opposed to Church teaching
         on capital punishment is unclear
2   Item expresses pro-Church viewpoint/support for Church
         teaching on capital punishment (i.e., item is anti-capital pun-
         ishment)
3   Item expresses anti-Church viewpoint/questions Church teach-
         ing on capital punishment (i.e., item is pro-capital punish-
         ment)

Variable: Death Penalty/Politics

Code   Description
0   Item does not address politics/public policy with regard to cap-
         ital punishment
1   Item addresses politics/public policy as it relates to capital pun-
         ishment

Variable: Death Penalty/Politics Direction

Code   Description
0   Item does not address politics/public policy with
         regard to capital punishment, or public policy/political pref-
         erence with regard to capital punishment is
         unclear
1   Item indicates that politics/public policy should do more
         to enforce/encourage adherence to Church teaching on
         capital punishment (i.e., should limit/abolish capital punish-
         ment)
2   Item indicates that politics/public policy should do less to en-
         courage or should not address Church teaching on capital pun-
         ishment (i.e., should maintain status quo on capital
         punishment)

Aid to the Poor

An item is considered to mention or to be about aid to the poor if there are references to helping the poor, disadvantaged, elderly, or disabled.

Variable: Aid to poor

Code	Description
0	No mention of aid to poor in item
1	Church's teaching on aid to poor is mentioned, but is not a key feature, in item
2	Church's teaching on aid to poor is a key subcomponent of the item
3	Church's teaching on aid to poor is the primary focus of the item

Variable: Aid/Church Direction

Code	Description
0	No mention of aid to poor in item
1	Whether item is supportive of or opposed to Church teaching on poor aid is unclear
2	Item expresses pro-Church viewpoint/support for Church teaching on poor aid (i.e., is pro-aid to poor)
3	Item expresses anti-Church viewpoint/questions Church teaching on poor aid (i.e., is anti-aid to poor)

Variable: Aid/Politics

Code	Description
0	Item does not address politics/public policy with regard to poor aid
1	Item addresses politics/public policy as they relate to poor aid

Variable: Aid/Politics Direction

Code	Description
0	Item does not address politics/public policy with regard to poor aid, or public policy/political preference with regard to poor aid is unclear
1	Item indicates that politics/public policy should do more to en-force/encourage adherence to Church teaching on aid to poor (i.e., public policy should be designed to aid the poor)

2   Item indicates that politics/public policy should do less to en-
         courage or should not address Church teaching on poor aid
         (i.e., government should do less/should not provide aid to
         poor)

International Aid

An item is considered to mention or to be about international aid if there
are references to helping the poor, disadvantaged, elderly, or disabled in foreign countries.

Variable: International Aid

Code	Description
0	No mention of international aid in item
1	Church's teaching on international aid is mentioned, but is not a key feature, in item
2	Church's teaching on international aid is a key subcomponent of the item
3	Church's teaching on international aid is the primary focus of the item

Variable: International Aid/Church Direction

Code	Description
0	No mention of international aid in item
1	Whether item is supportive of or opposed to Church teaching on international aid is unclear
2	Item expresses pro-Church viewpoint/support for Church teaching on international aid (i.e., is pro-international aid)
3	Item expresses anti-Church viewpoint/questions Church teaching on international aid (i.e., is anti-international aid)

Variable: International Aid/Politics

Code	Description
0	Item does not address politics/public policy with regard to international aid
1	Item addresses politics/public policy as they relate to international aid

Variable: International Aid/Politics Direction

Code	Description
0	Item does not address politics/public policy with regard to international aid, or public policy/political preference with regard to international aid is unclear
1	Item indicates that politics/public policy should do more to enforce/encourage adherence to Church teaching on international aid (i.e., public policy should be designed to promote international aid)
2	Item indicates that politics/public policy should do less to encourage or should not address Church teaching on international aid (i.e., government should do less/should not provide international aid)

Foreign Affairs

An item is said to mention or to be about foreign affairs to the extent that it addresses the war in Iraq, the war on terror, or military policy generally.

Variable: Foreign Affairs

Code	Description
0	No mention of foreign affairs in item
1	Church's teaching on foreign affairs is mentioned, but is not a key feature, in item
2	Church's teaching on foreign affairs is a key subcomponent of the item
3	Church's teaching on foreign affairs is the primary focus of the item

Variable: Foreign Affairs/Church Direction

Code	Description
0	No mention of foreign affairs in item
1	Whether item is supportive of or opposed to Church teaching on foreign affairs is unclear
2	Item expresses pro-Church viewpoint/support for Church teaching on foreign affairs (i.e., is antiwar)[1]

3   Item expresses anti-Church viewpoint/questions Church teaching on foreign affairs (i.e., is pro-war)

Variable: Foreign Affairs/Politics

Code	Description
0	Item does not address politics/public policy with regard to foreign affairs
1	Item addresses politics/public policy as they relate to foreign affairs

Variable: Foreign Affairs/Politics Direction

Code	Description
0	Item does not address politics/public policy with regard to foreign affairs, or public policy/political preference with regard to foreign affairs is unclear
1	Item indicates that politics/public policy should do more to enforce/encourage adherence to Church teaching on foreign affairs (i.e., public policy should be antiwar/more hesitant to use force)
2	Item indicates that politics/public policy should do less to encourage or should not address Church teaching on foreign affairs (i.e., government should be pro-war/willing to use force)

Voting

Variable: Vote

Code	Description
0	Item does not mention voting or voter registration
1	Item encourages parishioners to vote/register to vote

Definitions

"Church teaching on X is mentioned, but is not a key feature of item." By this is meant that Church teaching on X is mentioned in a clause, and may even be the subject of a sentence, but does not rise to the level of being the primary focus of several sentences.

"Church teaching on X is a key subcomponent of item." By this is meant that Church teaching on X is the primary focus of at least one sentence or of a substantial portion of the item, but the item in question addresses other or broader issues as well.

"Church teaching on X is the primary focus of the item." By this is meant that Church teaching on X is mentioned throughout the item and is the subject, at least indirectly, of the majority of sentences in the item. The item may touch on other subjects, but is substantially about Church teaching on X.

Line Counting

Titles are not counted, unless they are contained in the body of the announcement. Schedules and readings are not included in line counting.

Item Counting

Each separate bulletin announcement, except for schedules and readings, is included in the item count. In the instance where announcements are grouped under a single heading (for instance, Youth Group might be a heading in a box that contains three separate announcements), each announcement counts as an item (so the aforementioned situation would consist of three items).

Note

1. Of course, many Catholics and Catholic priests might dispute that the position of the Church is "antiwar." Pope John Paul II, however, made clear his opposition to the war in Iraq. In an address on January 13, 2003, for instance, he stated " 'No to war!' War is not always inevitable. It is always a defeat for humanity. . . . As the charter of the United Nations Organization and international law itself remind us, war cannot be decided upon, even when it is a matter of ensuring the common good, except as the very last option and in accordance with very strict conditions, without ignoring the consequences for the civilian population both during and after the military operations" (John Paul II 2003). Accordingly, Church teaching is considered here to be "antiwar."

Appendix C
2004 Survey of Priests

Instructions: For each question, please circle the most accurate response.

1. In the past few months, how often have you briefly touched on abortion in your homilies?
   1. Never
   2. A few times
   3. Several times per month
   4. Every week
2. In the past few months, how often have you spoken extensively about abortion in your homilies?
   1. Never
   2. A few times
   3. Several times per month
   4. Every week
3. If you have spoken about abortion in your homilies over the past few months, either by touching briefly on it or by discussing it more extensively, how have you done so? That is, have you concentrated mostly on public policy toward abortion or on the implications of abortion for individual morality, or both?
   1. Concentrated mostly on public policy toward abortion
   2. Concentrated mostly on abortion as it relates to individual morality
   3. Concentrated on both public policy and individual morality
   4. I have not addressed abortion in my homilies
   5. Other:_____

4. What about aid to the poor? In the past few months, how often have you briefly touched on aid to the poor in your homilies?
   1. Never
   2. A few times
   3. Several times per month
   4. Every week

5. In the past few months, how often have you spoken extensively about aid to the poor in your homilies?
   1. Never
   2. A few times
   3. Several times per month
   4. Every week

6. If you have spoken about aid to the poor in your homilies over the past few months, either by touching briefly on it or by discussing it more extensively, how have you done so? That is, have you concentrated mostly on public policy with regard to aid to the poor or have you concentrated mostly on encouraging individuals, in their private capacity, to provide assistance to the needy, or both?
   1. Concentrated mostly on public policy with regard to aid to the poor
   2. Concentrated mostly on encouraging individuals to provide aid to the poor
   3. Concentrated on both public policy and encouraging individuals to provide aid to the poor
   4. I have not addressed aid to the poor in my homilies
   5. Other:_____

7. What about capital punishment? In the past few months, how often have you briefly touched on capital punishment in your homilies?
   1. Never
   2. A few times
   3. Several times per month
   4. Every week

8. In the past few months, how often have you spoken extensively about capital punishment in your homilies?
   1. Never
   2. A few times
   3. Several times per month
   4. Every week

9. If you have spoken about capital punishment in your homilies over the past few months, either by touching briefly on it or by discussing it more extensively, how have you done so? That is, have you emphasized the Church's opposition to capital punishment, or have you pointed out that historically the Church has upheld the right of the state to enforce capital punishment under certain circumstances, or have you done both?
   1. Concentrated mostly on the Church's opposition to capital punishment
   2. Pointed out that capital punishment may sometimes be justifiable
   3. Stressed both the Church's opposition to capital punishment and pointed out that capital punishment may sometimes be justifiable
   4. I have not addressed capital punishment in my homilies
   5. Other:_____

10. What about foreign affairs, including the war in Iraq and the war on terror? In the past few months, how often have you briefly touched on foreign affairs in your homilies?
    1. Never
    2. A few times
    3. Several times per month
    4. Every week

11. In the past few months, how often have you spoken extensively about foreign affairs in your homilies?
    1. Never
    2. A few times
    3. Several times per month
    4. Every week

12. If you have spoken about foreign affairs in your homilies over the past few months, either by touching briefly on it or by discussing it more extensively, how have you done so? That is, have you concentrated mostly on the need to support the troops or have you concentrated mostly on the need to pray and work for peace, or both?
    1. Concentrated mostly on the need to support the troops
    2. Concentrated mostly on the need to pray and work for peace
    3. Concentrated on both the need to support the troops and the need to pray and work for peace
    4. I have not addressed foreign affairs in my homilies
    5. Other:_____

13. What about homosexuality and related issues, like same-sex marriage? In the past few months, how often have you briefly touched on homosexuality in your homilies?
    1. Never
    2. A few times
    3. Several times per month
    4. Every week

14. In the past few months, how often have you spoken extensively about homosexuality in your homilies?
    1. Never
    2. A few times
    3. Several times per month
    4. Every week

15. If you have spoken about homosexuality in your homilies over the past few months, either by touching briefly on it or by discussing it more extensively, how have you done so? That is, have you concentrated mostly on the need to have compassion towards those who might be of homosexual orientation or on the sinfulness of homosexual behavior, or both?
    1. Concentrated mostly on the need to have compassion for homosexuals
    2. Concentrated mostly on the sinfulness of homosexual behavior
    3. Concentrated both on the need to have compassion for homosexuals and the sinfulness of homosexual behavior
    4. I have not addressed homosexuality in my homilies
    5. Other:_____

16. Over the past few months, have you mentioned John Kerry by name in any of your homilies?
    1. Yes
    2. No (if No, SKIP to Question 21)

17. If you have mentioned John Kerry by name, did you point out that he is pro-choice on abortion?
    1. Yes
    2. No

18. If you have mentioned John Kerry by name, did you point out that he is in favor of government efforts to provide aid to the poor?
    1. Yes
    2. No

19. If you have mentioned John Kerry by name, did you point out that he has been critical of the war on terror and the war in Iraq?
    1. Yes
    2. No

20. If you have mentioned John Kerry by name, did you point out that he is in favor of allowing gays and lesbians to form civil unions?
    1. Yes
    2. No

21. Over the past few months, have you mentioned George W. Bush by name in any of your homilies?
    1. Yes
    2. No (if No, SKIP to Question 26)

22. If you have mentioned George W. Bush by name, did you point out that he is pro-life on abortion?
    1. Yes
    2. No

23. If you have mentioned George W. Bush by name, did you point out that he is in favor of reforming government spending on aid to the poor?
    1. Yes
    2. No

24. If you have mentioned George W. Bush by name, did you point out that he is responsible for prosecuting the war on terror and the war in Iraq?
    1. Yes
    2. No

25. If you have mentioned George W. Bush by name, did you point out that he is opposed to same-sex marriage?
    1. Yes
    2. No

26. Over the past few months, have you mentioned the Democratic Party by name in any of your homilies?
    1. Yes
    2. No (if No, SKIP to Question 31)

27. If you have mentioned the Democratic Party by name, did you point out that it is pro-choice on abortion?
    1. Yes
    2. No

28. If you have mentioned the Democratic Party by name, did you point out that it is in favor of government efforts to provide aid to the poor?
    1. Yes
    2. No
29. If you have mentioned the Democratic Party by name, did you point out that it has been critical of the war on terror and the war in Iraq?
    1. Yes
    2. No
30. If you have mentioned the Democratic Party by name, did you point out that it is in favor of allowing gays and lesbians to form civil unions?
    1. Yes
    2. No
31. Over the past few months, have you mentioned the Republican Party by name in any of your homilies?
    1. Yes
    2. No (If No, SKIP to Question 36)
32. If you have mentioned the Republican Party by name, did you point out that it is pro-life on abortion?
    1. Yes
    2. No
33. If you have mentioned the Republican Party by name, did you point out that it is in favor of reforming government spending on aid to the poor?
    1. Yes
    2. No
34. If you have mentioned the Republican Party by name, did you point out that it is responsible for prosecuting the war on terror and the war in Iraq?
    1. Yes
    2. No
35. If you have mentioned the Republican Party by name, did you point out that it is opposed to same-sex marriage?
    1. Yes
    2. No
36. Over the past few months, how often have you encouraged your parishioners to vote?
    1. Never
    2. A few times
    3. Several times per month
    4. Every week

37. In your homilies over the past few months, how often have you encouraged your parishioners to consider the abortion issue when they are deciding how to vote?
    1. Never—I have not explicitly encouraged my parishioners to consider the abortion issue when deciding how to vote.
    2. A few times
    3. Several times per month
    4. Every week

38. In your homilies over the past few months, how often have you encouraged your parishioners to consider the issue of aid to the poor when they are deciding how to vote?
    1. Never—I have not explicitly encouraged my parishioners to consider the aid to the poor issue when deciding how to vote.
    2. A few times
    3. Several times per month
    4. Every week

39. In your homilies over the past few months, how often have you encouraged your parishioners to consider the capital punishment issue when they are deciding how to vote?
    1. Never—I have not explicitly encouraged my parishioners to consider the capital punishment issue when deciding how to vote.
    2. A few times
    3. Several times per month
    4. Every week

40. In your homilies over the past few months, how often have you encouraged your parishioners to consider foreign affairs when they are deciding how to vote?
    1. Never—I have not explicitly encouraged my parishioners to consider foreign affairs when deciding how to vote.
    2. A few times
    3. Several times per month
    4. Every week

41. In your homilies over the past few months, how often have you encouraged your parishioners to consider the same-sex marriage issue when they are deciding how to vote?
    1. Never—I have not explicitly encouraged my parishioners to consider the same-sex marriage issue when deciding how to vote.
    2. A few times

3. Several times per month

4. Every week

42. In your parish over the past few months, about how often have the prayers of the faithful included a prayer about abortion (such as for an end to abortion)?

    1. Never

    2. A few times

    3. Several times per month

    4. Every week

43. In your parish over the past few months, about how often have the prayers of the faithful included a prayer for the poor and the disadvantaged?

    1. Never

    2. A few times

    3. Several times per month

    4. Every week

44. In your parish over the past few months, about how often have the prayers of the faithful included a prayer for an end to capital punishment or for those facing execution by the state?

    1. Never

    2. A few times

    3. Several times per month

    4. Every week

45. In your parish over the past few months, about how often have the prayers of the faithful included a prayer for the safety and support of American military personnel?

    1. Never

    2. A few times

    3. Several times per month

    4. Every week

46. In your parish over the past few months, about how often have the prayers of the faithful included a prayer for world peace or for peace in Iraq or the Middle East?

    1. Never

    2. A few times

    3. Several times per month

    4. Every week

47. In your parish over the past few months, about how often have the prayers of the faithful included a prayer for President George W. Bush?
    1. Never
    2. A few times
    3. Several times per month
    4. Every week
48. In your parish over the past few months, about how often have the prayers of the faithful included a prayer for John Kerry?
    1. Never
    2. A few times
    3. Several times per month
    4. Every week
49. In your parish over the past few months, about how often have the prayers of the faithful included a prayer that voters might cast a wise vote on election day?
    1. Never
    2. A few times
    3. Several times per month
    4. Every week
50. In your homilies and public statements over the past few months, have you mentioned the controversy over whether or not to provide communion to pro-abortion politicians?
    1. No, I have not publicly addressed this controversy.
    2. Yes, I have mentioned the controversy and said that priests should not provide communion to pro-abortion politicians.
    3. Yes, I have mentioned the controversy and said that priests should not deny communion to those who request it.
    4. Yes, I have mentioned the controversy, but in a different way (please specify):_____
    _____
    _____

51. Over the past few months, has your parish distributed the Bishops' statement on faithful citizenship to parishioners?
    1. No
    2. Yes

52. Over the past few months, has your parish distributed any other voter guides, pamphlets, or other political information to parishioners?
    1. No (if No, SKIP to Question 54)
    2. Yes
53. If your parish has distributed voter guides, pamphlets, or political information (other than the Bishops' statement on faithful citizenship), can you please tell me the name of the voter guide/pamphlet and how I might be able to obtain a copy?_____

    _____

    _____

54. Are there any other social or political issues that have come up in your homilies over the past few months that I have neglected to ask about here?
    1. No
    2. Yes (Please Specify):_____

    _____

    _____

Thank you for taking the time to complete this questionnaire, your assistance is greatly appreciated. If there is anything else that you would like to tell me, or if you have any comments about this survey, please feel free to write them in the space below.

Appendix D
Background on 2004
Survey of Parishioners

The survey was mailed to parishioners on November 1, 2004, so that it would be received on Election Day or immediately following the 2004 national elections, which were held on November 2. The survey was accompanied by a cover letter that described the project, solicited participation, and invited respondents either to complete the paper survey and return it via U.S. mail (in an addressed, stamped envelope that was provided), or to visit a website and complete the survey online. The survey was administered to a randomly selected sample of 150 parishioners at seven of the nine parishes that participated in the study (St. Anastasia, St. Barnabas, St. Cyrus, St. Leon, St. Norbert, St. Winifred, St. Yolanda). At St. Margaret Parish, which has fewer than 150 parishioners, surveys were sent to a randomly selected sample of 118 parishioners,[1] and at St. Zachary Parish, where there are 141 adult parishioners, surveys were sent to every parishioner. In most cases, parish directories, which contained the names and mailing addresses of registered parishioners, were provided to me by parish leadership. Using the directories and a random number generator (www.random.org), I selected a sample of households from each parish. For households with two resident adults, I randomly selected one adult (by flipping a coin) to receive the survey.

There were some exceptions to this method. Two parishes, St. Anastasia and St. Margaret, did not provide me with a complete parish directory. Instead, they informed me of the number of households contained in their directories; I, in turn, provided them with the (randomly selected) numbers of those households that would be included in the sample. These parishes then provided me with the names and addresses for only these sampled households. One parish, St. Norbert, did not provide contact information for parishioners at all. Instead, after determining the number of households contained in the St. Norbert directory, I provided the parish leadership there with the randomly selected numbers of those households to be included in the sample (along with directions as to which randomly selected adult, in the case of two-adult households, to whom to address the survey) and with 150 prepared survey mailings. The parish staff at St. Norbert then addressed the envelopes and mailed the surveys to parishioners. St. Barnabas Parish provided me with a largely unabridged parish directory that was altered only in that the addresses of a few well-known parishioners were removed. Finally, St. Leon Parish, before providing me with the parish directory, informed their parishioners of the project and asked them to come forward if they desired not to be contacted. These parishioners, of course, were not included in the population from which I sampled St. Leon parishioners. Though there were thus some idiosyncrasies in the sampling of parishioners and administration of surveys at the various parishes, I am very confident that the methods described here yielded a representative sample of registered parishioners at each parish.

To maximize the rate of response to the parishioner surveys, I followed (to the maximum extent possible) the methods for mail and internet surveys outlined by Dillman in *Mail and Internet Surveys: The Tailored Design Method* (2000). Although financial limitations made it impossible, as Dillman recommends, to begin survey administration by sending notification letters to the parishioners in the sample, I did ask the priests at each parish, just before I mailed the surveys, to announce this project to their parishioners and to request that parishioners, should they receive a survey, complete it and return it to me. The priests agreed to do so, and they also proved willing to place similar announcements in the parish bulletins. The cover letter that accompanied the survey was personalized to each recipient, and it directed respondents to a website at which they could complete the survey in lieu of completing and returning the paper survey. The survey consisted of a twelve-page booklet to facilitate ease of reading and completion, and the mailing included a pre-addressed, stamped envelope for parishioners to use to return completed questionnaires to me. To boost the response rate, postcards were mailed to all survey recipients approximately two weeks after the original surveys were mailed. The postcards thanked parishioners for participating in the project if they had already completed the survey, and requested that those who had not done so consider completing and returning the questionnaire.

Ultimately, surveys were mailed to 1,309 parishioners, and usable responses were obtained from 533 of these, with 512 responses returned via U.S. mail, and 21 surveys completed online. Thus, the final response rate for the survey was 40.7 percent.

Note

1. Originally, parish leaders estimated that St. Margaret Parish had in excess of 200 registered parishioners. Thus, as with most other parishes, 150 random numbers (corresponding to registered parishioners) were generated and provided to parish leadership. Ultimately, St. Margaret Parish turned out to have fewer than 150 registered parishioners, which meant that some of the randomly generated numbers did not have corresponding parishioners.

Appendix E
2004 Survey of Parishioners

Instructions: Please circle the response that comes closest to your own opinion.

1. In the space provided, please write the name of the parish where you most frequently attend Sunday/Saturday evening Mass:_____ __

2. About how long have you been attending this parish? (Please write): _____years

3. Do you live within the territorial boundaries of this parish (the one identified in question 1)?
   1. Yes → SKIP to Question 5
   2. No

4. (Answer ONLY if you answered "No" to question 3) Are there any special reasons why you attend Mass at this parish (the one you identified in question 1)?
   1. No
   2. Yes (Please write): _____

5. About how often do you attend Sunday/Saturday evening Mass at some other parish (other than the one you identified in Question 1)?
   1. Never/Rarely
   2. Occasionally
   3. Frequently

6. Some people don't pay much attention to political campaigns. How about you? How interested have you been in this fall's political campaigns?
   1. Very much interested
   2. Somewhat interested
   3. Not much interested

7. Did you vote in this year's presidential election?
   1. Yes
   2. No, I didn't vote this year.
8. Who did you vote for in this year's presidential election?
   1. George W. Bush
   2. John Kerry
   3. Other (Please write): _____
   4. I did not vote this year.
9. Generally speaking, would you say that you personally care a good deal who won the presidential election this fall, or that you don't care very much who won?
   1. Care a good deal
   2. Don't care very much
10. How many days in the past week did you watch the news on TV?
    1. None
    2. Between one and three days
    3. Between four and six days
    4. Every day
11. How many days in the past week did you read a newspaper?
    1. None
    2. Between one and three days
    3. Between four and six days
    4. Every day
12. I'd like to get your feelings toward some of our political leaders and other people who you might know or who are in the news these days. Beside the name of each person, I'd like you to rate that person using something we call the feeling thermometer. Ratings between 50 degrees and 100 degrees mean that you feel favorable and warm toward the person. Ratings between 0 degrees and 50 degrees mean that you don't feel favorable toward the person and that you don't care too much for that person. You would rate the person at the 50 degree mark if you don't feel particularly warm or cold toward the person. If you come to a person whose name you don't recognize, just leave the space for that person blank.
    a. George W. Bush: . . . .   _____Degrees
    b. John Kerry: . . . .   _____Degrees
    c. Dick Cheney: . . . .   _____Degrees
    d. John Edwards: . . . .   _____Degrees

e. Dennis Hastert: . . . .   _____Degrees

f. Nancy Pelosi: . . . .   _____Degrees

g. Bill Frist: . . . .   _____Degrees

h. Tom Daschle: . . . .   _____Degrees

i. John Paul II: . . . .   _____Degrees

j. Your Bishop: . . . .   _____Degrees

k. Your Parish Pastor: . . . .   _____Degrees

13. Do you approve or disapprove of the way George W. Bush is handling his job as president?
    1. Strongly approve
    2. Approve
    3. Disapprove
    4. Strongly disapprove

14. Would you say that you and your family are better off financially than you were a year ago, about the same, or worse off than you were a year ago?
    1. Better off
    2. Same
    3. Worse off

15. Would you say that over the past year the nation's economy has gotten better, stayed about the same, or gotten worse?
    1. Gotten better
    2. Stayed the same
    3. Gotten worse

16. We hear a lot of talk these days about liberals and conservatives. Here is a 5-point scale on which the political views that people might hold are arranged from very liberal to very conservative. Where would you place yourself on this scale?
    1. Very liberal
    2. Liberal
    3. Moderate/middle of the road
    4. Conservative
    5. Very conservative

17. Generally speaking, do you usually think of yourself as a Republican, a Democrat, an Independent, or what?
    1. Strong Democrat
    2. Weak Democrat
    3. Independent, but lean Democratic

4. Independent
5. Independent, but lean Republican
6. Weak Republican
7. Strong Republican
8. Other (Please write):_____

18. Some people think the government should provide fewer services, even in areas such as health and education in order to reduce spending. Other people feel it is important for the government to provide many more services even if it means an increase in spending. Which of the statements below comes closest to your own view on this issue?
    1. Government should provide fewer services to reduce spending.
    2. Government should stick with what it is doing now, no more and no less.
    3. Government should provide more services even if it has to increase spending.

19. Some people believe that we should spend less money for defense. Others feel that defense spending should be increased. Which of the statements below comes closest to your own view on defense spending?
    1. Decrease defense spending
    2. Keep defense spending where it is now
    3. Increase defense spending

20. Some people feel there should be a government insurance plan which would cover all medical and hospital expenses for everyone. Others feel that all medical expenses should be paid by individuals and through private insurance plans like Blue Cross or other company paid plans. Which of the statements below comes closest to your own view on this issue?
    1. Favor government insurance plan
    2. Favor a mixture of government and private insurance plans
    3. Favor private insurance plans only

21. Some people feel the government in Washington should see to it that every person has a good standard of living. Others think the government should just let each person get ahead on their own. Which of the statements below comes closest to your own view on this issue?
    1. Government should see to it that every person has a good standard of living.
    2. We should have a mixture of government help and individual initiative.
    3. Government should let each person get ahead on their own.

22. In your opinion, should government spending on welfare programs to help the needy be increased, decreased, or kept about the same?
    1. Increased
    2. Kept about the same
    3. Decreased
23. In your opinion, should government spending on solving the problem of the homeless be increased, decreased, or kept about the same?
    1. Increased
    2. Kept about the same
    3. Decreased
24. Which one of these statements best agrees with your view about abortion?
    1. By law, abortion should never be permitted.
    2. The law should permit abortion only in case of rape, incest, or when the woman's life is in danger.
    3. The law should permit abortion for reasons other than rape, incest, or danger to the woman's life, but only after the need for the abortion has been clearly established.
    4. By law, a woman should always be able to obtain an abortion as a matter of personal choice.
25. Do you favor or oppose the death penalty for persons convicted of murder?
    1. Strongly favor
    2. Favor
    3. Oppose
    4. Strongly oppose
26. Thinking about foreign affairs generally, in the future, how willing should the United States be to use military force to solve international problems?
    1. Very willing
    2. Somewhat willing
    3. Not very willing
    4. Never willing
27. Thinking specifically about terrorism, how willing should the United States be to use military force to fight terrorism?
    1. Very willing
    2. Somewhat willing
    3. Not very willing
    4. Never willing

28. Do you think the U.S. made the right decision or the wrong decision in using military force against Iraq?
    1. Right decision
    2. Wrong decision
    3. Unsure
29. Do you believe gays and lesbians should be allowed to get legally married, allowed to enter a legal partnership similar to (but not called) marriage, or should there be no legal recognition given to gay and lesbian relationships?
    1. Gays and lesbians should be allowed to get legally married.
    2. Gays and lesbians should be allowed to enter a legal partnership similar to marriage.
    3. There should be no legal recognition of gay and lesbian relationships.
30. Generally speaking, do you favor or oppose allowing research on embryonic stem cells?
    1. Strongly favor
    2. Favor
    3. Oppose
    4. Strongly oppose
31. In the presidential election campaign, what would you say was the single most important issue to you? (Circle one)
    1. The economy
    2. National security/war in Iraq/war on terror
    3. Taxes
    4. Abortion
    5. Welfare
    6. Health care
    7. The values and integrity of the candidates
    8. Gay marriage/civil unions
    9. Other (Please write):_____
32. In the presidential election campaign, what would you say was the second most important issue to you? (Circle one)
    1. The economy
    2. National security/war in Iraq/war on terror
    3. Taxes
    4. Abortion
    5. Welfare
    6. Health care

7. The values and integrity of the candidates
8. Gay marriage/civil unions
9. Other (Please write):_____

33. In the presidential election campaign, what would you say was the third most important issue to you? (Circle one)
    1. The economy
    2. National security/war in Iraq/war on terror
    3. Taxes
    4. Abortion
    5. Welfare
    6. Health care
    7. The values and integrity of the candidates
    8. Gay marriage/civil unions
    9. Other (Please Write):_____

34. Do you happen to know which party had the most members in the House of Representatives in Washington immediately before the recent election? Which one?
    1. Democrats
    2. Republicans
    3. Don't know/can't remember

35. Do you happen to know which party had the most members in the U.S. Senate in Washington immediately before the recent election? Which one?
    1. Democrats
    2. Republicans
    3. Don't know/can't remember

36. I would like to ask you some questions now about your involvement in your parish. With so many demands on our time, it is often difficult to get involved in many activities, committees, or ministries in a parish. Overall, how many parish groups/activities are you involved in?
    1. I don't have time to participate in parish groups/activities outside of Mass.
    2. One or two groups/activities
    3. Three or four groups/activities
    4. Five or more groups/activities

37. On the average, how many total hours per month do you spend participating in parish groups and activities?_____

38. In general, how attached to your parish do you feel?
    1. Not at all attached
    2. Somewhat attached
    3. Very attached
39. How often do you have longer conversations with one or more of the priests at your parish during the course of an "average" month?
    1. Never
    2. Seldom
    3. Frequently
    4. Daily
40. How often do you have longer conversations with other parish members during the course of an "average" month?
    1. Never
    2. Seldom
    3. Frequently
    4. Daily
41. In general, how well does this parish meet your spiritual needs?
    1. Completely
    2. Very well
    3. Not very well
    4. Not at all
42. How often do you attend Mass?
    1. Never/Rarely
    2. Once or twice a year
    3. Several times a year
    4. Once a month
    5. Two or three times a month
    6. Once a week
    7. Several times a week
    8. Every day
43. When you attend weekend Mass, what time do you usually go?
    1. Saturday evening
    2. Sunday morning
    3. Sunday evening
    4. It varies from week to week

44. Is your decision about which Mass to attend influenced by knowing which priest will be saying that Mass?
    1. No, at my parish we only have one priest who presides at all of the Masses.
    2. No, at my parish, we have no way of knowing who will preside at any given Mass.
    3. No, even though my parish announces who will preside at each Mass, this does not figure into my decision.
    4. Yes, I usually attend Mass with Father (please write in):_____

45. How would you describe a typical homily that is given during Sunday/ Saturday evening Mass at your parish church? Is it inspiring or uninspiring?
    1. Very uninspiring
    2. Uninspiring
    3. Not really uninspiring or inspiring
    4. Inspiring
    5. Very inspiring

46. Is a typical homily that is given during Sunday/Saturday evening Mass at your parish church dull or interesting?
    1. Very dull
    2. Dull
    3. Not really dull or interesting
    4. Interesting
    5. Very interesting

47. Is a typical homily that is given during Sunday/Saturday evening Mass at your parish church informative or uninformative?
    1. Very uninformative
    2. Uninformative
    3. Not really uninformative or informative
    4. Informative
    5. Very informative

48. Please indicate whether people who engage in the following activities should be considered "true Catholics." For each item (a–f), circle Yes if they should be considered true Catholics, and No if they should not be considered true Catholics.

a. Someone who rarely goes to Mass?. . . . .   YES   NO
b. People who live together outside of marriage?. . . . .   YES   NO
c. People who get married outside the Church?. . . . .   YES   NO
d. People who urge or undergo abortion?. . . . .   YES   NO
e. People who practice homosexuality?. . . . .   YES   NO
f. People who use artificial birth control?. . . . .   YES   NO

49. How often do you read or study the Bible on your own?
     1. Never
     2. At least once a year
     3. At least once a month
     4. At least once a week
     5. Daily

50. How often do you pray with friends or with members of your household, other than grace at meals?
     1. Never
     2. At least once a year
     3. At least once a month
     4. At least once a week
     5. Daily

51. Please indicate whether you agree or disagree with the following statement: The Church should remain firm in its opposition to the use of contraceptives.
     1. Strongly disagree
     2. Disagree
     3. Agree
     4. Strongly agree

52. To what degree do you feel your religious beliefs and values guide or influence your voting decisions?
     1. Not at all
     2. Only to a small degree
     3. To a large degree
     4. My voting decisions are completely determined by my religious beliefs and values.

53. The Catholic Church offers guidance and teaching on current issues in a number of ways. The pope may issue an encyclical, bishops may issue statements, priests may preach sermons, or the issue might be left up to individual Catholics to make their own judgment. For each of the issues

below (a–h), please indicate whether you think it is appropriate for the pope to speak out on that matter. If you think the pope should speak about that particular issue, circle "Pope Should Speak." If you think the pope should not speak about that particular issue, circle "Pope Should Not Speak."

a. Aid to poor countries	Pope Should Speak	Pope Should Not Speak
b. Fighting poverty in U.S.	Pope Should Speak	Pope Should Not Speak
c. Birth control	Pope Should Speak	Pope Should Not Speak
d. War on Terror	Pope Should Speak	Pope Should Not Speak
e. Death penalty	Pope Should Speak	Pope Should Not Speak
f. Abortion	Pope Should Speak	Pope Should Not Speak
g. Foreign affairs/war	Pope Should Speak	Pope Should Not Speak
h. Gay marriage/civil unions	Pope Should Speak	Pope Should Not Speak

54. Now, for each of the issues (a–h) below, please indicate whether you think it is appropriate for the U.S. bishops to speak out on that matter.

a. Aid to poor countries	Bishops Should Speak	Bishops Should Not Speak
b. Fighting poverty in U.S.	Bishops Should Speak	Bishops Should Not Speak
c. Birth control	Bishops Should Speak	Bishops Should Not Speak
d. War on Terror	Bishops Should Speak	Bishops Should Not Speak
e. Death penalty	Bishops Should Speak	Bishops Should Not Speak
f. Abortion	Bishops Should Speak	Bishops Should Not Speak
g. Foreign affairs/war	Bishops Should Speak	Bishops Should Not Speak
h. Gay marriage/civil unions	Bishops Should Speak	Bishops Should Not Speak

55. Now, for each of the issues (a–h) below, please indicate whether you think it is appropriate for parish priests to speak out on that matter.

a. Aid to poor countries	Priests Should Speak	Priests Should Not Speak
b. Fighting poverty in U.S.	Priests Should Speak	Priests Should Not Speak
c. Birth control	Priests Should Speak	Priests Should Not Speak
d. War on Terror	Priests Should Speak	Priests Should Not Speak
e. Death penalty	Priests Should Speak	Priests Should Not Speak
f. Abortion	Priests Should Speak	Priests Should Not Speak
g. Foreign affairs/war	Priests Should Speak	Priests Should Not Speak
h. Gay marriage/civil unions	Priests Should Speak	Priests Should Not Speak

56. For each of the items (a–f) listed below, please indicate how much of the time you think you can trust them to do what is right by circling almost always, most of the time, or only some of the time for each individual or organization.

a. Federal government	almost always	most of time	some of time
b. Corporations/business	almost always	most of time	some of time
c. The pope	almost always	most of time	some of time
d. The bishops	almost always	most of time	some of time
e. Priests in general	almost always	most of time	some of time
f. Your parish priests	almost always	most of time	some of time

57. In what year were you born? 19_____

58. Are you married now, or are you widowed, divorced, separated, or have you never married?
    1. Married
    2. Never married
    3. Divorced
    4. Separated
    5. Widowed

59. What is the highest grade of school or year of college you have completed?
    1. Some high school or less
    2. High school diploma or equivalency test
    3. Some college, but no degree
    4. Junior or community college degree
    5. Bachelor's level degree
    6. Some postgraduate education, but no postgraduate degree
    7. Advanced degree (such as a master's or doctorate)

60. What is your gender?
    1. Male
    2. Female

61. What is your race?
    1. White
    2. Black
    3. Hispanic
    4. Asian
    5. Other

62. From the list below, please give an estimate of your annual total family income, before taxes.
    1. Less than $25,000
    2. $25,000–$50,000
    3. $50,000–$75,000
    4. $75,000–$100,000
    5. $100,000–$125,000
    6. More than $125,000
63. Do you have any children?
    1. No
    2. Yes, I have a child/children, at least one of whom lives with me.
    3. Yes, I have a child/children, but they do not live with me.
64. What is your religious denomination?
    1. Catholic
    2. Protestant
    3. Jewish
    4. Other (Please write):_____   _____

Thank you for taking the time to complete this questionnaire, your assistance is greatly appreciated. If there is anything else that you would like to tell me, or if you have any comments about this survey, please feel free to write them in the space below.

References

Abramson, Paul R., John H. Aldrich, Phil Paolino, and David W. Rohde. 1992. " 'Sophisticated' Voting in the 1988 Presidential Primaries." *American Political Science Review* 86:55–69.

Achen, Christopher H. 1975. "Mass Political Attitudes and the Survey Response." *American Political Science Review* 69:1218–31.

Allen, Charlotte. 2004. "For Catholic Politicians, a Hard Line." *Washington Post*, April 11. www.washingtonpost.com/ac2/wp-dyn?pagename=article&node=&contentId=A766-2004Apr9&notFound=true (accessed January 12, 2007).

Althaus, Scott. 1998. "Information Effects in Collective Preferences." *American Political Science Review* 92:545–58.

Bartels, Larry M. 1996. "Uninformed Votes: Information Effects in Presidential Elections." *American Journal of Political Science* 40:194–230.

Beatty, Kathleen Murphy, and Oliver Walter. 1989. "A Group Theory of Religion and Politics: The Clergy as Group Leaders." *Western Political Quarterly* 42:129–46.

Berelson, Bernard R., Paul F. Lazarsfeld, and William N. McPhee. 1954. *Voting*. Chicago: University of Chicago Press.

Bernardin, Joseph Cardinal. 1983. *Gannon Lecture—A Consistent Ethic of Life: An American Catholic Dialogue*. http://archives.archchicago.org/JCBpdfs/JCBatconsistentethicfordhamu.pdf (accessed February 19, 2007).

Bjarnason, Thoroddur, and Michael R. Welch. 2004. "Father Knows Best: Parishes, Priests, and American Catholic Parishioners' Attitudes toward Capital Punishment." *Journal for the Scientific Study of Religion* 43:103–18.

Brewer, Mark D. 2003. *Relevant No More? The Catholic/Protestant Divide in American Politics*. Lanham, MD: Lexington Books.

Byrnes, Timothy A. 1991. *Catholic Bishops in American Politics*. Princeton: Princeton University Press.

Campbell, Angus, Philip E. Converse, Warren E. Miller, and Donald E. Stokes. 1960. *The American Voter*. New York: Wiley.

Campbell, David E., and J. Quin Monson. 2005. "The Religion Card: Evangelicals, Catholics, and Gay Marriage in the 2004 Presidential Election." Paper presented at the annual meeting of the American Political Science Association, September 1–4, Washington, DC.

Castelli, Jim, and Joseph Gremillion. 1987. *The Emerging Parish: The Notre Dame Study of Catholic Life since Vatican II*. San Francisco: Harper & Row.

Catechism of the Catholic Church, with Modifications from the Editio Typica. 1997. New York: Doubleday.

Center for Applied Research in the Apostolate. 2005. "Self-Reported Mass Attendance of U.S. Catholics Unchanged during Last Five Years." http://cara.georgetown.edu/AttendPR.pdf (accessed January 18, 2007).

Converse, Philip E. 1964. "The Nature of Belief Systems in Mass Publics." In *Ideology and Discontent*, ed. D. E. Apter, 206–61. New York: Free Press.

Dalton, Russell J., Paul A. Beck, and Robert Huckfeldt. 1998. "Partisan Cues and the Media: Information Flows in the 1992 Presidential Election." *American Political Science Review* 92:111–26.

D'Antonio, William V., James D. Davidson, Dean R. Hoge, and Katherine Meyer. 2001. *American Catholics: Gender, Generation, and Commitment*. Walnut Creek: Altamira Press.

D'Antonio, William V., James D. Davidson, Dean R. Hoge, and Ruth A. Wallace. 1996. *Laity, American and Catholic: Transforming the Church*. Kansas City: Sheed and Ward.

Delli Carpini, Michael X., and Scott Keeter. 1996. *What Americans Know about Politics and Why It Matters*. New Haven: Yale University Press.

de Tocqueville, Alexis. 1833. *Democracy in America*. Trans. George Lawrence. Ed. J. P. Mayer. New York: HarperPerennial.

Dillman, Don A. 2000. *Mail and Internet Surveys: The Tailored Design Method*. New York: J. Wiley.

Djupe, Paul A., and Christopher P. Gilbert. 2002a. "The Construction of Political Mobilization in Churches." Paper presented at the annual meeting of the Society for the Scientific Study of Religion, Salt Lake City, UT.

———. 2002b. "The Nature of Religious Influence on Political Behavior: Perception and Reception." Paper presented at the annual meeting of the Midwest Political Science Association, Chicago.

———. 2002c. "The Political Voice of Clergy." *Journal of Politics* 64:596–609.

———. 2003. *The Prophetic Pulpit: Clergy, Churches, and Communities in American Politics*. Lanham, MD: Rowman & Littlefield.

———. 2006. "The Resourceful Believer: Generating Civic Skills in Church." *Journal of Politics* 68:116–27.

Entman, Robert. 1989. "How the Media Affect What People Think: An Information Processing Approach." *Journal of Politics* 51:347–70.

Fetzer, Joel S. 2001. "Shaping Pacificism: The Role of the Local Anabaptist Pastor." In *Christian Clergy in American Politics*, ed. Sue E. S. Crawford and Laura R. Olson, 177–87. Baltimore: Johns Hopkins University Press.

Finifter, Ada. 1974. "The Friendship Group as a Protective Environment for Political Deviants." *American Political Science Review* 68:607–25.

Freedman, Paul. 2004. "The Gay Marriage Myth: Terrorism, Not Values, Drove Bush's Re-election." *Slate*, November 5. www.slate.com/id/2109275/ (accessed February 15, 2006).

Froehle, Bryan T., and Mary L. Gautier. 2000. *Catholicism USA: A Portrait of the Catholic Church in the United States*. Maryknoll, NY: Orbis Books.

Gallup Poll of Catholics. 1999. www.thearda.com/Archive/Files/Codebooks/GALLUP99_CB.asp (accessed January 18, 2007).

"Gay Marriage": A Catholic Answers Special Report. 2004. San Diego: Catholic Answers.

Gerner, George W. 1995. "Catholics and the Religious Right: We Are Being Wooed." *Commonweal*, May 1995, 15–20.

Gilbert, Christopher P. 1993. *The Impact of Churches on Political Behavior: An Empirical Study*. Westport, CT: Greenwood Press.

Goodstein, Laurie. 2004. "Communion Issue Creates Split among U.S. Bishops." *The New York Times*, June 6, 2004.

Green, John C., James L. Guth, Corwin E. Smidt, and Lyman A. Kellstedt. 1996. *Religion and the Culture Wars: Dispatches from the Front*. Lanham, MD: Rowman and Littlefield.

Guth, James L. 2001. "Reflections on the Status of Research on Clergy in Politics." In *Christian Clergy in American Politics*, ed. Sue E. S. Crawford and Laura R. Olson, 30–43. Baltimore: Johns Hopkins University Press.

Guth, James L., Lyman A. Kellstedt, Corwin E. Smidt, and John C. Green. 2005. "Religious Mobilization in the 2004 Presidential Election." Paper presented at the annual meeting of the American Political Science Association, September 1–4, Washington, DC.

Hoge, Dean R., and Jacqueline E. Wenger. 2003. *Evolving Visions of the Priesthood: Changes from Vatican II to the Turn of the New Century*. Collegeville, MN: Liturgical Press.

Huckfeldt, Robert, and John Sprague. 1995. *Citizens, Politics, and Social Communication: Information and Influence in an Election Campaign*. New York: Cambridge University Press.

Huckfeldt, Robert, Eric Plutzer, and John Sprague. 1993. "Alternative Contexts of Political Behavior: Churches, Neighborhoods, and Individuals." *Journal of Politics* 55:365–81.

Hunter, James Davison. 1991. *Culture Wars: The Struggle to Define America.* New York: BasicBooks.

Iyengar, Shanto. 1991. *Is Anyone Responsible? How Television Frames Political Issues.* Chicago: University of Chicago Press.

Iyengar, Shanto, and Donald R. Kinder. 1987. *News that Matters: Television and American Opinion.* Chicago: University of Chicago Press.

Jelen, Ted G. 1984. "Respect for Life, Sexual Morality, and Opposition to Abortion." *Review of Religious Research* 25:220–31.

———. 1992. "Political Christianity: A Contextual Analysis." *American Journal of Political Science* 36:692–714.

———. 1993. *The Political World of the Clergy.* Westport, CT: Praeger.

———. 2001. "Notes for a Theory of Clergy as Political Leaders." In *Christian Clergy in American Politics*, ed. Sue E. S. Crawford and Laura R. Olson, 15–29. Baltimore: Johns Hopkins University Press.

———. 2003. "Catholic Priests and the Political Order: The Political Behavior of Catholic Pastors." *Journal for the Scientific Study of Religion* 42:591–604.

John XXIII. 1961. "Mater et Magistra: Christianity and Social Progress." In *Human Dignity and the Common Good*, ed. Richard W. Rousseau, 133–208. 2001. Westport, CT: Greenwood Press.

———. 1963. "Pacem in Terris: Peace on Earth." In *Human Dignity and the Common Good*, ed. Richard W. Rousseau. 2001, 209–62. Westport, CT: Greenwood Press.

John Paul II. 1981. "Laborem Exercens: On Human Work." In *Human Dignity and the Common Good*, ed. Richard W. Rousseau, 301–64. 2001. Westport, CT: Greenwood Press.

———. 1991. "Centesimus Annus: On the Hundredth Anniversary of Rerum Novarum." In *Human Dignity and the Common Good*, ed. Richard W. Rousseau. 2001, 433–512. Westport, CT: Greenwood Press.

———. 1995. *Evangelium vitae.* www.vatican.va/holy_father/john_paul_ii/encyclicals/documents/hf_jp-ii_enc_25031995_evangelium-vitae-en.html (accessed February 19, 2007).

———. 2003. *Address of His Holiness Pope John Paul II to the Diplomatic Corps.* www.vatican.va/holy_father/john_paul_ii/speeches/2003/january/documents/hf_jp-ii_spe_20030113_diplomatic-corps_en.html (accessed February 19, 2007).

Keeter, Scott. 1985. "Public Opinion in 1984." In *The Elections of 1984*, ed. Gerald Pomper with colleagues, 91–111. Chatham, NJ: Chatham House.

Kellstedt, Lyman A., and Corwin E. Smidt. 1993. "Doctrinal Beliefs and Political Behavior." In *Rediscovering the Religion Factor in American Politics*, ed. David C. Leege and Lyman A. Kellstedt, 177–99. Armonk, NY: M. E. Sharpe.

Kenski, Henry C., and William Lockwood. 1989. "The Catholic Vote from 1980 to 1986." In *Religion and Political Behavior in the United States*, ed. Ted G. Jelen, 109–38. Westport, CT: Praeger.

Kinder, Donald R., and Lynn M. Sanders. 1996. *Divided by Color: Racial Politics and Democratic Ideals.* Chicago: University of Chicago Press.

Klapper, Joseph T. 1960. *The Effects of Mass Communication.* New York: Free Press.

Kohut, Andrew, John C. Green, Scott Keeter, and Robert C. Toth. 2000. *The Diminishing Divide: Religion's Changing Role in American Politics.* Washington, D.C.: Brookings Institution Press.

Kreft, Ita G. G. 2000. "Using Random Coefficient Linear Models for the Analysis of Hierarchically Nested Data." In *Handbook of Applied Multivariate Statistics and Mathematical Modeling,* ed. Howard E. A. Tinsley and Steven D. Brown, 613–43. San Diego: Academic Press.

Krosnick, Jon A., and Donald R. Kinder. 1990. "Altering the Foundations of Support for the President Trough Priming." *American Political Science Review* 84:497–512.

Kuklinski, James H., and Paul J. Quirk. 2000. "Reconsidering the Rational Public: Cognition, Heuristics, and Mass Opinion." In *Elements of Reason: Cognition, Choice, and the Bounds of Rationality,* ed. Arthur Lupia, Mathew D. McCubbins, and Samuel L. Popkin, 153–82. Cambridge: Cambridge University Press.

Kuklinski, James H., Paul J. Quirk, Jennifer Jerit, David Schwieder, and Robert F. Rich. 2000. "Misinformation and the Currency of Democratic Citizenship." *Journal of Politics* 62:790–816.

Layman, Geoffrey. 2001. *The Great Divide: Religious and Cultural Conflict in American Party Politics.* New York: Columbia University Press.

Layman, Geoffrey C., and John C. Green. 2006. "Wars and Rumours of Wars: The Contexts of Cultural Conflict in American Political Behavior." *British Journal of Political Science* 36:61–89.

Lazarsfeld, Paul F., Bernard Berelson, and Hazel Gaudet. 1944. *The People's Choice.* New York: Columbia University Press.

Leege, David C. 1988. "Catholics and the Civic Order: Parish Participation, Politics, and Civic Participation." *Review of Politics* 50:704–36.

———. 1996. "The Catholic Vote in '96: Can It Be Found in Church?" *Commonweal*, September 1996, 11–18.

Leege, David C., and Lyman A. Kellstedt. 1993. "Religious Worldviews and

Political Philosophies: Capturing Theory in the Grand Manner through Empirical Data." In *Rediscovering the Religious Factor in American Politics*, ed. David C. Leege and Lyman A. Kellstedt, 216–31. Armonk, NY: M. E. Sharpe.

Leege, David C., and Michael R. Welch. 1989. "Religious Roots of Political Orientations: Variations among American Catholic Parishioners." *Journal of Politics* 51:137–62.

Leege, David C., Kenneth D. Wald, Brian S. Krueger, and Paul D. Mueller. 2002. *The Politics of Cultural Differences: Social Change and Voter Mobilization Strategies in the Post-New Deal Period*. Princeton, NJ: Princeton University Press.

Lenski, Gerhard. 1961. *The Religious Factor: A Sociological Study of Religion's Impact on Politics, Economics, and Family Life*. Garden City, NY: Anchor Books.

Leo XIII. 1891. "Rerum Novarum: On Capital and Labor." In *Human Dignity and the Common Good*, ed. Richard W. Rousseau, 9–54. 2001. Westport, CT: Greenwood Press.

Lodge, Milton, and Marco R. Steenbergen, with Shawn Brau. 1995. "The Responsive Voter: Campaign Information and the Dynamics of Candidate Evaluation." *American Political Science Review* 89:309–26.

Long, J. Scott. 1997. *Regression Models for Categorical and Limited Dependent Variables*. Thousand Oaks, CA: Sage Publications.

Loverde, Paul S. 2004. "Pre-Election Letter to the People of Arlington." *Arlington Catholic Herald*, October 28, 2004.

Luke, Douglas A. 2004. *Multilevel Modeling*. Thousand Oaks, CA: Sage Publications.

McCombs, M. E., and D. Shaw. 1972. "The Agenda-Setting Function of the Mass Media." *Public Opinion Quarterly* 36:176–87.

Mendelsohn, Matthew. 1996. "The Media and Interpersonal Communications: The Priming of Issues, Leaders, and Party Identification." *Journal of Politics* 58:112–25.

Nelson, Thomas E. 2004. "Policy Goals, Public Rhetoric, and Political Attitudes." *Journal of Politics* 66:581–605.

Nelson, Thomas E., and Donald R. Kinder. 1996. "Issue Frames and Group-Centrism in American Public Opinion." *Journal of Politics* 58:1055–78.

Nolan, Hugh J., ed. 1984. *Pastoral Letters of the United States Catholic Bishops: Volume IV, 1975–1983*. Washington, D.C.: United States Catholic Conference.

———. 1989. *Pastoral Letters of the United States Catholic Bishops: Volume V, 1983–1988*. Washington, D.C.: United States Catholic Conference.

Page, Benjamin I., and Robert Y. Shapiro. 1992. *The Rational Public: Fifty*

Years of Trends in Americans' Policy Preferences. Chicago: University of Chicago Press.

Penning, James M. 1986. "Changing Partisanship and Issue Stands among American Catholics." *Sociological Analysis* 47:29–49.

Perl, Paul, and Jamie S. McClintock. 2001. "The Catholic 'Consistent Life Ethic' and Attitudes toward Capital Punishment and Welfare Reform." *Sociology of Religion* 62:275–99.

Pew Research Center for the People and the Press. 2002. "Americans Struggle with Religion's Role at Home and Abroad." http://people-press.org/reports/display.php3?ReportID=150 (accessed January 18, 2007).

———. 2004. "Voters Liked Campaign 2004, But Too Much Mudslinging—Moral Values: How Important?" http://people-press.org/reports/pdf/233.pdf (accessed February 15, 2006).

———. 2005a. "Religion a Strength and a Weakness for Both Parties: Public Divided on Origins of Life." http://people-press.org/reports/display.php3?ReportID=254 (accessed January 18, 2007).

———. 2005b. "Beyond Red vs. Blue: Republicans Divided about Role of Government—Democrats by Social and Personal Values." http://people-press.org/reports/pdf/242.pdf (accessed January 18, 2007).

———. 2006a. "Pragmatic Americans Liberal and Conservative on Social Issues: Most Want Middle Ground on Abortion." http://people-press.org/reports/display.php3?ReportID=283 (accessed January 18, 2007).

———. 2006b. "Strong Public Support for Right to Die: Most Americans Discussing—and Planning—End of Life Treatment." http://people-press.org/reports/display.php3?ReportID=266 (accessed January 18, 2007).

Plotkin, Henry A. 1985. "Issues in the Campaign." In *The Elections of 1984,* ed. Gerald Pomper with colleagues, 35–59. Chatham, NJ: Chatham House.

Pomper, Gerald M. 2005. "The Presidential Election: The Ills of American Politics after 9/11." In *The Elections of 2004,* ed. Michael Nelson, 42–68. Washington, D.C.: CQ Press.

Popkin, Samuel L. 1994. *The Reasoning Voter: Communication and Persuasion in Presidential Campaigns.* Chicago: University of Chicago Press.

Prendergast, William B. 1999. *The Catholic Voter in American Politics: The Passing of the Democratic Monolith.* Washington, D.C.: Georgetown University Press.

Raudenbush, Stephen W., and Anthony S. Bryk. 2002. *Hierarchical Linear Models: Applications and Data Analysis Methods, Second Edition.* Thousand Oaks, CA: Sage Publications.

Reichley, James A. 1986. "Religion and the Future of American Politics." *Political Science Quarterly* 101:23–47.

Rousseau, Richard W., ed. 2001. *Human Dignity and the Common Good: The Great Papal Social Encyclicals from Leo XIII to John Paul II*. Westport, CT: Greenwood Press.

Singer, Judith D. 1998. "Using SAS PROC MIXED to Fit Multilevel Models, Hierarchical Models, and Individual Growth Models." *Journal of Educational and Behavioral Statistics* 23:323–55.

Smith, Gregory A. 2005. "The Influence of Priests on the Political Attitudes of Roman Catholics." *Journal for the Scientific Study of Religion* 44:291–306.

Sniderman, Paul M., Richard A. Brody, and Philip E. Tetlock. 1991. *Reasoning and Choice: Explorations in Political Psychology*. Cambridge: Cambridge University Press.

Steenbergen, Marco R., and Bradford S. Jones. 2002. "Modeling Multilevel Data Structures." *American Journal of Political Science* 46:218–37.

Steinfels, Peter. 2003. *A People Adrift: The Crisis of the Roman Catholic Church in America*. New York: Simon and Schuster.

Sullivan, John L., James Piereson, and George E. Marcus. 1978. "Ideological Constraint in the Mass Public: A Methodological Critique and Some New Findings." *American Journal of Political Science* 22:233–49.

Taber, Charles S. 2003. "Information Processing and Public Opinion." In *Oxford Handbook of Political Psychology*, ed. David O. Sears, Leonie Huddy, and Robert Jervis, 433–76. Oxford: Oxford University Press.

Thigpen, Paul. 2004. *What Every Catholic Needs to Know about Voting*. Huntington, IN. In *Our Sunday Visitor*. www.osv.com/peridodicals/show-article.asp?pid=1025 (accessed November 8, 2004).

Torraco, Stephen F. 2003. *A Brief Catechism for Catholic Voters*. St. Paul, MN: Leaflet Missal Company.

Tumulty, Karen, and Perry Bacon Jr. 2004. "A Test of Kerry's Faith." *Time*, April 5. www.time.com/time/magazine/article/0,9171,605436,00.html (accessed January 12, 2006).

United States Conference of Catholic Bishops. 1983. *The Challenge of Peace: God's Promise and Our Response*. Washington, D.C.: United States Conference of Catholic Bishops.

———. 1986. "Economic Justice for All: Pastoral Letter on Catholic Social Teaching and the U.S. Economy." In *Tenth Anniversary Edition of Economic Justice for All*, 13–141. 2000. Washington, D.C.: United States Catholic Conference.

———. 2003. *Faithful Citizenship: A Catholic Call to Political Responsibility*. www.usccb.org/faithfulcitizenship/bishopStatement.html (accessed February 21, 2007).

Valentino, Nicholas A. 1999. "Crime News and the Priming of Racial Attitudes during Evaluations of the President." *Public Opinion Quarterly* 63:293–320.

Valentino, Nicholas A., Vincent L. Hutchings, and Ismail K. White. 2002. "Cues That Matter: How Political Ads Prime Racial Attitudes during Campaigns." *American Political Science Review* 96:75–90.

Voter's Guide for Serious Catholics. 2004. El Cajon, CA: Catholic Answers.

Wald, Kenneth D. 1992. "Religious Elites and Public Opinion: The Impact of the Bishops' Peace Pastoral." *Review of Politics* 54:112–43.

———. 1997. *Religion and Politics in the United States.* Washington, D.C.: CQ Press.

Wald, Kenneth D., Lyman A. Kellstedt, and David C. Leege. 1993. "Church Involvement and Political Behavior." In *Rediscovering the Religious Factor in American Politics,* ed. David C. Leege and Lyman A. Kellstedt. Armonk, NY: M. E. Sharpe.

Wald, Kenneth D., Dennis E. Owen, and Samuel S. Hill, Jr. 1988. "Churches as Political Communities." *American Political Science Review* 82:531–48.

Welch, Michael R., and David C. Leege. 1988. "Religious Predictors of Catholic Parishioners' Sociopolitical Attitudes: Devotional Style, Closeness to God, Imagery, and Agentic/Communal Religious Identity." *Journal for the Scientific Study of Religion* 27:536–52.

———. 1991. "Dual Reference Groups and Political Orientations: An Examination of Evangelically Oriented Catholics." *American Journal of Political Science* 35:28–56.

Welch, Michael R., David C. Leege, and James C. Cavendish. 1995. "Attitudes toward Abortion Among U.S. Catholics: Another Case of Symbolic Politics?" *Social Science Quarterly* 76:142–57.

Wilcox, Clyde, Ted G. Jelen, and David C. Leege. 1993. "Religious Group Identifications: Toward a Cognitive Theory of Religious Mobilization." In *Rediscovering the Religious Factor in American Politics,* ed. David C. Leege and Lyman A. Kellstedt, 72–99. Armonk, NY: M. E. Sharpe.

Wuthnow, Robert. 1988. *The Restructuring of American Religion. Society and Faith since World War II.* Princeton, NJ: Princeton University Press.

Zaller, John. 1992. *The Nature and Origins of Mass Opinion.* Cambridge: Cambridge University Press.

———. 1996. "The Myth of Massive Media Impact Revived: New Support for a Discredited Idea." In *Political Persuasion and Attitude Change,* ed. Diana C. Mutz, Paul M. Sniderman, and Richard A. Brody, 17–78. Ann Arbor: University of Michigan Press.

Index

Note: Page numbers in italics followed by "t" or "f" indicate tables or figures in the text.